AF361421

# COMPOSING TEACHER-RESEARCH

SUNY Series, Teacher Preparation and Development
Alan R. Tom, Editor

# Composing Teacher-Research

## A Prosaic History

CATHY FLEISCHER

State University
of New York
Press

Published by
State University of New York Press, Albany



Production by Susan Geraghty
Marketing by Dana Yanulavich

Printed in the United States of America



For information, address State University of New York
Press, State University Plaza, Albany, N.Y., 12246

**Library of Congress Cataloging-in-Publication Data**

Fleischer, Cathy.
    Composing teacher-research : a prosaic history / Cathy Fleischer.
        p.   cm. – (SUNY series, teacher preparation and development)
    Includes bibliographical references and index.
    ISBN 0-7914-2361-1. – ISBN 0-7914-2362-X (pbk.)
    1. Action research in education.   2. Teaching.   I. Title.
  II. Series: SUNY series in teacher preparation and development.
  LB1028.24.F54 1995
  370′.78–dc20                                                    94-13681
                                                                       CIP

10 9 8 7 6 5 4 3 2 1

*In memory of my mother,*
*Clare Fleischer,*
*my first, best teacher*

*And for my sons,*
*Seth and Jesse Fleischer Buchsbaum,*
*who teach me every day*

# CONTENTS

# ACKNOWLEDGMENTS

Teacher-research, I argue in the pages that follow, relies on composing collaborators to create new knowledge as they come together to rethink, to research, and to write about their individual and shared understandings. It is in the spirit of this collaboration that I would like to acknowledge some of those who have created the ideas of this book with me.

I have been fortunate to have had the opportunity to research with a number of students and teachers over the past decade, some of whom figure quite prominently in my work here. My thanks go to the students of fourth-hour English at Arthur Hill High School whose work is depicted in chapter 4, the students of my Argumentative Writing class at The University of Michigan whose work is discussed in chapter 5, and the students of my Introductory Composition class at Eastern Michigan University whose work is referred to in chapter 6. Specifically, I want to acknowledge the contributions of four students—Akemi Johnson, Sarah Swallow, John Choi and Susan French—whose words will teach you just as they taught me. As you read, you will see how integral their voices are to this book. I'd also like to thank two teachers who have added much to my developing insights about literacy and research: Sheila Smith of Arthur Hill High School, who graciously opened up her class to let me teach and learn alongside her, and Russ Larson of Eastern Michigan University, who added to his own load by coming into my class every day for an entire semester for our collaborative research project.

I have been fortunate as well to have had colleagues over the last several years who share my interest in literacy instruction and teacher-research. Our formal and informal talks, our work together on various projects, and our sharing and critiquing of each other's papers have helped me immensely. Among those I'd like to thank: Loren Barritt, Anne Ruggles Gere, Valerie Polakow, Carol Winkelman, and the many teachers of the Eastern Michigan Writing Project who read and critiqued drafts of the first chapter.

I'd also like to thank Priscilla Ross and her colleagues at State University of New York Press who have encouraged me and helped me through the process of turning my ideas into this book.

Finally, I'd like to acknowledge four individuals whose help in different ways has been invaluable to me. Many of the ideas which form the center of this book found their beginnings in my work with Jay Robinson. He has been mentor and friend, encouraging me to do the kind of work I want to do; helping me, through his position as Director of the Center for Educational Improvement through Collaboration, to find the sites in which to do it; and pushing me to think my own best thoughts. My friend David Schaafsma and I have been talking, writing, and sharing our ideas since the day we met, our first day of graduate school. He continues to set an example for me in the work he undertakes and the sensitive way in which he writes about people and communities. My professional and personal friendship with Patricia Lambert Stock has served as an important inspiration for my work. Over the past eight years, we have spent countless hours talking about the ideas that eventually came together to form this book, and she has spent more hours than she has to give helping me clarify my positions and my writing. I am grateful to her for her loving friendship and emotional support as well as her critical eye and insistence that I work through what always seem to me impossible tasks.

My final thanks are to my husband, Andy Buchsbaum. In our years together he has encouraged me in many ways to do the kind of work I do: reading and talking to me about every word that I write; adjusting his schedule so that I can spend long hours in the schools and at my writing; helping me through discouraging moments; and, most of all, providing me with a model for what it means to base your work and your life in the ethical stands which are at the center of this book. Without his unqualified love and support, I could neither do this work nor understand its importance.

# CHAPTER 1

# *A Practitioner's Retrospective*[1]

## INTRODUCTION: THE PICTURE ALBUMS
## OF A PROSAIC HISTORY

Later on today, I will get up from my computer and begin a task I look forward to as both joy and drudgery: sifting through the piles of photographs that have accumulated in a box in the corner of my study. Each time I collect developed film from my local pharmacy, I vow this will be the time I will put the pictures immediately in an album. I even buy albums occasionally, and they sit forlornly next to the box stuffed with yellow envelopes that hold the visions of my memories of the past few years. Once I begin the task of reviewing those snapshots, I know I will respond as I have responded before: oohing and aahing over a particularly cute picture of my sons, saying, "I can't believe how much they've changed!"; noticing for the first time an acquaintance relegated to the background of a shot who has since become an important friend; wondering why I ever took five shots of that particular tree, unsure as to where it is and why it was important to me at the time; but mostly conjuring up a wealth of memories and emotions, amazed as ever that these still pictures can produce such strong reactions in me. Often, when I look through a particular set of pictures taken randomly over the course of some months, I see connections among the shots, themes that emerge as I arrange the pictures in an album. I can see, for example, the development of my older son's motor skills across these stills: He's grasping a spoon, sitting up against our dog, standing and holding onto a chair, climbing into his kiddie pool, jumping into a pile of leaves. Individual moments suggest a moving scenario for me, and I remember far more than the pictures can show: the tears as he fell over when the dog moved; the thirty-three steps taken in a row on the first day he really started walking; the time he slid down the slide in his kiddie pool, landing flat on

---

[1]An earlier version of this chapter appears in *English Education,* May 1993.

his back, screaming for us to rescue him from the four inches of water.

As I imagine the task that lies ahead, it gives me a way to think about the one at hand: explaining my forays into teacher-research and my shifting understanding of that work over the past seven years. The picture album becomes an apt metaphor for me: As a teacher, I have accumulated memories of my classrooms much as I accumulate pictures. The fragmented stills—a snippet of a conversation with a student, a particularly memorable paper, musings in a personal journal about a certain lesson or occasion in the classroom—alone remain a jumble of memories, at times leaving me perplexed as to why the vision still intrudes upon my memory. It is only when I have taken the time to reflect, to rethink, and to rearrange these images that I begin to understand their significance. Over the years, I have taken time to do that with my teaching, composing these images into stories of my classrooms, stories which pull together the fragments as I have tried to connect what at first may have seemed disconnected, as I have searched for the patterns which impose meaning on the individual images.

What I write about in this volume builds and extends upon this metaphor. Just as I have shelves of already completed picture groups arranged chronologically in appropriately titled albums ("Wedding," "Trip to England," "Seth's First Year"), I have composed over the past several years a series of case studies based in my own experiences as a teacher-researcher in various classrooms ("Sarah's Story," "Akemi's Story," "A Collaboratively Taught Class," "A Collaborative Research Project with Susan and John"). Until quite recently, these studies have sat quietly in their files on my computer or have been presented to others in the abridged form of articles and presentations, as separate from each other as those individual albums on the book shelf. Lately, however, I've been thinking about the connections across those case studies, across those albums. Given the perspective that time allows, when I look across my picture albums now, I resee these events whose meaning I created in my painstaking arrangement of particular photographs. I begin to understand in new ways why I put certain pictures together as I did, and, in so doing, I begin to understand some new things about myself as photographer and chronicler of these events. In like manner, as I review the various case studies I have written, I see new things about myself as writer and researcher: themes which emerge across cases, themes which emerge about the act of research itself, growth and change in myself as a researcher. It is only in this act of looking *across* the case studies that I can begin to identify both patterns about the research methodology which I took for granted at the time of conducting the research and also those patterns about myself as researcher, a look which helps me continue my own growth and development.

My colleague Patti Stock suggested that my reflections on my experiences as a classroom researcher sound and read like a history of teacher-research in this country, as many of us who practice research in our own classrooms have changed over time and developed our understandings of what classroom-based research can be. In light of that connection between my story and others, in this book, I try to sift through the photo albums of my classroom research over the past seven years to make a particular point: The practice of teacher-research has a history, a history which can be found in the practices of the individuals who apply its art. I'm not talking here about the history of the movement as described by Susan Lytle and Marilyn Cochran-Smith and others, a history which explains to us the development of teacher-research from Stenhouse onward, a history focused in what the leaders of the movement have inscribed for other practitioners (Cochran-Smith and Lytle, "Research on Teaching"). This history, an important history, seems to me to focus primarily on the theoretical development of teacher-research from Stenhouse to Britton to Goswami: on the theoreticians who work with teachers, look at what the teachers have said, and help to create a theoretical construct from that. As a teacher-researcher, I celebrate this history which has helped shape my own vision of classroom research in vital ways.

But in this essay, I'm talking about another kind of history, a *prosaic* history of teacher-research (to borrow from Louise Phelps)—a history that has been inscribed by those of us who have been doing it even when we didn't always know what we were doing, a down-in-the-trenches discussion of the development of those of us who practice teacher-research and have been influenced by what we read and what we do in the classroom. Important books exist in our history, books which contain a series of practical projects, such as those undertaken by Glenda Bissex, by Nancie Atwell, by the teachers whose work is found in the critical volumes by Goswami and Stillman, Lytle and Cochran-Smith, and

Branscombe, Goswami, and Schwartz. These projects can be seen as the picture albums of the teacher-research movement, the everyday collections of stories and projects that teachers have conducted to make sense of the worlds of the classrooms in which they live. What I will argue here is that projects such as those described in these books, projects conducted by teachers, when seen over time, represent the fascinating change and development of this grass-roots movement in another way, in a way that creates its own history and theory. What I am attempting to do here is reread across one teacher's picture albums—my own—in order to represent some of that history, as I demonstrate the growth and change I have experienced as a member of the teacher-research movement.

Because teacher-research is more than a method—is, in fact, a way of thinking about issues of power and representation and storytelling and much more—its very existence and development are dependent upon our understanding not only of the particular issue we are researching but also of the complexities of the research process itself. My own dynamic development as a teacher-researcher, in other words, has depended not only on my interest in my students' literacy (the subject I have chosen to pursue) but also on my constant reevaluation and rethinking of what it means to conduct research in the way that I do. For many of us who practice classroom-based research, the pertinent issue is no longer one of the relative value of qualitative versus quantitative research, although this debate is an important one and represented a starting point for discussion for many of us. The question is no longer simply a matter of how to make our voices as teacher-researchers more powerful, although that, again, is an important debate and one that many of us see as vital to our work. The issues have changed dramatically over the past few years, to the point where many of us now are looking to the fields of anthropology and various philosophies in order to investigate the very nature of the research experience. As we seek to discover what it means to be a researcher and represent the experience of another, many of us have begun to wonder how this role of representer is integrally tied to issues of power.

Like many teacher-researchers, I believe that our continual posing of new questions in order to develop our understanding of the research process depends largely on the integration of our practical projects with our program of reading. The projects in which I have been involved over the past seven years have taken me into a variety of settings, from rural to urban, and given me the opportunity to work with a number of different students, from high school to college level, from those labeled "basic" to those labeled "gifted." The progam of reading in which I have been simultaneously engaged has taken me into a variety of theoretical discourses: theories in the social sciences, theories in literacy learning and literacy use, theories in feminist studies, as well as theories in teacher-research. My interactions with the people with whom I have been working and the texts I have been reading informed each other: As teacher-researcher I read theoretical texts from a practical perspective; as reader of theoretical texts, I practiced teacher-research from a theoretical perspective.

And so in this book—and particularly in this first chapter—I will share a number of pictures taken from my own albums of teacher-research over the past several years. As I have arranged these images, I have attempted to trace my reflections about teacher-research, both at the time each particular image was inscribed in my memory and at the present time as I see each image in its overall place in my own growth and development. In order to do so, I look at both the practical projects in which I have been involved and the program of reading which paralleled that involvement. Looking carefully now at these understandings, I can see changes particularly in three areas: first, in my shifting comprehension of literacy and literacy education, and especially in how these politically charged terms take shape for students, their teachers, and researchers in terms of form and genre; second, in my shifting stance toward the methods I took on as researcher in order to learn how students understand their literacy and their literacy learning which they described to me in terms of form and genre; and third, in my shifting conceptions of what teacher-research can and—I will argue—should be.

In this first chapter, then, I will overview my experiences as a teacher-researcher, briefly exposing the reader to the classrooms in which I worked, the questions which arose out of my experience in each classroom, and the changes in my own understanding which grew out of my reflections on each project, mingled with the reading I was doing at the time. In subsequent chapters, I offer two additional means for the reader to look with me at these experiences: First, the bulk of each chapter is an actual write-up of a teacher-research project, composed at the time I ended work in each classroom, write-ups which, warts and all, can show the reader the details of my method at various moments in my history as well as the thought processes which informed such method. Second, in pre- and postscripts to each chapter, I point out to the reader certain issues to notice in her reading: issues that I can see *now* as informing ones, issues about method and theory which are reflected in the words of the texts and which have helped me see the complexities of the research process I have undertaken. By exposing readers to both the actual write-ups and my reflections, I hope to show that teacher-research is, more than anything else, an evolving process. The write-ups of the teacher-research studies that we all read (and admire immensely for their depth and confidence) represent a moment in time for their researchers, carefully crafted renditions of the research experience as it seems at the moment. Seldom as teacher-researchers do we have the opportunity to publicly revisit such research: to re-see how we looked at a particular issue, to re-vise the methodology, to re-define the important terms, to be able to say, "Hey, I think differently about that now." But all of us who are reflective about our classroom practices and who take the time to compose our adventures into prose do grow and change and rethink our approaches—such reflection is the very basis of teacher-research. We are not satisfied ultimately with each attempt; we return to the very basis of our method with each new project in our neverending quest to "do better next time," to get close to capturing the spirit of the teaching and learning enterprise in our classroom. By laying out for you here my series of attempts at teacher-research along with my hindsight commentary about what I learned in order to change, I hope to model a way of thinking about classroom research, a model of constant reevaluation that we all need to adopt, I believe, in order to keep this movement alive and evolving.

I ask the reader to see my story, then, as a reflection of the story of many teacher-researchers and to recognize the changes I have made as constitutive of some of the developments many of us have made in this important movement of research and teaching. My hope is that, as you read through these pictures, you will respond in kind with pictures of your own and, in so doing, expand these reflections to make sense in your own lives and worlds.

# THE MANTLE OF RESEARCH: LEARNING TO REMOVE THE ARMOR

A first memory of teaching: August 31, 1980. I am 23 years old. I walk into my first day of high school teaching an hour early, well armed with lesson plans, "Big Blue" (the curriculum guide for the school district), practical ideas gleaned from years of academic training preparing me for this day. As a former English major with a master's degree specializing in the teaching of writing, I know about The Writing Process, New Criticism, Reliability and Validity, Techniques to Reduce the Paperload, and Performance and Behavioral Objectives. Like all new teachers, though, I don't know much about the living and breathing adolescents whom I will meet in 60 short minutes. Soon I will face five different classes of students, all aware that I am The New Teacher. They all know each other well, having survived ten years of other teachers, living in a connected community, a community in which I don't yet have an apartment. I ransacked the closet earlier this morning, changing clothes five times as I searched for the outfit that would best cover my fears and help me project that professional yet friendly persona I kept reading about in college. I have been awake since 4:30 . . . after having fallen asleep at 1:15. I am running on adrenaline and caffeine and I have my carefully prepared lesson plans clutched in my trembling hands as I stand in front of my room, *my room,* with its meager assortment of books and hastily assembled bulletin boards. I am filled with panic.

Every teacher I know now can relate a first-day scenario much like this one which remains indelibly stamped in her brain. Veteran teachers often recall with rueful laughter those first days when the gulf between the theories of academia and the practices of the classroom seemed too wide to ever span. When I think back now to my first years of teaching, the metaphor of armor seems appropriate. As a new teacher, I sank into the safe protection that the armor of my academic training provided. I wore that armor proudly: I had spent energy and time learning the latest techniques and the theoretical rationales, and I kept that knowledge in the forefront, relying on that knowledge to help me through difficult moments in the classroom.

As an undergraduate and graduate student in English Education, I had learned about teaching through the lenses of what Garth Boomer called "Big R research." In course after course I was exposed to studies about teaching and learning conducted by outsiders to the classroom—usually university researchers who used what seemed to me at the time a logical scientific method to conduct their studies. Reading between the lines of their rather dense write-ups, I eventually came to detect a pattern as to how the research was conducted: University professors would start from a hypothesis about how students learn and then look in on some clearly defined slice of the students' school lives for a specific period of time in order to draw some conclusions and suggest some generalizations. Then, after having collected their data, these researchers would return to their own settings—usually the university or some research agency—and write up their results in the form of a study or a grant. Eventually, some of these studies would be translated into teacher texts, how-to books or exercise exchanges loosely based on the original studies.

As an eager devourer of these studies and texts, I took their conclusions to heart, trying to learn as much as I could about these ideas before I began teaching, appreciating the work that had gone into such studies and anxious to try out all that I was learning. I read in detail studies which used control groups and experimental groups to determine the feasibility of one teaching technique over another; I studied papers in which researchers watched children through mirrors so that they would be unobtrusive in their observations so as not to skew the results. And so, as I began teaching, my head was filled with visions of T units and pause time, sentence combining and IRE questioning techniques, all based in sound scientific research. I felt as if I had all the right stuff—now all I had to do was fill the kids up with these great ideas and exercises.

Through all this training I never once thought of myself as someone capable of contributing to this body of research. Mostly I learned how to respond to what was already out there awaiting my consumption. I dutifully memorized the five parts of a research study; I became proficient in distinguishing the reliability and validity of a study; I learned to say "interesting but flawed" when confronted with what I was told were less objective measures of research; I began to speak of contamination as I was taught about the importance of purity of samplings in control and experimental groups. Research, I decided, was something only well-trained, statistics-minded persons (i.e., not me) could conduct.

Within this training, I remember in particular my response when I read for the first time a different kind of research: Janet Emig's *The Composing Processes of Twelfth Graders*. What I saw in that work was Emig's attempt to talk *with* students about their writing, rather than merely to observe them in the ways I had been taught. I saw Emig using the students' own responses as the basis of her unfolding understanding, rather than relying solely on her own reactions. For the first time in these courses filled with statistics and quantitative measurements, I immersed myself in some research that spoke to me in meaningful ways about literacy, in ways I could understand and respond to in kind—but I masked that reaction in keeping with the perspective of the research world in which I was being educated. I convinced myself that Emig's study was an exception, an interesting exception, but certainly not in keeping with the knowledge I was acquiring in my other Ed. school courses.

When I graduated, I was grateful that I was leaving the world of research for one of teaching. Practical measures were more up my alley, I thought. Those studies were interesting and had helped me acquire a battery of techniques, but my interest was in the practice and not the theory. And, as had been drummed into my head, both at a conscious and a subconscious level, ne'er the twain shall meet.

An early introduction to research: December 1982. A note from my supervisor arrives in my classroom asking me to come down to her office during my free period next hour. As my class ends and I walk down the hall, I think about the progress these students are making. In this, my second year of teaching literature and writing, mostly to classes of severely learning-disabled students, I have been trying to adapt the "regular curriculm" in writing to these students whose writing skills are far different from anything I ever studied at the university. I teach 4 classes a day of 10–15 students each, serve as an advisor and counselor to 7 of these students, preparing their IEPs, taking them on field trips, meeting regularly with their families. In addition, I teach an advanced composition course for 30 of the "regular kids." I love this mix of assignments. While my lack of training in learning disabilities appalls me, my training in the teaching of writing has helped me adjust, adapt, introduce these kids to more than the formulaic, mind-dulling curriculum they have been used to in their English classes: filling in forms, writing resumes, answering multiple-choice questions about their reading. I think about the growth Jill and Charlie are making, and I can't wait to tell my supervisor about it. I burst into her office full of excitement. "You'll never guess what Jill did today! She actually participated in a peer group with Charlie and helped him revise his essay. She did a great job asking questions about sentences she didn't understand, and Charlie actually took the critiscism well! And, you know how I got that class of seniors reading *Ordinary People?* Well, yesterday I showed them the movie version of the book and Frank—you know Frank who has never read a book in his life— told me that the movie wasn't nearly as good as the book, because he really imagined the characters differently. So now he's going to write about the differences and why the book characters seemed more real!" My supervisor smiles. "Slow down, Cathy! You know I'm really pleased with the progress you're making with those kids. In fact that's one of the reasons I asked you in here today. I'm thinking about putting together a book about teaching students with learning disabilities, and I was wondering if you'd be interested in writing the section on teaching writing?" I am immediately overwhelmed and panicked. What do I know about this subject? What could I possibly write that anyone else would want to read? I've never even taken a course in learning disabilities; I've just adapted and adjusted as best I could what I know about teaching writing. I plan my approach: After school that day, I 'll drive to the district curriculum library and ask the librarians to help me run an ERIC search about learning disabilities and writing. I know that once I have the ERIC search grasped tightly in my hands, I will feel less panicked. The research skills I learned in my own training will pay off: The studies I'll read will help me formulate some thesis and discussion about the subject, much like those papers I had written that had been emblazoned with *A*'s in my undergraduate and graduate experience.

Looking for research in all the right places had been impressed on me for my entire educational life. And so, when asked to compose an essay about learning-disabled students, I never even considered writing about my own experiences with those forty students whose lives had become now so intertwined with mine. ERIC, I knew, represented "real" research, and I duly believed that the studies I uncovered would tell me more "truth" than anything I might learn from Charlie and Jill and Frank and all the other students I worked with hour after hour, day after day. Like many teachers, I denigrated the reliability of my own lived experience, my own perspective, in favor of the work of researchers who clearly had never set foot in my classroom.

This perspective remained at the forefront of all my teaching in those days. As I continued to teach writing to all levels of students, I tried to put into effect many of the techniques I had learned. When students had trouble writing complex sentences, I pulled out a book of sentence-combining exercises to give them practice. Because I knew about The Writing Process, I required kids to complete a five-step process for every paper, complete with a check list for each step. I pulled out the exercise exchange list that I had developed over the years from the books and journals I had read, and practiced a variety of techniques that I had been told were tried and true.

Some students seemed to "get it"; some students didn't. Some classes were turned on to reading and writing; some weren't. At first, along with many of my colleagues, when a lesson didn't work, I blamed the kids: either they weren't trying hard enough or else they had forgotten everything they had been taught by other teachers. I had worked through these great plans to entertain and instruct; so what was wrong with them that they didn't/wouldn't/couldn't respond?

Blaming the kids got me nowhere, so I turned to blaming teachers: first the other teachers and then myself. "Why didn't the tenth-grade teacher prepare the students better?" I would moan to my sympathetic colleagues. "How can I possibly get students to believe in the writing process when all their other teachers don't even ask them to write?" Finally, I began blaming myself: If I could just write more exciting plans, if I just worked harder preparing good lessons, if I could just write perfect comments on their papers, I could inspire these kids. And I turned back to the lessons I had been taught, desperately desiring that missing element which all the teachers in the books I read seemed to possess.

Eventually, my search for blame shifted to the theorists themselves. I was in good company as I began to develop a them-versus-us mentality. "They" were the ones who developed the theories; "we" were the ones who put the theories into practice. "They" were the ones who got time, grants, and research assistants to conduct their research; "we" were the ones who ran our own dittos, developed lesson plans in the wee hours of the morning, and faced kids hour after hour, day after day. "They," we said in the teachers' lounge quite often, "have no idea what happens in the real world of school. Let them try teaching their theories for a few weeks and they'll see what it's really like."

Not surprisingly, blaming this group did me little good. Even though I felt let down by the theory they had given me, I had nowhere to turn for new theory. As an overwhelmed beginning teacher who poured all my energy into surviving my day, I had no time to read journals or books or to attend conferences, to try to find new theories to replace the ones I was working from. And so, like many of my colleagues, I complained and I cried . . . but I mostly stayed within the ways I had been taught to teach. I felt I had no other choice.

Frustrated by my experiences but still committed to the teaching of writing and anxious to understand how I could do better, I returned to graduate school in 1985. Once there, I began to realize that I did have a choice. As I was introduced to the notion of teacher-research, I saw some hope for connecting the worlds of theory and practice which, up to that point, had seemed closed down to me. I began to see myself as a "kidwatcher," to use Goodman's term, learning to be a theory maker myself as I started to reflect on my own practice and to rely on those reflections to help me understand the unique contexts of the classrooms in which I taught. I learned not to toss out the studies and research on which I had cut my teeth but, rather, to place that research where it belongs: as part of a whole rather than *the* whole, as useful background which might help me begin my own reflection and study of my own local circumstances.

As I learned more about teacher-research, I began to see just how much it differed from the kind of research which had become second nature to me. I learned that more traditional research had been named in a variety of ways by a number of people over the years—as the positivist paradigm, as the natural scientific research model, as decontextualized or separatist research, as "Big R research,"—and had been criticized in an equal number of ways from a variety of stances.[2] For my purposes here, I limit my objections to methodology: to the paradigm's reliance on decontex-

---

[2]Among those who lay out serious critiques of this paradigm from varying perspectives are Donald Schon in *The Reflective Practitioner,* Loren Barritt in "Reflections on a Change of Mind," Valerie Suransky in *The Erosion of Childhood,* and Marcia Westkott in "Feminist Criticisms of the Social Sciences."

ualized studies. Traditional researchers, in order to fulfill their research mission, always seemed to limit what they could talk about in the classrooms they visited. Because they had to strip away as much context as possible in order to isolate some kind of variable (which would then be used to separate a control group from an experimental group), these researchers seemed to focus on one specific or another—in striking contrast to the teachers I knew who had to see the classroom in its contextual fullness. Because classroom teachers recognize that students are multidimensional people who are more than the sum of discrete, isolable variables, they often cannot see the connection between the traditional research of these outsiders and the reality that exists within their classrooms. This fullness of teacher-research appealed to me. Teachers who spend innumerable hours with their students and are responsible and responsive to the teaching and learning which occurs in the classroom seemed to me to be in a better position than visiting researchers to see their students and their classrooms as they really exist: Thus, they are able to complicate and problematize the settings in which they work, able to look into the depth and degree of difference which exist in classrooms.

I began to recognize as well that compounding the problem presented by the difference in understanding between outside researchers and classroom teachers is the value placed on the knowledge each group is able to produce, a difference discussed by Steve North in *The Making of Knowledge in the Field of Composition*. North believes that theory and practice, at least in composition studies, are too often disparate entities: Theory is molded by theorists and researchers who see themselves (and are seen by much of the world) as separate from teachers. Theorists and researchers are granted a status in the world quite different from that of classroom teachers: Theorists and researchers unfortunately are seen as more knowledgeable, more sophisticated, more reliable than teachers, as North tells the story. Teachers' knowledge has too often been relegated to the world of lore, and this world is seen as inhospitable to and intolerant of activities that support legitimate research and theory building.[3]

Teacher-research, with its emphasis on *context-full* study, works toward debunking this notion. Convinced that educational

---

[3]For an intriguing discussion of the connection between theory and practice and its relation to teacher-research, see Ruth Ray's *The Practice of Theory: Teacher Research in Composition*.

research must account for the multidimensional and multifaceted nature of teaching and learning, the movement believes that classroom teachers are uniquely positioned to conduct such studies. Present day in and day out, teachers are able to observe classrooms in their fullness: They are able to observe their teaching and their students' learning, and are able to reflect productively on the relationships between that teaching and that learning. When teachers observe at a local level the situations of concern for them in their own lived worlds, they call their own horizons into question. By first looking critically at their particular experiences as teachers in particular classrooms, and by then reflecting on recurring themes in those particular experiences in order to make sense of the complex world that exists in their classrooms, teacher-researchers prepare themselves to create worthwhile learning environments, to develop purposeful curricula, to devise productive methods of teaching. Such practice is what Paulo Freire calls "praxis": critical reflection and action that changes conditions of being in the world.

The teacher-research movement looks to define the research paradigm differently from the separatist scenario: Teachers in classrooms research themselves and their students, and accordingly make appropriate changes in their own classrooms. The assumption underlying this stance is that teachers who are intimately involved in the complex context of the classroom are best able to see into the dynamics in it. The implication of such a stance, then, is one that elevates the status of teachers and equates their theory-making ability with that of researchers.[4]

After my initial excitement about discovering this new movement, I was surprised to find out it was not such a new movement after all. I learned teacher-research had a history of its own, first becoming popular among teachers in Great Britain in the 1960s. I read Jon Nixon's important book, *A Teacher's Guide to Action Research,* and in particular John Eliot's foreword, which chronicles the rise of what he calls the teachers-as-researchers or action research movement and which credits Lawrence Stenhouse as the "formative influence" behind such movement.[5] Stenhouse became

---

[4]The issues raised here are discussed further in Patricia Stock's forthcoming book *The Rhetoric and Poetics of Education.*

[5]Cochran-Smith and Lytle, in their discussion of the history of the teacher-research movement, note its roots in action research in the 1950s and 1960s. They mention in particular Lewin and Corey as two whose work "presented an implicit

a champion of teachers in schools as he directed a number of projects which celebrated the presence of teachers as contributors to the research community. He encouraged teachers to study curriculum issues in their own schools and to publish papers and speak at conferences about their findings. Stenhouse critiqued the control of educational research by outside researchers practicing what he termed the "psycholostatistical paradigm"; he called instead for the establishment of a different kind of paradigm, that of action-oriented research. In his view, action research promoted the role of teachers as theory makers because of their intimate knowledge of the inner workings of the classroom, leading to teachers taking on new roles as the driving forces for change in the schools. He believed the relationship between teachers and researchers, then, had to change as well as the relationship between theory and practice. He believed that "teachers must inevitably be intimately involved in the research process. . . . [R]esearchers must justify themselves to practitioners, not practitioners to researchers" (Ruddock and Hopkins 19). In addition, he saw the new role of research as that of "producing theory which can enrich action" (28), action which benefits both teachers and students. As Stenhouse says, "Action research in education rests upon the designing of procedures in schools which meet both action criteria and research criteria, that is, experiments which can be justified both on the grounds of what they teach teachers and researchers and on the grounds of what they teach pupils" (29).

As I read about Stenhouse, I turned with growing enthusiasm to his counterparts in the United States: Goswami and Berthoff, Shaughnessy and Heath, Paley and Atwell. I learned about the networks of teacher-researchers that had arisen in this country: the National Writing Project, the Bread Loaf School of English, Marion Mohr's program for teacher-researchers at George Mason University, and, more recently, Janet Miller's work with teachers in the New York area. I was particularly struck by Goswami's survey of teacher-research which led her to notice certain common characteristics among those teachers who conduct research in their own classrooms:

---

critique of the usefulness of basic research for social change," although they acknowledge Stenhouse as one of the most "influential" interpreters of action research (4–5).

1.  Their teaching is transformed in important ways: they become theorists, articulating their intentions, testing their assumptions, and finding connections with practice.
2.  Their perceptions of themselves as writers and teachers are transformed. They step up their use of resources; they form networks; and professionally they become more active.
3.  They become rich resources who can provide the profession with information it simply doesn't have. They can observe closely, over long periods of time, with special insights and knowledge . . .
4.  They become critical, responsive readers and users of current research, less apt to accept uncritically others' theories, less vulnerable to fads, and more authoritative in their assessment of curricula, methods, and materials.
5.  They can study writing and learning and report their findings without spending large sums of money (although they must have support and recognition) . . .
6.  They collaborate with their students to answer questions important to both, drawing on community resources in new and unexpected ways . . .  (Goswami and Stillman, preface)

I was sold. As I read these articles and articles by other authors, I began to think carefully about how I, too, might become a teacher-researcher. Ann Berthoff, for example, taught me to see the value in pronouncing " 'research' the way the southerners do: REsearch,"; she taught me the value of rejecting ERIC as the primary source of understanding my students and to look instead in a serious manner at the information I had gathered from the students themselves. She writes, "REsearch, like REcognition, is a REflexive act. It means looking—and looking again. This new kind of REsearch would not mean going out after new 'data' but rather REconsidering what is at hand" (Goswami and Stillman 30).

Lucy Calkins taught me the difficulty but importance of trying to make the familiarity of the classroom unfamiliar in order that I might see what was occurring before my eyes. She recalls her first occasion as a researcher in a classroom, an incident which became quite real for me during my first few attempts at making the familiar unfamiliar:

On my second day as a researcher, Don Graves joined me in Pat Howard's third-grade classroom. The children weren't writing, but Graves suggested we stay. I paced up and down the rows. The kids were all copying things out of their math books. I anxiously waited for someone to *do something* so I could gather some data. But no, they just kept on copying out of those math books. I went to the back of the room and leaned against the radiator to wait for some data to appear. Nothing. Finally I signaled to Graves, who'd been scurrying about, and we left.

Before I could let out a quiet groan, Graves burst out with, "What a gold mine! Wasn't it amazing? How'd you suppose that one kid up front could write with a two-inch pencil? And that guy with the golf ball eraser on the end of his pen. Zowie." In his enthusiasm, Graves didn't notice my silence. . . .

I had learned a big lesson. The task of case-study research is to make the familiar unfamiliar. (9–10)

Vivian Paley taught me to try to see the world through the eyes of my students, to accept and explore their logic, their "magical thinking," as a key to understanding their perceptions of the classroom. She tells us about the "remarkable point of view" to which children can expose us—if we care enough to listen and watch:

WALLY: People don't feel the same as grown-ups.
TEACHER: Do you mean "Children don't"?
WALLY: Because grown-ups don't remember when they were little. They're already an old person. Only if you have a picture of you doing that. Then you could remember.
EDDIE: But not thinking.
WALLY: You never can take a picture of thinking. Of course not. (4)

Reflecting on this exchange, Paley writes:

You can, however, write a book about thinking—by recording the conversations, stories, and playacting that take place as events and problems are encountered. A wide variety of thinking emerges, as morality, science, and society share the stage with fantasy. If magical thinking seems most conspicuous, it is because it is the common footpath from which new trails are explored. I have learned not to resist this magic but to seek it out as a legitimate part of "real" school. (4)

Nancie Atwell taught me to have the courage to allow what I learned from this kind of research to be a catalyst for change in my classroom. She recounts her first exposure, and first resistance, to some ideas shared with her by another teacher-researcher, Susan Sowers:

> I kept Susan at our school much later that day than she intended
> to stay, explaining the reasons her findings couldn't possibly
> apply to me and my students. All that week I continued to ex-
> plain, to anyone who would listen, how Sowers advocated topic
> anarchy. But on my free periods and in the evening, I read and
> reread the manuscripts she'd shared. And I saw through my
> defenses to the truth: I didn't know how to share responsibility
> with my students, and I wasn't too sure I wanted to. . . .
>
> What I did, finally, was to put the question to my students:
> "Children in an elementary school in New Hampshire are choos-
> ing their own topics for writing. Could you do this? Would you
> like to?" Resoundingly, they said yes, and the underground cur-
> riculum surfaced. (*In The Middle* 179–180)

Through these and other works, I learned to appreciate teachers' depictions and analyses of their classrooms as well as the variety of genres in which teachers shared the results of their research
with others. From Paley's not-so-simple telling of stories to Calkins'
analytical case-study research, to Atwell's curriculum design,
teachers inscribed their "study of cases," as Stenhouse suggested
they might. In their various and accumulating presentations, these
teacher-researchers helped me to form the beginnings of an argument: that context-based studies could provide a vision of classrooms and students that teachers to this point had been unable to
glean from studies conducted by professional researchers in classrooms. Research conducted by teachers, I discovered, might lead
quickly to soundly reasoned changes in pedagogy; teachers can
empower themselves intellectually and politically as they present
their research in the academic community. Instead of the separatist
research scenario I had been trained to embrace, I began to imagine my classroom as a place where theory and practice might become one, where teachers might become researchers and researchers might become teachers to the benefit of them both and,
more importantly, to the the benefit of students.


## LEARNING NEW WAYS: THE WINKS UPON WINKS UPON
## WINKS OF ETHNOGRAPHY

When I began graduate school in English and Education, I assumed that I would be reading into fields traditionally associated
with that subject area: composition studies, critical theory, reading

development, and literary theory, for example. Because of my growing interest in teacher-research and through the encouragement of my professors, I began to read in areas that at first seemed strange to me: philosophy, anthropology, and feminist studies, among others. I was surprised to find strong connections between the methodologies which informed these fields of study and teacher-research. And so, like many learning teacher-researchers, I became intrigued by the variety of disciplines that were influencing its development as a research movement. Like other teachers interested in doing context-based research, I began to read into interpretive anthropology and to explore ethnographic research methods because such methods emphasize the value of local knowledge and thick description, of coming to understand an event from the point of view of the participants in that event. I did so mindful of Mohr and Maclean's caution about the differences that exist between the methodology of ethnography and that employed by teacher-researchers:

> Ethnographers are new to and separate from the situations they enter. For them distance is the starting point. . . . Teacher-researchers deal with the same participant-observer role tension, but for them the starting point is one of participation, not observation—immersion, not distance. (55)

My caution attracted me to the kind of ethnography practiced by one of anthropology's leading—if controversial—spokesmen, Clifford Geertz, who offered me much in the way of understanding how to do contextual study.

I learned that cultural anthropologists like Geertz believe that the best means of learning about a particular culture is through intimate involvement in that culture, by listening to the people who make up a particular community and by trying to represent their voices in as complete a fashion as possible, always highlighting the complicated contextual nature of such local knowledge. Traditionally, these anthropologists rely on the researcher becoming a participant-observer in a particular world and learning—somehow—to balance the attempt to establish a close relationship with those one is observing in order to truly understand the world from their point of view, with the attempt to retain enough distance from those informants in order to comment on them as others. Traditionally, then, ethnographic research becomes a constant ping-pong game of getting close and stepping back, getting close and stepping back, as one carefully tries to maintain that balance. Geertz talks of this distinction in terms of experience-near and experience-distant concepts:

> An experience-near concept is, roughly, one that someone—a patient, a subject, in our case an informant—might himself naturally and effortlessly use to define what he or his fellows see, feel, think, imagine, and so on, and which he would readily understand when similarly applied by others. An experience-distant concept is one that specialists of one sort or another—an analyst, an experimenter, an ethnographer, even a priest or an ideologist—employ to forward their scientific, philosophical, or practical aims. (*Local Knowledge* 57)

Geertz believes in the blending of the two roles, but he stresses that in order to come to "see things from the native's point of view," one needs to consider the implication of each role. He continues:

> Confinement to experience-near concepts leaves an ethnographer awash in immediacies, as well as entangled in vernacular. Confinement to experience-distant ones leaves him stranded in abstractions and smothered in jargon. . . . To grasp concepts that, for another people, are experience-near, and to do so well enough to place them in illuminating connection with experience-distant concepts theorists have fashioned to capture the general features of social life, is clearly a task at least as delicate, if not a bit less magical, as putting oneself into someone else's skin. The trick is not to get yourself into some inner correspondence of spirit with your informants. . . . The trick is to figure out what the devil they think they are up to. (*Local Knowledge* 57–58)

This figuring out "what the devil they think they are up to" becomes essentially the ethnographer's task.

In order to perform this task, Geertz rejects the usual description of ethnography as merely methodology. Instead he refers to this process of "doing ethnography" as a kind of "intellectual effort . . . an elaborate adventure" (*Works and Lives* 6), a way of inscribing social discourse—that is, reading the situation and then writing down events in human lives as they occur. "Doing ethnography is like trying to read . . . a manuscript," he believes, "foreign, faded, full of ellipses, incoherences, suspicious emendations, and tendentious commentaries, but written not in conventionalized graphs of sound but in transient examples of shaped behavior" (*Interpretation of Cultures* 10). Ethnography in this sense is a process of coming to understand not merely what the people of a community say but rather what they mean—a distinction that is often difficult to ascertain.

As an English teacher well-trained in the reading of literary texts, I was struck by those ethnographers who talked about their work as an elaborate adventure and as more than the usual ethnographic tactics I saw outlined in many of the numerous volumes proclaiming the answer to "how to become an ethnographer": selecting informants, establishing rapport with them, keeping field notes, transcribing conversations, and so on. Geertz, in contrast, helped me see that doing ethnography is a semiotic undertaking, well-described for me in two terms he has popularized: "deep play" and "thick description." Deep play, in Geertz's terms, is a metaphor for the meanings which lie beneath the surface of some everyday event, the deep meanings which can only be gotten at through looking and relooking and relooking at the actions and talk of a particular group of people. In other words, the words and actions of the people one is observing carry meaning other than what one would grasp from a surface reading. To use Geertz's own example, borrowed from Gilbert Ryle, one has to look beneath the surface to come to understand the difference between a twitch and a wink. Thick description becomes the means of getting at such deep play, the way in which an ethnographer looks and relooks at a particular setting. By thickly describing in minute detail an everyday phenomenon—such as a wink—and thus placing that phenomenon in its full context, one is constantly looking beneath surface meanings, continually analyzing, thematizing, and explicating. As Geertz tells us,

> the point is that between . . . the "thin description" of doing what the rehearser (parodist, winker, twitcher) . . . is doing ("rapidly contracting his right eyelid") and the "thick description" of what he is doing ("practicing a burlesque of a friend faking a wink to deceive an innocent into thinking a conspiracy is in motion") lies the object of ethnography: a stratified hierarchy of meaningful structures in terms of which twitches, winks, fake-winks, parodies, rehearsals of parodies are produced, perceived, and interpreted, and without which they would not . . . in fact exist. (*Interpretation of Cultures* 7)

Enough of this kind of thick description allows ethnographers to begin to construct a rich if partial picture of a culture. Because we always assign meaning to events in the everyday lives of ourselves and others, Geertz believes there is, in fact, no other way to look at a culture: "Right down at the factual bone, the hard rock, in so far as there is any, of the whole enterprise, we are already explicating: and worse, explicating explications. Winks upon winks upon winks" (*Interpretation of Cultures* 9).

As I read and responded to the ideas raised in my reading into ethnography, I began to imagine myself as a particular kind of teacher-researcher, trying as best I could to understand the winks upon winks upon winks that occurred in the classrooms in which I was involved. And as a graduate student, I was fortunate enough to be involved in a number of classrooms, from my own introductory composition class at the university where I was studying to several classrooms in the two Saginaw, Michigan, high schools whose teachers and administrators were participating in a unique university–school collaboration.[6] In the winter of 1986, I began in earnest an initial research project in one of the Saginaw schools. In this project I became a participant-observer, shadowing a high school sophomore named Akemi, attending classes with her and observing her responses to the varied writing tasks she was asked to complete. Akemi, a bright young woman, volunteered to take part in this project to help me see her school world. As someone accustomed to being in classrooms, I was pretty confident when I entered her school world that I would recognize what I saw there and have an easy time interpreting it. After all, I thought, schools are schools. But as I describe more completely in chapter 2, Akemi's school world was a far cry from the schools I had attended as a student and taught in as a teacher: 95 percent minority students, understaffed, understocked, filled with students and teachers whose culture was in many ways quite different from mine. Not only was my familiar world of school made unfamiliar by my attempt to see through the eyes of a student rather than as a teacher, it was made unfamiliar merely by the traditions and expecta-

---

[6]This farreaching collaborative project, under the auspices of the Center for Educational Improvement through Collaboration at the University of Michigan, has influenced the Saginaw schools in a number of ways. Teachers and administrators from Saginaw have worked with teachers and administrators from the University of Michigan since 1985 and have formed ongoing teacher-research groups which have revised the English curriculum in the schools and reconceived the ways of assessing student literacy among other projects. For more information on this collaboration, see Jay L. Robinson's *Conversations on the Written Word* and Patricia L. Stock's forthcoming book *The Dialogic Curriculum*.

tions which differed from those which surrounded my own school experiences.

And so, as I entered these classrooms with Akemi, I was quite conscious of embracing the notions of teacher-research and ethnography to which I had been exposed: I formulated a research question but let the question change as I became better versed in the deep play in the particular school setting in which this particular student and I moved around together; as I wrote in my log, I focused on context and tried to thickly describe in vivid detail one student's world; I gathered data from multiple sources, such as Akemi's own writing, my own observation notes, transcripts of our discussions, and transcripts of the classes we attended in order to create a new semiotic space—the school as seen through the eyes of a student. Although I was not a teacher of the student I shadowed—and some would say therefore not a teacher-researcher—I thought myself at that point in my work to be a teacher-as-researcher. I looked at Akemi's world from the perspective of a teacher who was trying to see through the eyes of a student, from the perspective of a committed teacher who was pausing for the moment to learn more about the experiences of a student like the students she had taught. My stance was that of teacher-researchers I had been reading, even if my role was not quite theirs.

When I began to look to Akemi's school world, I began to do REsearch as Ann Berthoff suggested it should be done. I saw into Akemi's world from perspectives gained in my own worlds: the world I had occupied as a high school teacher of language arts, the world I occupied as a college teacher of introductory composition courses, and the world I occupied as a graduate student. What surprised me perhaps should not have done so. When Berthoff told me that my research would have me "REconsider . . . what is at hand," I assumed I would reconsider the world I moved through with Akemi. And, of course, I did that. But I also reconsidered the worlds of my high school teaching, my university teaching, and my reading program. In light of my research experience with Akemi, I found ways to think about my own exposure to issues of literacy in the terms I was remembering from my past experience and discovering from my reading program as a graduate student. As Akemi spoke to me about the writing she was doing, her definitions of the various kinds of writing she practiced seemed to fall into generic categories. Although the ways in which she named the forms of expression she composed differed from my own prior thinking about ways of naming pieces of writing, I began to see connections between her experience in school and my own teaching.

As a high school teacher, I had been involved in the design of a new curriculum for the two writing courses to which all teachers and students in my large district had to subscribe. In that design I worked hard with other teachers to lay out a program of study which moved students from what we named as descriptive and narrative essays, to summary-analyses, followed by compare/contrast essays, and eventually to the research paper—in other words, to lay out a writing program which required students to exercise specifically defined forms of writing. As a teaching assistant when I was a graduate student, I started to rethink this design. Required, as all first year TA's were, to use a particular textbook, one which advanced a conception of writing instruction in similar—in fact, more rigidly defined—categorizations, I found myself hesitant and unprepared when students pushed me to explain the difference between an Analysis Essay and a Synthesis Essay, the two final types of writing I was supposed to teach. The more I looked at these forms, the less convinced I was that inviting writing in response to these categories was an appropriate means of expanding students' literacy. Furthermore, the program of reading which I had begun in my graduate studies was reinforcing my uneasiness. When Ann Berthoff labeled such instruction as "the muffin tin" approach, (*The Making of Meaning*) and Knoblauch and Brannon called form merely "ceremonial discourse," (*Rhetorical Traditions*) I found their claims persuasive in light of my own experience, and I found their terms unsettling. Was the teaching I and others were doing as impoverished as their terms implied? I grew increasingly convinced that form-based writing instruction was not a generative way of teaching for the students who had experienced it. I saw this kind of form-based instruction as limiting and limited, forcing students to package ideas in particular ways and discouraging them from using writing as a way toward discovering new meanings.

It was just at this time, when I was questioning a form-based definition of writing instruction, that I began to work with Akemi. The terms in which she described her writing experiences to me reinforced my own experience and reading. Akemi talked to me about the distinctions she saw between the writing she did at home for herself and that which she did at school for others, and about still other distinctions among the kinds of writing she did for different teachers within the school day. As I lay out in the case study I have written of Akemi in chapter 2, these differences became quite complicated for her, but the terms in which she was able to talk about them were formal terms, generic terms. Akemi spoke of writing in school as essays, reports, summaries, and outlines, forms she identified as constraining exploration and thinking; she spoke of writing at home as stories, poems, letters, and diaries, forms she identified as inviting exploration and thinking. Some might protest that what Akemi was seeing in a negative light as differences resulting in limitations was in actuality a reflection of her clear understanding of the rhetorical nature of all writing tasks: how one writes depends on the particular audience, purpose, and occasion of that writing, and students who learn to make shifts in writing for different teachers and from home to school are becoming well prepared as writers. I would be the first to argue that students do need to be sensitive to the rhetorical constraints that define all writing tasks, that they do need to write differently for different occasions, different audiences, different purposes. What Akemi helped me to see, though, through her own depictions of her writing, were not the constraints but the restraints that school instruction placed on her writing and how those restraints led her to think that school writing was different in kind from the writing she did at home. At home she wrote to explore, to make sense of her lived world, to accomplish certain real tasks she set for herself, the kinds of uses for writing one would expect schools and school teachers to require. Instead, Akemi showed me how most students were being told that they were only capable of writing in the specific ways their teachers had already modeled for them and that to move beyond a certain prescribed form, even for good reasons, was out of the question. On one occasion, for example, Akemi's English teacher instructed the class to write a four-paragraph essay with an introduction and three paragraphs of proof but to leave out a concluding paragraph since "you haven't yet learned how to write those." For Akemi, this kind of message struck deeply; as I explore in my case study, her separation of in-school writing and out-of-school writing forced her to devalue the former if it broke across the rigid line she had erected between the two. In other words, the perception of form-based writing she began to learn was one that disallowed much variation and not only restricted her opportunities for expanding her literacy in school but also led her to form a limited notion of the literacy she might exercise for personal reasons.

## ONE FOOT IN EACH WORLD: WHAT KIND OF RESEARCHER AM I ANYWAY?

If my work with Akemi was supporting the lessons I had learned from my experience and my reading about the relationship of form to literacy instruction, my actual experience as teacher-as-researcher was not supporting in similar ways my reading in that field, nor was it supporting my best intentions of what teacher-research could be. While I realized that some of the problems arose from my role of teacher-as-researcher, other problems emerged from the very nature of the research that I and many other teacher-researchers were espousing. These problems resulted, it seemed to me, from the gap that existed between the research principles Stenhouse, Geertz, and others were advocating and the research principles we teachers have inherited from more traditional researchers in education. It began to become clear to me that the old ways of thinking don't die easily. For a time I found myself with one foot in each world, concerned about telling the story of my experience with Akemi but mindful of issues of validity and reliability. I believed this new kind of research I was doing was important for me, but I wondered how it would "count," not only in the real world of Big R research, but also in the small world of my own teaching and colleagues. Would what I learned from this experience help me in teaching other students to write, or was this first "study of cases" too isolated an undertaking to do any real good?

> An early bout of insecurity, May 1987: I am writing about my work with Akemi as the written portion of one of my doctoral exams, an exam in the area of research methods. I thought this exam would be easy, given the amount of reading I've been doing and my hands-on experiences as a beginning researcher with Akemi. But as I write the exam, filling the pages with uplifting words about the power of teacher-research, one moment with Akemi that happened a few weeks ago keeps haunting me. She was writing for a district wide assement on the subject of stress, and I was sitting right next to her, observing her and anxious to

read what she wrote. Immediately after the assessment session ended, Akemi handed me her essay, a piece I read with increasing glee as I saw her breaking down some of the form barriers she had been constructing for herself over the term, barriers we had talked about in some depth as I've been striving to understand why these barriers exist for her. Ready to clap her on the back for this work, I turned for a moment to the content of the piece, content which mostly revolved around her difficulty in responding to this prompt since she claimed that she really rarely, if ever, feels stress, except, that is, for the present occasion. "Right now I do have a small fear," she wrote. "The fear is that I am sitting here and writing on stress and I have absolutely nothing to write about. Cathy . . . is sitting here ready to read what I have wrote and yet I have written nothing." I panicked. Did my presence there actually contribute to Akemi's blocking on her assessment? Despite the close relationship we have begun to develop, did Akemi still see herself as the object of my scrutiny, an object whose meaning-making role is clearly denied? And now as I get ready for this exam, I am angry. Why haven't I read about anything like this in all those books about teacher-research I have pored over for over a year? Why do the issues which seem so clear to the researchers in those books become so confusing for me? As I turn back to the exam, I reflect upon this confusion I am feeling about my own role as researcher, and the words flow out of my pen:

> . . . This, of course, feeds into a larger theoretical issue of the observer's intrusion into the participant's life and the situation we create by that entrance. If I as a researcher ask Akemi about her drafts, she may feel compelled to change her normal writing process to measure up to some standards she thinks I hold. . . . How aware can we be as researchers that the results of our hard work are not borne almost solely for our benefit? How can we distinguish between what the student would "normally" do and what the student does while we are present?

Factored into this is that we do have an underlying purpose in any research that we undertake in the schools. As a literacy worker and student of composition, I believe there are some better ways than others to teach students to write. As a "neutral" observer, that notion obviously colors my perspective; as a new friend of Akemi, it sometimes makes our "professional" relationship difficult: I want to "suggest" ways to help her improve her writing (and she sometimes looks to me to help in that role), which makes me feel torn about my own

> purpose in conducting this research. Is my job simply to sup-
> ply an anecdotal description of the literacy environment in
> this high school from Akemi and Cathy's perspective? Or is it
> to effect change in one student? or in an entire system? . . .
> How can I separate my participant self from my observer self
> to write about the experience in ways which will be read
> kindly and seriously and help effect some change?

I later began to see more clearly that the issues I had raised that spring are some of the issues basic to teacher-research. Like many teacher-researchers, I began to wonder about the very nature of the methodology I was practicing. My two concerns at that point seemed to be these: First, was I getting too close to Akemi, and was our developing relationship somehow contaminating my research findings? Did my eagerness to see how she was progressing actually hinder her ability to write an essay for the assessment? And second, should the research I was practicing be isolated from her world? If she did write that assessment essay in a different form from her usual approach because of the questions I had been asking her, was that appropriate? Should any change appropriately arise from the work I had so painstakingly done? And I felt torn as I worked to answer my own questions: I knew that talking with Akemi about her writing was important, whether that changed her subsequent writing or not; and, yes, underneath the mask of re-searcher I had donned, I hoped that our talk would effect some positive changes for Akemi. I also knew that if I talked with other teachers in Akemi's school about what I was learning from Akemi, this talk might result in changes in some classrooms, but it might also result in less desirable consequences as well. These teachers had graciously opened the doors of their classrooms to me, and many of them had become my friends. How could I then critique what I had seen? Despite assurances from a number of the sources I had read that teacher-research should result in change and that I should stop thinking not only in terms of contamination, re-liability, and validity but also in terms of the potential displeasure of colleagues, I found myself still questioning the integrity of the research I was doing.

What began to trouble me was what seemed to be a mixed message in much of what I was learning from my reading of books and essays written about teacher-research. I was convinced that many of the so-called teacher-researchers were, like me, still situated in two worlds. Despite the almost inspirational tone of the messages delivered by the believers in the power of teacher-research and despite their insistence on contextual study, much of the movement remained mired in both the attitudes and assumptions, if not the methods, of the world of decontextualized research.

Consider for a moment these passages from Miles Myers's 1985 book *The Teacher-Researcher: How to Study Writing in the Classroom:*

> A matrix or diagram can also be used to plan process/procedure studies. In figure 2, for example, a writing sample can be located at four different points on the matrix. The vertical line represents time for composing and prewriting, two different points, and the horizontal line represents processing strategies, one point to the left for the size of sentence encoding and one point to the right for the size of discourse encoding. (11)

> The write-up of the study should begin with some background about why the issue or question of the study became important to you in your classroom. It is important at this point to cite the insights of other classroom teachers whose previous work, whether in the form of teacher research, lunchroom conversation, or ditto sheets, has been helpful. . . . In addition, the write-up should explicitly describe the design of the study, and enough data should be made available so that the reader can make some kind of independent judgment of the results. If possible, always attach samples of student work. (24–25)

To this day I can recall the confusion I felt upon reading these passages and others in Myers' book. As an avid reader and fan of the important work Myers had contributed to composition studies, I searched for ways to resolve the disparity between what I was reading here and my developing understanding of what teacher-research could be. Myers' language here and in other passages reminds me now, as it did then, of the separatist research scenario which most teacher-researchers say they are trying to move away from. How could I fit these recommendations in with the critique those like Stenhouse had posed? I saw Myers' language as contradictory to the other lessons I was learning, as he described writing up a piece of teacher research according to the genres and forms made popular by the psychostatistical paradigm: a research report, complete with a section reviewing the literature, explaining the design and identifying "the limitations and unanswered questions in the study" (25). Myers' work, at that moment in time, ignored the alternative ways of thinking about research advocated by Stenhouse, Berthoff, Geertz, and others. And because his work was (and still is) a well-known NCTE publication, and thus presumably much read by teachers like me attempting to try out such work on our own, it promoted a kind of teacher research which conformed to the conduct and presentation of the more traditional educational research paradigm. Where did this leave conscientious teacher-researchers struggling to find other meaningful genres in which to present their own studies, genres that allow for context-full presentations in the forms and language such presentations imply?[7]

As I came to see this inherent contradiction in the work of some teacher-researchers, I began to ask why this kind of double-speak existed in our language and ultimately in our practice. Why was it that those of us who were striving to create a new kind of knowledge in a new way continued (and still continue) to find ourselves so often a part of the two worlds? Would we not end up being voiceless in each? I began to see that what Knoblauch and Brannon call "the claims to authority" rested then in the hands of those whose very language and mode of presentation conformed to genres and conventions reminiscent of decontextualized research. Even today, those who are most often "allowed" to contribute to "the making of knowledge in composition" are those researchers who present their findings in familiar genres. McDermott and Hood discuss this problem in terms of those who claim to practice educational ethnography, claiming that although many ethnographic researchers in education are committed in name to the goals of capturing reality by contextualizing the subjects and objects of their study, they are limited in what they can even see. Following the argument of various social constructionists, McDermott and Hood claim the language community of which we are a part constructs for us a view of the world. They argue that many educational researchers who work as ethnographers are stuck in polarized positions because the language of educational psychology in which they have been trained and which has thus become

---

[7]I must reiterate that Myers continues to contribute an exceptional amount to composition studies; despite my disgruntled response to this publication, I remain a big fan of his work.

second nature to them shapes what they can see and know and say. Thus, "ethnographers continue to allow educational psychology to define research problems, to set limits on what can be studied competently by ethnographers, and even to dictate some key theoretical concepts" (232). McDermott and Hood critique those engaged in ethnographic studies of schools from the perspective of educational psychology. Such researchers attempt the irreconcilable: They consider the problem, see the data, and write up their studies in terms that cannot represent their understanding. In fact, their efforts are confounded from the outset, because the language of educational psychology from which they begin does not enable them to employ purposefully the ethnographic methods of study they say they are adopting. Similarly, when those of us committed to the ideas of teacher-research allow the psychostatistical paradigm to influence our approach to thinking about issues of composition, we are bound to feel a split. Those who try to take on the language and the stance of context-full researchers must constantly wage a battle within themselves: to stop thinking like Big R researchers.

In addition to the educational training of those conducting it, there are other reasons for the mixed methods and metaphors of teacher-research, particularly at the time. Most published research in education in the 1980s was composed by researchers practicing in the psychostatistical tradition. Furthermore, classroom teachers at the secondary school level, working with 150 students a day in addition to performing bus duty, hall duty, lunchroom duty, and so forth, who did manage to find the time to compose the findings of their research for publication, had a difficult time getting published if they didn't shape their research in the forms familiar to conference planners and journal editors. The mismatch between the conduct and substance of teachers' research and the established forms and genres for presenting research both discouraged and prevented classroom teachers from publishing. Steve North points out that "the format and length of Research journal articles have been determined by the Experimental tradition. Knowledge has to be packaged, as it were, in paradigmatically acceptable units, a form to which Ethnography's fictions obviously don't lend themselves" (313). North aptly names a number of studies described as ethnographies by their authors that were compromised by the authors' presentations of their findings. In this situation, it is not surprising that a thirty-page narrative in which a teacher thickly describes her classroom, raises more questions than she answers, and fails to achieve closure in terms of "suggestions for further research" was a rarity in journals or conferences at the time.[8]

Even more serious perhaps than the fact that teacher-researchers found it difficult to find forms and forums in which to publish their work at this time were conditions that hindered their potential to develop and grow as a research community. In their vitriolic article, "Knowing Our Knowledge: A Phenomenological Basis for Teacher Research," Knoblauch and Brannon show how the separatist researchers who controlled the creation of knowledge in education maintained that control. They recount the occasion of one group's proposal to house the Center for the Study of Writing several years ago, a proposal asking for funds to support teacher-based inquiry. In the National Institute of Education's refusal of that proposal, the NIE explained its reasoning:

> "The conception of practitioners as researchers," the NIE letter read, "and of the related activities involved in empowering teachers and practitioners is an untested idea, one that is labeled an 'ideology.' As such, reviewers feel it to be a suitable subject for research but not appropriate as the guiding assumption on which to conceive a research center." (7)

Knoblauch and Brannon go on:

> In other words, teachers' activities in the classroom can legitimately be scrutinized by "research experts" who possess the requisite methodological sophistication and "objectivity," but teachers themselves have no equivalent expertise in the making of knowledge or ability to reflect on their teaching practices. (7)

And again they quote from the NIE letter: "The feasibility of theory and model-building with such a practitioner-oriented approach is, thus, questioned. Discussions about 'research into practice' issues lack sufficient understanding of the complexities associated with improving teacher knowledge, creating . . . change, and improving practice" (7).

---

[8]Some happy exceptions to this generalization are arising more and more: two excellent examples are found in recent issues of *English Education:* the first an 84-page ethnographic study of teachers and students by Denny Taylor, the second a personal journey by Jenifer Smith.

As Knoblauch and Brannon point out, this letter reveals a number of "appalling assumptions":

> that "real" science is comprised of "model-building" and "testing"; that only "real" scientists, not teachers, understand the complexities of the world they study (even if they then proceed to overlook those complexities by stripping context from their carefully controlled experiments); and that teachers are merely "ideological" when they speak of making knowledge from their classroom experience, while "real" science is intrinsically un-ideological because its methods and conclusions lie . . . beyond even the messy phenomenal world it undertakes to observe. (7)

NIE's review of this proposal, the problems of publication raised by North and by McDermott and Hood, and my concerns about my own teacher-research awakened me to the issues of power involved in the creation and dissemination of information in education. Is it any wonder that classroom teachers like me felt unable to participate in research in education when the NIE didn't believe that teachers have the ability to be theory-makers and when educational ethnographers believed that their work had to be composed in terms and formats inconsistent with its purposes if it were to be published? I still remember, for example, my dismay and confusion when, newly excited by the potential for teacher-research, I opened up Arthur Applebee's "Musings" in the February 1987 issue of *Research in the Teaching of English,* a journal he co-edited:

> The classroom teacher is inevitably an imperfect researcher—the agendas of the classroom are too different, and the daily demands too pressing, to expect most of us to be both researcher and teacher at the same time. When we try, the two roles may even conflict—the detached, observational stance of the researcher intruding upon the teacher's need to make immediate decisions about how to respond to and shape the emerging life of the classroom. (7)

I continue to feel that same dismay when I talk to a number of researchers, parents, school board members, and even teachers, about the issue of "what counts" as research, "what counts" as theory, "what counts" as a basis for our restructuring and reseeing curriculum. Inevitably, what counts is what has been traditionally seen as "real research."

## FUSING HORIZONS: RESEARCH *WITH*—NOT RESEARCH *ON*

As a developing teacher-researcher and erstwhile graduate student confused by these issues, I found myself once more open to the understanding my program in reading could offer me. I began with the essay by Knoblauch and Brannon citing the example of the NIE, an essay which seemed to speak to the confusion I was experiencing. It helped me see a way out of this schizophrenic split. Knoblauch and Brannon suggest that if teacher-researchers would become more knowledgeable about research in general, they would recognize that an alternative tradition exists out of which teacher-research might more appropriately find its roots. Once teachers come to understand that their work, too, derives from a historically recognized philosophical tradition different from the psychostatistical one, they may find it easier to simply opt out of that separatist research scenario. Knoblauch and Brannon advocate teacher-research based in phenomenological principles in which researchers seek to uncover the "life worlds" of those they are researching, often in narrative retellings of classroom experiences. They look to research that

> aims not at selectivity or simplification but at richness of texture and intentional complexity. The telling does not seek to highlight problems and solutions, or causes and effects, or stimuli and responses, or success and failures, or heroes and villains, but seeks instead to depict, to evoke, what phenomenologists such as Heidegger and Gadamer have called "the life-world"—that palpable, sensual, kaleidoscopic, mysterious reality that constitutes our material rather than merely intellectual existence . . . : a close observation of the phenomenal reality of the classroom, what it looks like, the objects that define it as a material and social space, how the people in it look, talk, move, relate to each other, the emotional contours of their life together, the things that happen, intellectual exchanges, social understandings and misunderstandings, what the teacher knows, plans, hopes for, and discovers, how different students react, the subtle textures of the teaching experience, the subtle textures of the learning experience. (12–13)

I could see in their description some connections to the ethnographic tradition which had appealed to me: the focus on close observation of how people act and talk and move, a way of writing which supported narrative versions of understanding. Feeling inspired by, and more than a little apprehensive about, this description of what research could be, I began to take their advice and to read into phenomenological research, searching for connections to both my prior reading and experience and my developing vision of what I imagined for the research I hoped to undertake. What I discovered in my reading showed me a way out of the split that was causing me so much anguish and which seemed to be causing others much theoretical confusion. The principles upon which phenomenology is based showed me the soundness of a tradition other than the separatist scenario, a tradition in sympathy with the ideals which inspired teacher-research. The deep-rootedness of this tradition with its articulate theorists provided me a pathway past the barrier I faced in the conduct and language of decontextualized research method. Phenomenology let me open the door to a new way of conceptualizing knowledge about my students and to envisioning a new way of creating knowledge in composition studies.

The tradition itself derives from a philosophy whose theoreticians distinguish themselves from one another but who are joined by a common belief that if one wishes to describe the life worlds of human beings, one must go back to "the things themselves." From the transcendental musings of Brentano and Husserl to the existential approaches of Merleau-Ponty, Sartre and Heidegger to the hermeneutics of Gadamer, all believe to some extent that by focusing on the lived world experience of people, the *lebenswelt,* we can approach understanding.

Like those who subscribe to the more familiar notions of social construction theorists, phenomenologists believe that human beings are intentional actors and that the reality people create is not an outside truth awaiting discovery but rather a constructed event, constructed by those participating in an event. Thus, meaning becomes a blend of the intentionality of an individual actor in the world and the intentionality of other people and other social institutions, that is, shared intersubjective experience. The original phenomenologists posited this conception of meaning to contrast it with the principles of logical positivism which posit reality as a static truth that can be discovered and individuals as clean slates whose understanding is or can be common occurrence.

The significance of phenomenology for me as a researcher is captured most clearly in Gadamer's notion of a *fusion of horizons.*

For Gadamer, understanding is not a reconstruction of events, a re-creation of a given reality, but rather a mediation between subjects. Each person's creation of meaning is necessarily limited by the background and incumbent prejudices she brings to a situation. When individuals' meanings come together, though, to form a kind of "comprehensive horizon" (Linge, in Gadamer, xix)—an event marked by a fusion of those horizons—understanding can result. Understanding, then, is dialogical in nature. It follows that we cannot gain further understanding of a situation simply by looking at others' horizons—that is, by standing on the outside and looking in as traditional research suggests we can—but rather by looking together critically with others, at their horizons and our own. In order to look in this way, we must be enough a part of each other's horizons that we can begin a mediation.

A fusion of horizons, then, means not seeing the world through others' eyes, but making sense of the world with others, each seeing through his or her own eyes. It implies a vision of meaning and understanding based in dialogue, based in mediation and interpretation—and reinterpretation and reinterpretation—as the conditions, and thus the horizons each participant brings with her, constantly change. It shows us a view of the world in which there is no single truth situated outside the self, waiting to be discovered, but a world in which meaning is something that is created, not solipsistically or relativistically, but dialogically and socially.

Such a stance implies a particular approach to research in which meaning and understanding become events, arrived at by all of those participating. In order to create meaning, in order to come to understanding, the researcher first has to come to see the world from the perspective of each participant in that research—including her own. This is essential if the researchers are to uncover the core phenomenon or essence of human experience for all participants. If we believe that the researched (i.e., the students) and the researchers (i.e., the teachers) together create knowledge, we cannot conduct research *on* students in the customary ways, ways which legitimate previously formed hypotheses in statistically sound fashion and which leave out meaning-making individuals as constructors of their own horizons.

In one of his own studies, George Hillocks provides an example of research that leaves out the student as a meaning maker:

> The results of this experiment indicated that focused comments
> coupled with the assignment and revision produced a significant
> quality gain, as did this assignment with no revision. However,
> the gain for students doing revision (1.57) was nearly twice that
> for students receiving comments but doing no revision (.89).
> Further, analysis of covariance revealed a significant interaction
> between comment length and instructional pattern ($p$ .009).
> (167)

Maintaining his emphasis on statistical facts throughout his influential book, *Research on Written Composition,* Hillocks searches for an exactness in composition research: more carefully thought out hypotheses, more use of control groups, and better reporting of data, all methodological means, among other things, of shutting out students as meaning makers. Gadamer, in contrast, suggests that statistical facts such as these conceal by abstraction and, as McDermott and Hood point out, thus limit other possibilities for questioning: Gadamer writes, "What is established by statistics seems to be a language of facts, but which questions these facts answer and which facts would begin to speak if other questions were asked are hermeneutical questions" (11).

For phenomenological researchers what counts is coming as close as possible to the point of view of those we are researching, recognizing the meaning-making potential of each individual. Ton Beekman, a phenomenological researcher of children, for example, talks about this approach in terms of "immersing ourselves in the culture of childhood" (44). He argues that researchers need to go beyond closely observing a child's world, working instead toward having "a close and intimate rapport with her." He explains,

> As long as we see the actions of little children through the models
> of our shared adult conventionality we are not likely to see the
> world as children, in their own uniqueness, see it. Nor are we
> likely to see children, themselves, very clearly. (40)

I, too, was beginning to see: In order to understand the notions of literacy which were important to the students with whom I was working, I needed to do more than simply drop my statistical frame of reference. I had to find a way to see through their lenses in addition to looking more clearly through my own, realizing that the knowledge we created together would be more significant than any numbers and charts could ever be: The students I taught needed to be the subjects, not the objects, of the studies in which we were engaged.

My study of phenomenology also provided a much-needed connection for me between the world of research and the world of teaching. I was heartened to discover an active branch of phenomenology which connected its philosophies in immediate ways to classroom practice. Phenomenological pedagogy as described in the work of M. J. Langeveld, founder of the Utrecht School, represents a research/teaching philosophy in which the research and the pedagogy are completely intertwined. For Langeveld and his followers, all research must tie in the true aims of classroom pedagogy, which they describe as emancipatory education. Those who practice phenomenological pedagogy believe that research is an important—in fact, an integral—part of teaching, but that phenomenological descriptions alone are not sufficient for research in the schools. Instead, they believe,

> phenomenological descriptions always are constructed within the integrity of an ongoing interpretation of the meaning and purpose of what it means to educate, i.e., to interact with the child towards emancipatory goals. In short, educational research must always be structured pedagogically; that is, it should be grounded reflectively in the *emancipatory norms* toward which all education is oriented. (van Mannen 4–5)

In other words, phenomenological description is important in that it helps the teacher come closer to analyzing and then understanding the world of the student, which in turn results in practical action, the teacher striving to make the world of schools work better for them both. Neither phenomenological description nor practical action, believe the phenomenological pedagogues, can work in isolation, but instead are integral components for an improved pedagogy.

These phenomenological descriptions lead to action in a broader context as well, according to Langeveld. He talks of the impact of such description for other researchers, by inviting others "to insert [their] own experiences in a reflective dialogue" (van Mannen 22). Unlike positivist researchers who make explicit or implicit claims that their work can help uncover some absolute truth, phenomenological description and pedagogy suggest that through reflective dialogue "the reader [is] invited to collaborate in the construction of the analytic descriptions" (22). In this way, the full-fledged portrayals of individual classrooms become valuable to other teachers as they insert their own experience into the reading of another description, raising questions and creating connections across classrooms, and ultimately helping to effect change.

The connections educational phenomenologists make between pedagogy and research were connections I, too, wished to make. If a teacher believes that the basis of understanding is a fused horizon, gleaned perhaps by thick description, she can neither conduct research nor teach in a way that supports what Paulo Freire calls the "banking concept" of education (*Pedagogy of the Oppressed*). Students cannot be seen as empty vessels waiting to be filled. Instead of the kind of subject–object relationship between teachers and students which the banking concept supports, teachers instead must coexist with their students in a kind of subject–subject relationship. In Paulo Freire's view, it is only through a dialogue with others, a dialogue which involves critical thinking, that a word can become true. Those who come together in this dialogue become actors or agents of the world; as agents, they become subjects in the world rather than objects of it. In his view, pedagogy which aims toward this kind of subject–subject relationship, rather than a subject–object one, in which teacher-students and student-teachers converse on a more equal footing, is one that is truly liberatory in nature. When all those who are involved in the classroom are conversing subjects, true dialogue through true words can result. This is not to say that the dialogic relationship implies a total equality of roles: No relationship ever exists as such because of the innate power relationships in any community. An emphasis on dialogue, though, can help us consciously attempt to keep the roles of teacher and student from being polarities—as it helps us recognize the potential for meaning making and theory making, from the fused perspectives of teacher-students and student-teachers.

As I continued to inform myself about these traditions of research and pedagogy, I began to see that teacher-research is indeed more aptly based in these than in the context-free program of the separatist scenario or in a philosophically unsettled program which draws sometimes upon ethnography, sometimes upon psychostatistical research, sometimes upon nothing. The notions arising from phenomenology, it seemed to me, are what Stenhouse, Goswami, Berthoff, and others intended and would support. But I also came to realize that even the forms of teacher-research which seemed to be based in this tradition leave out a significant part of its inherent philosophy: that is, if the most promising research in education is research in which we seek to achieve a fused horizon between teachers and students, we must seek to conduct research *with* rather than research *on* our students. If we look at research in this way, we necessarily must reject that last vestige of Big R research in which outsiders to the classroom attempt in a short visit to understand the essence of the classroom, the perspective of the students who inhabit that world. At the same time, we have to reject the forms of teacher-research which, although they emphasize context, action, and local understanding, continue to view students as objects of study rather than subjects with whom teachers can conduct research collaboratively.

It was with this phenomenological understanding of teacher-research that I began to rethink my case study of Akemi, recognizing that many of the problems that had plagued me could be solved satisfactorily when I thought of my work in terms of this phenomenological approach. Once I discovered a meaningful research perspective which accurately reflected my own pedagogy and research interests, I realized the extent to which my own background in educational research had made me doubt my intuitions. I also recognized the extent to which I had conducted research *on* Akemi, seeing her as the object of my study rather than as a co-researching subject of her own study. My increasing understanding and excitement about what research could be began to inform my approach to a project with which I was then already immersed, a case study of a young woman named Sarah that I conducted over a period of four years.

I began my work with Sarah in 1987 when I was her teacher in a summer writing program known as the Huron Shores Summer Writing Project.[9] She subsequently attended the university where I was a graduate student, and I was able to continue my work with her over the next two years of her undergraduate studies. And, although as we worked together over the next years I could see

---

[9]The Huron Shores Summer Writing Project was a collaboratively conceived and executed program between some of us from the University of Michigan and the community of Rogers City, Michigan. Teachers from both sites came together with secondary students for a three-week "writing camp" in which students interviewed community members, researched town history, and composed and published a series of books based on these oral histories.

some changes in my stance as researcher, my initial encounters still reeked of that split I felt.

An early encounter with Sarah: December 1987. I curl my feet up under me as I sit on the couch and pass Sarah some crackers and cheese. "Finally, we get a chance to talk," I exclaim. "We've both been too busy running around this term. So, tell me, Sarah, how is it going? Do you love college? Are you wowing all your teachers with your writing?" As I pose these questions, Sarah knows, as I do, that I have a mixed agenda in inviting her over for dinner tonight. She and I plan to catch up on mutual friends, our families, our lives—an exciting prospect for both of us who forged a strong friendship in our summers of working together in her part of the world, when I was her teacher and she was my student, a friendship that went beyond the normal bounds of teacher–student relationships. But Sarah has also agreed to let me study with her the writing she does as a first-year college student, as we both hope to see how her strong background and interest in writing help her make it through the first year in an honors program at a highly academic school. After all the reading I've been doing about researching *with* rather than researching *on,* I have created this wonderful scenario in my mind of us working side by side, sharing ideas and creating a true attempt at phenomenological research. "Partners" is the word I've used with Sarah, and she has enthusiastically agreed. Forging a partnership with Sarah would be easy, I had thought: Sarah is one of those students who is a teacher's dream: someone who spends hours writing and revising, a passionate composer who knows that she will be a professional writer some day, a writer who has discovered her own style and method and excels at producing imaginative and compelling pieces of prose. The research would be a benefit to both of us, we had decided when we first talked about the project. For me, working with such an articulate student would help me see just how feasible this notion of co-researchers might be. For her, looking together at her writing would be an empowering and exciting undertaking.

And so, I am unprepared when Sarah seems on the edge of tears after my questions. What's the matter, I ask? And Sarah begins a tale of woe, in which she talks about the B's and C's she received on her papers last term, how she's lost confidence in her writing, is rarely writing on her own anymore, and lacks the passion for the written word which at one time consumed her. She tells me, "Even when I'm writing, I don't feel like I'm writing . . . I'm fulfilling a requirement . . . doing something I don't want to do. It's really strange because I've never not wanted to write—*never*—and now, with every paper, I just want to cringe."

I sit back, stunned, unsure how to proceed. My immediate inclination is to hug Sarah, talk with her, offer advice, and help her work through this problem of writing, but the researcher voice I thought I had banished screams, "Get a tape recorder; this is great stuff for your research." While Sarah rants, I find myself working through this new-found researcher role, immediately realizing that I don't really know yet what my response is supposed to be as a "researching partner." Am I her friend? her teacher? her counselor? her researcher? This would be so much easier if I were merely a researcher, separate from my subject and able to record her responses without this investment that arises when you've worked hard to understand each other's perspectives. As she cries, I relive my own experience as a college freshman, the disastrous class I had with a professor who hated my writing and told me I should switch majors immediately. Should I share that with Sarah? Will that help her get through this or will it interfere with the research I'm gathering?

Sarah takes a breath, and so do I. The conflict is ridiculous, I tell myself. Sarah is a person, not a project, and with my emerging understanding of what research can be, I try to convince myself those two roles are not in conflict. I tell myself I can offer advice and suggestions about her writing and still look with her at what is going on within her composing self. As I share with her my story about my freshman year, I feel better, but even as the words come out, I recognize that the old researcher mode is going to be hard to bury. Reading about this stuff is easy; reimagining my role is much more difficult.

As I met with Sarah over the next two years, I tried to resolve the inner conflict which was still a part of me. From that first tearful meeting on my couch, Sarah and I continued to meet and talk and to audiotape our conversations, and I continued the log about her writing that I had begun in the summer project. Over that time, I felt myself starting to think more in the manner of a phenomenological researcher, trying to keep uppermost in my mind that Sarah's investment in this project, that her own recognition of her role as a subject of the study, was a key element to its success as a representation of her understanding about issues of form and their relationship to literacy. Toward that end, I spent hours talking with her, showing her what I had written, asking her to critique and help me to represent her understanding as closely as possible. I became less concerned about our new-found friendship "skewing" the results of the study; in fact, I celebrated the idea that our talk might very likely change how she approached writing. I felt our time together furthered the emancipatory goals which had become so important to me.

I was aided in this growing understanding by the reading I was doing at the time, reading which took me into the area of feminist research methodologies. Even assuming there is a thing called feminist research implies more agreement among researchers than currently exists; still, there is a growing consensus about certain issues of methodology and content among those who proclaim themselves researchers of issues about women. More often than not, feminist research methodologies, like phenomenological methods, begin with a critique of standard research techniques, especially in social science research. Some of the critique focuses on issues raised by phenomenologists in particular, those issues that led to a rejection of decontextualized research, a celebration of local knowledge, a movement toward blurring the lines between the knower and the known, but feminist researchers add another problematic to the critique: They insist that researchers concern themselves with how their research impacts specifically on the lives of researching and researched women. Researchers as diverse as Carol Gilligan, Kathleen Weiler, and Marcia Westkott document both the historical exclusion of women's experiences from much of the research in their particular disciplines as well as the viewing of women's experiences, when it is even included, through the lenses of a masculine perspective.[10] For them, a feminist research tradition "calls into question the methodology, assumptions and language itself of the male intellectual tradition" (Weiler 58). These researchers and others, then, speak to the inherent problems in a patriarchal view of research which limits women's perspective to how it fits (or more often how it doesn't fit) with male experience, that is, assuming male experience as the norm and seeing women's experience in terms of that norm.

---

[10]Gilligan speaks of both the exclusion of women and the viewing of women in male terms in the field of psychology in her book *In a Different Voice;* Weiler considers this in the area of education in her book *Women Teaching for Change,* and Westkott summarizes the issue in the field of social science in her essay "Feminist Criticism of the Social Sciences."

A second kind of feminist critique of traditional research arises from what may be called the "myth of objectivity." While some feminist researchers go so far as to claim that a positivist view of reality is inherently male-oriented (i.e., with its resulting emphasis on numbers and figures and hard statistical data), most would say that a positivist view ignores individual experience and, as such, tends to ignore large groups of people, especially minorities and women. Westkott, citing the work of Dorothy Smith, explains the problem with positivist research in terms of women in this way:

> The methodological norm of objectivity is itself socially and historically constituted, rooted in an ideology that attempts to mystify the social relations of the knower and the known through procedures that appear anonymous and impersonal. This aura of objectivity can be maintained so long as the object of knowledge, the "known," can be an "other," an alien object that does not reflect back on the knower. Considering women only as *objects* of social knowledge fails to challenge this disassociation. . . . It is only where women are also brought in as the *subjects* of knowledge that the separation between subject and object breaks down. (425)

Similar to the intersubjective approach to the creation of knowledge for which phenomenologists argue, Westkott's approach suggests that issues raised by the positivist paradigm, while both inaccurate and detrimental to all people, are even more worrisome in terms of research on and by women. Because there still exists in much research a view of the world that continues to see women's experiences as other, as alien, as not fitting into the neat categories of experience already designed and established in terms of the experience of males, it remains easy to keep women in the object position and thus to maintain the positivist notions of categorized, predetermined understandings of peoples' lives. But when the "knower," the researcher, begins to see the experience of women in terms of her own experience, the categories are bound to break down, resulting in a new and perhaps unpredictable kind of knowledge. As Westkott continues,

> Thus, the questions that the investigator asks of the object of knowledge grow out of her own concerns and experiences. The answers that she may discover emerge not only from the ways that the objects of knowledge confirm and expand these experiences, but also from the ways that they oppose or remain silent

about them. Hence, the intersubjectivity of meaning takes the form of dialogue from which knowledge is an unpredictable emergent rather than a controlled outcome. (426)

Drawing upon these critiques of variously conceived and practiced patriarchal research paradigms, many widely diverse feminist researchers seem to come together to identify what they consider to be the basic contours of a feminist research paradigm, what DuBois calls "a passionate scholarship: necessary heresy" (112). First, a feminist research paradigm depends upon a grounding of inquiry in concrete experience and actual language, in the lived lives of women, rather than in preconceived, abstract categories. This seeking to understand the lives of actual women in their own terms necessarily implies an end to both the myths of objectivity and to the tendency that exists to see women "as data-gathering objects of research, . . . as . . . passive recorder[s] of social reality" (Westkott 428). Knowledge about women's lives, seen in this light, relies on the local and the individual rather than the global; the concrete experience of particular women, often captured in narrative or anecdotal retellings, can tell more about the worlds in which women live than those context-free studies which relegate women's experiences to generalized data.

Such an emphasis on grounded research leads understandably to the other two major goals of the feminist research paradigm. Once we reject the myths of objectivism and distant generalizability, we open a door to a different sort of research—a research that closes the gap between those who are doing the searching and those who are the objects of the search, calling instead for an interactive approach. "Feminist scholarship," DuBois tells us, "reveals a different animating assumption: that the knower and the known are of the same universe, that they are not separable" (111). The argument continues in this way: Because women share the experience of marginalization simply because they are women, a research which draws upon the personal necessarily ties the researcher to the researched in important ways. Their creation of knowledge results from certain common understandings, despite their original roles as researcher and researched: a knowledge which emerges from an intentionally created dialogic relationship. Such a relationship calls for a blurring of lines in the roles of the researcher and the researched so that each learns from the other as, together, they come to understand anew the world they are co-researching. The many feminist researchers who draw heavily upon the works of Paulo Freire add to this position a commitment to the transformative or emancipatory nature of such dialogic feminist research, seeing research as "a process of 'conscientization,' both for the so-called 'research subjects' (social scientists) and for the 'research objects' (women as target groups)" (Mies 125). Because the object of feminist research is to self-consciously support the feminist agenda of political change for women, its practitioners believe that the goal of any study that involves women must be one in which some sort of social or personal transformation occurs. Thus, the kind of research that simply studies women as a means of filling in gaps of understanding—what Gerda Lerner has referred to as "a feminist cocktail" ("add women and stir")—is not truly feminist in nature (qtd. in Bezucha 91). Westkott eloquently identifies this goal of feminist research in this way:

> A social science for women does not exclude information about women, but informs the knowledge it seeks with an intention for the future rather than a resignation to the present. The intention is not an historical inevitability but a vision, an imaginative alternative that stands in opposition to the present conditions of the cultural domination of women and is indeed rooted in these conditions. This dialogue with a future suggests a social science that is not simply a doleful catalogue of the facts of patriarchy, but an opposition to the very facts that it discovers. . . . The difference between social science about women and a social science for women, between the possibilities of self-exploitation and those of liberation, is an imaginative capacity to inform our understandings of the world with a commitment to overcoming the subordination and devaluation of women. (428–30)

The "dialogue with a future" that Westkott envisions implies these two goals of feminist research: making new knowledge through an interaction between the self and other (the researcher and the researched) and transforming existent knowledge through the emergence of imaginative alternatives which result in change for both parties in the research.

## PRONOUNS AS A POLITICAL PROBLEM; OR WHAT DO WE MEAN WHEN WE SAY "WE"?

As a researcher, I found the lessons gleaned from feminist research to be valuable: When I looked at Sarah's writing with her, I was able to learn much more about her understanding of form and its relation to literacy than I had from my approach to Akemi, resulting in a fuller, more detailed portrait of a young writer at work. In my work with Akemi, my voice took precedence: My perspective stood as the authoritative one. In contrast, in my work with Sarah, I made some small moves toward becoming a new kind of researcher: When Sarah disagreed with me on an interpretation of her work, when our perpsectives did not mesh, I listened carefully to her voice. The most obvious example of this occurred when I revised the text of my case study after Sarah set me straight on a particular point. In the final case study I wrote, "At first I believed . . . But Sarah took exception to the characterization," going on to explain how her interpretation makes better sense. What shows up less specifically in the text, though, is the kind of changed attitude I held while working with Sarah. As I began to analyze Sarah's writing, I initiated talk with her about what I saw, relaying to her my early understandings of what I believed was going on with her writing. She responded by explaining to me her understandings of the problems she was having with her writing and eventually reading and critiquing the text of the case study as a whole, a critique which resulted in its major revisions. Sarah continued to turn to me, not as a researcher, but as a teacher and friend in whom to confide her new fears of writing for her college courses. I found myself increasingly confident that the suggestions and advice I offered were not only appropriate ones for a researcher to make but completely justifiable by the standards of the phenomenological and feminist research agenda I was trying to undertake. I came to believe that this increasingly collaborative—and in some ways emancipatory—approach to researching and writing Sarah's story became a small start toward both a truer representation of Sarah and an attempt to have her place herself in a subject position.

Yet this small start did not go far enough. I see now the product as quite firmly a creation of the researcher and not the researched. While Sarah's words are featured more prominently and treated more seriously in this text than were Akemi's in that case study, Sarah is still objectified in ways quite similar to the ways Akemi was objectified. Even though the piece resounds with both of our voices, the overriding metaphors, structures, and even selection of transcripts and writing still belong to me. I initiated the study; I did the research; I wrote up the findings; Sarah served primarily as a critical reader of my work. I still thought of the work as *my* research study, in spite of my attempts to include Sarah in its production. I still found myself hiding behind the royal *we*, either self-consciously in the text itself or more subtly in the persona I created for myself as an author. When I reread the case now, such statements jump out at me: "By looking at a paper Sarah wrote . . . we can clearly see how her preoccupation with correct content and correct form affected her writing," a clear indication that some we (me? my university colleagues who might read this? teachers in general?) might understand Sarah's writing better than Sarah possibly could; or, "Thus, Sarah . . . was ripe for [this] experience." Did I see myself as shopping researcher, carefully examining a productive student's work to see if there were any spoiled spots on it? Over time, I came to believe that, despite the value I found in this piece, I was still failing to achieve a "fusion of horizons" with my students . . . but I wasn't really sure if such a thing were possible or how it might be achieved.

The problem, I began to discover, had to do with the nature of representation itself. At the time I was working with Sarah, I was introduced to an essay by Adrienne Rich, a piece that continues to have a profound effect on my thinking about research and on the assumptions I had made about my ability to represent the shared and constructed knowledge I felt I had formed with Sarah (and with others). In "Notes Toward a Politics of Location," Rich rethinks her position on the subject of representation, questioning her own ability, of which she was at one time convinced, to adequately speak for all women. She begins her essay in this way:

> A few years ago I would have spoken of the common oppression of women, the gathering movement of women around the globe. . . . I would have spoken these words as a feminist who "happened" to be a white United States citizen . . . quoting without second thoughts Virginia Woolf's statement in *Three Guineas* that "As a woman I have no country. As a woman I want no country. As a woman my country is the whole world." (7)

Rich sets her task in this essay and beyond as a "need to understand how a place on the map is also a place in history, within which as a woman, a Jew, a lesbian, a feminist, I am created and trying to create" (8), a questioning of the tendency by scholarly feminist women like herself, who have had easy access to authorship, to lay claim to the representation of others. She says, "The problem was that we did not know who we meant when we said 'we'" (11). Throughout her essay she plays with this notion; while she feels a responsibility to limit her presumption of understanding of the lives of others and thus to think in terms of "we" less often in her writing, she recognizes the paradox of this stance since "there is no liberation that only knows how to say 'I.' And so even ordinary pronouns become a political problem" (16).

The paradox Rich feels in representing the world of women is in many ways similar to the paradox I feel as a teacher-researcher when I take on authorship and represent those students with whom I've researched. Like Rich, the interrelatedness of common interests and purposes between myself and those with whom I research, as well as the commitment to discover with those Others the threads which bind us, seems to allow me in some ways to speak for those who neither have the access nor the desire to voice our discoveries in a public forum. Rich recognizes the power of that "we," to be able to present a seemingly unitary front that says, "Look at us, look at how we're treated, look at how change can happen." Teacher-researchers who have long bemoaned the tendency of outsiders to explain to us what is happening in our own classrooms easily recognize the power of that same "we": to be able to proclaim, "We teachers and students together have discovered this about ourselves." At the same time, the uniqueness of each of our positions and the power implications inherent in those positions create a chasm that, despite our best efforts, may be impossible to span. When Rich says "we," she recognizes that she may not really be speaking for others in the complete and complicated sense that an "I" implies. And thus, the paradox results: Speaking for others gives us the needed power in the public world to effect change, but it also reduces and may misrepresent the power of the individual life upon which we originated our research.

As I reviewed my own research with Sarah and others, I began to wonder a lot about the actual purposes of such representational research. As I did so, I asked myself a number of questions: Can I as a researcher, even if I join with my students, ever adequately understand another's world view? Even if I show my students the research I've composed, even if I describe their worlds with them, even if they take on responsibility for parts of the research, can I as author ever really do justice to a representation of someone else's world? For whom do we really do these research projects? Whom does the research most benefit?

## FUSING HORIZONS: CONNECTING LITERACY, PEDAGOGY, AND RESEARCH

If the fusion of horizons I was striving to create with Sarah remained somewhat problematic, the fusion I was creating between my practical program and my reading program was a continuing enlightenment. At the same time that my work as a teacher-researcher with Sarah was informed by my own reading into theoretical understandings of research, my understanding of how form functioned in Sarah's developing literacy was informed by another set of readings, arising mostly from my study of the works of Bakhtin. As I was working with Sarah, I was intently reading into Bakhtin, and I found in his writings a way to think about Sarah's depiction of her own literacy, just as I found her understandings of literacy enhancing my reading of Bakhtin. Bakhtin's intriguing ideas about how an individual's relationship to the varying discourses in her life shapes her formation of a unique perspective on the world gave me a way to think about the relationship of the reading I was doing about form and discourse to the reading I was doing about literacy and literacy instruction; it gave me a way to think about the terms in which Akemi and Sarah spoke to me about writing and the practice of reading and writing instruction in schools and universities. As I discuss more fully elsewhere, I started to rename what Bakhtin in *The Dialogic Imagination* termed "internally persuasive discourse" and "authoritative discourse" in terms of issues of literacy: as an *in-forming literacy*, the literacy students bring to bear on school forms from their own backgrounds and experiences, and as a *conforming literacy*, the literacy formally reified in school work.[11] I began to think about how such literacies play off each other in the worlds of schools, bearing in mind Bakhtin's notions that the struggle that necessarily occurs between internally persuasive and authoritative discourses is vital to the development of an individual ideology. As Bakhtin tells us, our own words are constantly formulated in a social dia-

[11]See my essay in Robinson's *Conversations on the Written Word*.

logue; it is the constant interaction of our own multivoiced words with the more unchanging words of an authoritative discourse that allows us to develop an individual perspective on the world.

Keeping in mind my recasting of Bakhtin's ideas, I began to look at Sarah's understanding of literacy and literacy instruction differently from how I had looked at Akemi's. Rather than seeing issues of literacy from an in-school/out-of-school perspective as I had with Akemi, naming in-school writing as formally restrained and out-of-school writing as freeing, my reading of Bakhtin allowed me to recognize the complexity of the formal nature of composing in all settings. If the development of an individual ideology is dependent upon an interplay between the two formations of literacy, in-forming and conforming, the shape of literacy instruction in the schools becomes of paramount importance, as a site where the two kinds might interact, leading to the creation of another kind of literacy, a re-forming one. For Sarah, however, the interplay in school settings between an in-forming and a conforming literacy became a struggle, in fact a battle. For reasons I explore in my study of Sarah, she was unable to visualize a way to connect the two types of literacy in most of the school settings in which she participated. Her inability to resolve the conflict led her toward writing blocks, dissatisfaction with her writing, and discouragement in seeing herself as an author.

I entitled the work involving Sarah as I had the work involving Akemi—with the words "Forming Literacy." I chose my terms carefully as a way to reflect my position as a learner in the work I took on as a teacher-researcher and to make clear that in both cases the focus would be on the formation of literacy—a reflection of the world of discourse as both Akemi and Sarah saw it. In both cases, I was struggling through my reading and my practice to understand how the students themselves were viewing their literacy and literacy instruction. Together, we were trying to understand how literacy itself was formed, both for them as individuals and for them as students in classrooms in which literacy instruction was ongoing. As I embarked upon my next project I felt that, while I still needed to learn more about how literacy was formulated by the students I would meet, it was time for me to consider as well how we might re-form the definitions of literacy and the literacy instruction that were operational in the classrooms I encountered. My next two projects reflect those attempts, and I think of them as more appropriately titled "Re-forming Literacy." When I once more entered the world of the classroom as a collaborating teacher, I was intent upon using the occasions as a way to re-form my own notions of literacy instruction and of research, committing myself to think hard about both issues as I taught. The classrooms I entered offered a perfect opportunity to think about such reform.

In the first classroom, which you will read about in chapter 4, two of us collaborated as teacher-researchers: two teachers committed to emancipatory notions of pedagogy, working with a group of high school students for whom conventional measures of teaching writing had failed, and a somewhat flexible curriculum. After talking about our goals for teaching this class, my coteacher, Sheila Smith, and I decided to try out some ideas: to think about re-forming notions of literacy instruction by studying form and genre in writing as an integral part of the curriculum of the class; to think about re-forming notions of research by relying on the students to be the primary researchers of their own and their peers' writing. We structured this student-designed research program quite simply: We asked students to use the occasion of this class to study the writing of themselves and their peers. Beginning with lots of writing and talk about how they felt about writing, we moved through the term toward studying specific pieces of their own writing composed for a variety of in- and out-of-school occassions. We believed that this approach might give us a new insight into how these "nonwriting" students write, as well as provide students with an occasion to become invested in the curriculum of the course and, by the very nature of what they might discover, to help us to make appropriate recommendations for changing the curriculum. We were, in other words, committed to seeing the students in subject rather than object positions—both as learners and as researchers. The resulting study allowed me to feel, for the first time in my research program, that the research in the classroom was integral to the content of the course: A curriculum gleaned from the students' collaborative research with Sheila and me began to emerge. We students and teachers were working within Freire's notion of praxis; through critical reflection on their own writing, students began to take some action.

As they became co-researchers with Sheila and me and began to study their own writing, they played roles that often have been reserved for teacher-researchers: Student-researchers became authorities in the classroom as they studied their own writing and the writing of their classmates. In order to do this, they wrote reflective pieces about their writing processes, they interviewed peers to see differences in others' writing processes, they reviewed the kinds of writing assignments they were regularly given in all their classes (including this one), and they analyzed the differences in the resulting pieces of writing. In short, they followed the procedures that any good teacher-researcher might, using their own experiences as the basis of their understanding and as the catalyst to effect change in their approach to writing. As Sheila says, students became "proud of themselves as researchers," while at the same time they became involved "in their own learning . . . creating definitions and becoming conscious of several facets of their own education" (1). The notion inherent in such research—that of the researcher and the researched collaborating—came to change, for all of us in that class, many of our prior ideas about teaching and learning. I believe we effected together the kind of research for which many phenomenological and ethnographic researchers argue.

And while I believe in the value of this particular study, the experience of one student in that class managed to keep me from feeling overly proud of our work.

> A failure?: June 1988. I am reviewing my notes from the term, feeling very good about the work Sheila and I did together, feeling very good about the progress the students made. As I read through my teaching log and my assortment of student papers, projects, and transcripts of interviews, my enthusiasm continues to grow. These students seem to me to now understand so much more about writing than they had prior to this semester; given the chance to study writing, they seem to be less fearful of it, more in control of it, ready to take on more writing tasks in many contexts as they express their understanding. I come across my notes on Fred and slowly my happy grin begins to fade.

> Fred had become one of my "projects" that term, a student who told me up front that he hated writing yet who showed incredible insight in the writing tasks he chose to complete for the class. At times motivated to participate in our class project, Fred would share with me and his peers his responses toward writing: mostly reiterating that he hated writing because he couldn't do it, explaining that he wouldn't even write letters back to girls because he didn't know what to say, bemoaning how "stupid" the kinds of writing were that he was asked to do in his

other classes (mostly endless outlines of chapters, he told us). At the same time, he told us, "People can write when they feel like it. When they do they do a good job of it." Despite our work all term long, we could never really determine what might make Fred feel like it—and, in fact, as the term ended I was told that he had failed his social studies course for the second time, because he refused to do the "endless outlines" that were the basis of that class.

Despite our attempts to achieve an emancipatory research with him and with the other students, research that was intended to spur students to action, Fred still failed a class that term, primarily because he refused to do his writing assignments for that class. Clearly, all students have failures; not even emancipatory student-teacher-research can change that. Still, Fred's experience set me to wondering again about the research in which I was engaged. After all our discussions about writing, why did Fred fail to complete the assignments for that class? Would other students recall what we had learned when they went on to other classes? As one of my university students who later read an abridged version of this study asked me, would these students be prepared to take the new understandings about issues of form they had gained from this experience and apply them to the more traditional settings they would encounter in the rest of their high school experience? I think her question gets at the heart of this work: Was the project a one-time undertaking, a satisfying but limited exercise for the students, or a real beginning for them to change their understandings of their own literacy and to act upon that change in subsequent settings? Again, I wondered: For whom do we really do this research? Whom does the research most benefit? Who is really being empowered here?

In part, the issue becomes one of separating the process of research from its product. The students in this case were intimately involved in the process—in fact, the research process became the emergent curriculum for the class. But the resulting product remained quite separate. Despite the students' inclusion in the research process, the final composition of this case study, a writing that does incorporate their voices in prominent ways, was done by me. As the writer, I assumed the power to decide what of their research was significant as well as who should be the recipients of this judgment. The audience for this work remained not those who participated, who might have benefited from a writing which would be directed toward them, but rather outsiders to the situation who can learn from this study to other, admittedly important, ends. In many ways, then, I, too, named these students as writers, but not Authors, telling them that their work was significant only in how it fed into my reading of it. Is this perhaps why this experience was ultimately not an empowering one for Fred? Did he recognize in some way the disparity between a research process in which he could take some authority and a product in which he had none? I began to ask myself whether by recognizing the students as meaning makers but by leaving them out of this final step—composing the experience—I necessarily reduced their significance in the process?

Perhaps, I began to think, the essence of the problem goes back to Adrienne Rich's response to the use of a "we." What does it mean to try to understand and then represent through writing someone else's perspective on the world? Can we as researchers, even if we join with our students, ever adequately understand another's worldview? Even if we show our students the research we compose, even if we describe their life-worlds with them, even if they are responsible for the research, is it ever possible that we, as solitary authors, can represent someone else's understanding?

## BEYOND REPRESENTATIONAL RESEARCH

Once more, as Knoblauch and Brannon had suggested, I turned to the philosophy increasingly informing my work, and as I began to read into current perspectives on ethnography, I found that these questions are the same questions asked by many anthropologists today. Geertz, in particular, separates the issues surrounding the ethnographic methods with which I was struggling into two basic but far-reaching questions: Is it decent? Is it possible?—questions which he admits have led to a crisis of conscience among contemporary ethnographers. Geertz connects the idea of decency, of the ethical implications of ethnographic methods, to questions of audience. Historically, he tells us, the writing of ethnographies has been exclusively for academic audiences, complete outsiders to the community under investigation. In fact, as he explains, "One of the major assumptions upon which anthropological writing rested until only yesterday [was] that its subjects and its audience were not only separable but morally disconnected, that the first were to be described but not addressed, the second informed but not implicated" (*Works and Lives* 132). Certainly, I had been largely guilty of this same assumption. My own writing about the students was not intended for them, nor for their teachers with whom I worked most directly, for that matter; instead it was directed toward readers of proposals for conferences and editors of journals as well as my own professors. If I believed in the power of readers coming to share my understanding as they read into my "study of cases," how could I justify this exclusion?

The related question Geertz asks is whether ethnographic representation is even possible. Ethnographers are beginning to ask how, in a postmodern society which, from a number of philosophical stances, is concerned with the centrality of interpretation, any ethnographer can possibly lay claim to representing accurately a particular group of people. Such wonderings lead to the now commonplace notions that surround contemporary ethnography: that "ethnographic truths are inherently partial" (Clifford and Marcus 7); that ethnographies may, indeed, be inherently fictions. James Clifford asks some important questions about representation, questions which seemed appropriate to my work: in an ethnography, "who speaks? who writes? when and where? with or to whom? under what institutional and historical constraints?" (13) Such questions tend to remind us not only of the difficulty—some would say the impossibility—of representing others fairly and accurately but also of the political implications of even trying to do so.

Geertz connects the questions of audience and representation in somewhat different terms. For him, the major problem ethnographers face—that of persuading their audiences—has resulted in what he calls issues of one's signature entering the writing. That is, how an author enters a text, who the author of the text is, what an author does to convince a readership that she has "been there" are questions that concern him. This implies more than simply the question of whether or not the author is a trustworthy spokesperson. The "moral certainty" involved with such questions lead Geertz to a specific conclusion: in today's world, he tells us, "the burden of authorship seems suddenly heavier" (*Works and Lives* 138). He goes on to say,

> How you know you know is not a question they [anthropologists] have been used to asking in other than practical, empiricist terms. . . . How words attach to the world, texts to experience,

works to lives, is not one they have been used to asking at all.
(*Works and Lives* 135)

In other words, "Is it decent? . . . Is it possible?" (135)

His answer at least partly lies in what he believes is the underlying purpose of this kind of research. He believes ethnography cannot and should not be viewed as an exact science in which the ethnographer provides factual answers; rather, readers of ethnographies should recognize them for what they really are: texts constructed in the imagination, situated "between author-saturated texts like *David Copperfield* and author-evacuated ones like 'On the Electrodynamics of Moving Bodies'" (*Works and Lives* 141). Recognizing that ethnographies, then, are always "the describer's description" (145) and that they are a very particular kind of discourse allows him to posit this purpose for ethnography: "enabling conversation across societal lines . . . to enlarge the possibility of discourse between people quite different from one another . . . and yet contained in a world where . . . it is increasingly difficult to get out of each other's way" (147).

I share Geertz's sentiment here, and I see the importance of his perspective for teacher-research. Teacher-researchers who subscribe to this view must see their work as emerging from a new community of researchers whose purpose is to expand knowledge and conversation among a cadre of other teacher-researchers by thickly describing, for example, in the ways I have done in these case studies. As teachers in widely different settings begin to share with others the descriptions of their own classrooms, the "possibility of intelligible discourse" is vastly increased, resulting— perhaps—in both important camaraderie and effective understanding of multiple situations as we find both commonality and difference across these settings. As I read Geertz's words, I recalled the similar sentiment expressed by the phenomenological pedagogues, a sentiment whose full implications had escaped me at the time of my initial reading. Both Geertz and those of the Utrecht School recognize the need for teachers to enter a "reflective dialogue" through the reading of others' portrayals of their classrooms. By actively reading these cases, teachers respond in an "aha!" fashion: An incident depicted in the written text reminds them of the struggles of a particular student in fourth hour; a classroom crisis brought to life in descriptive words by a teacher-researcher helps them make sense of a similar crisis they experienced last semester. Such teachers, then, become participants in some ways in the actual creations of a text: The text on the pages is constructed in terms of the texts of the teachers' experiences. Stenhouse would see this kind of "study of cases" as exactly what he intended.

While this emphasis on seeing teacher-research as central to expanding the conversation among teachers answered in some ways my questions about the ethics of my undertaking, I still found myself worried about the impact my own research had on the students with whom I was working. As long as I focused on representing their perspectives, despite my struggle to get as close as possible to the students in order to understand those perspectives, I found myself caught in a trap. The very nature of such research depends on someone representing somebody else, a task which had begun to seem to me not only impossible, but also in conflict with my goals of participating in an emacipatory, advocacy mode of research with my students.

I eventually came upon the work of Stephen Tyler, an ethnographer who offered me a radical way of rethinking representational research. Tyler believes there is no point in trying to make a better representation; instead, we should try "to avoid representation altogether" (128). Tyler instead calls for a "postmodern ethnography," what he sees as "the mutual dialogical production of a discourse . . . a polyphonic text" (126). He explains the postmodern ethnography in this way:

> It foregrounds dialogue as opposed to monologue, and emphasizes the cooperative and collaborative nature of the ethnographic situation in contrast to the ideology of the transcendental observer. In fact, it rejects the ideology of "observer-observed," there being nothing observed and no one who is observer. There is instead the mutual, dialogical production of a discourse, of a story of sorts. We better understand the ethnographic context as one of cooperative story making that, in one of its ideal forms, would result in a polyphonic text, none of whose participants would have the final word in the form of a framing story or encompassing synthesis—a discourse on the discourse. It might be just the dialogue itself, or possibly a series of juxtaposed paratactic tellings of a shared circumstance . . . or perhaps only a sequence of separate tellings in search of a common theme, or even a contrapuntal interweaving of tellings, or of a theme and variations. (126)

This "mutual dialogic production" for Tyler relies on *evocation* rather than representation, on text that evokes experience rather than representing it. What might this mean, then, to focus on evocation rather than representation? Evocation, as I began to understand it, seemed to me what Bakhtin might call a self-consciously heteroglossic version of a culture, a piece that resounds with the many voices involved in its making, without any one person situating herself as author and thus as representer of the experiences of others. Evocation implied, for me, a way in which all those participating in a research project would become true collaborators, participating in the process from start to finish, speaking in their own voices in the inevitable product that resulted. My developing thinking then led me to wonder what a postmodern ethnography, what evocational research, might actually look like. What would happen if I no longer was the representer, if students and I truly became composing collaborators, involved together in the research process from start to finish: determining the issues for the research, issues which ultimately would affect how we all looked at an aspect of our own lives; looking deeply into our own experience and the experience of others in order to better understand our chosen topic; writing collaboratively with each other to make concrete the issues we raised; choosing together what to do with our written piece, in order to help others toward increased understanding of our experience.

With these notions in mind, I invited a group of students to undertake such a project. This project began as a way for students in a college writing course I taught to think through the connections of form and the perceived literacies of male and female students, that is, their own literacies reconceived in gendered terms. Calling upon the understandings of forming literacy I had gained from my reading of Bakhtin and others and from my experiences with Sarah, Akemi, and others, I began by setting up a class that I hoped would immediately challenge some of my students' preconceived notions of a conforming literacy: a class in argumentative writing which resisted categorizations of argumentation into preordained formal classifications and which attempted to create a space where those formal definitions might come up against other notions of form the students knew from their backgrounds and experiences. As ten volunteer students joined with me outside class time to study these same notions in terms of a topic they chose—

that of gender issues and their relationship to their own writing—we together set the stage for what I had imagined a truly emancipatory research project could be.

For an entire term, the eleven of us met weekly, reading essays, talking about issues of literacy and gender, and setting the stage for them to conduct research into an issue of literacy that captured their individual imaginations. Students produced a variety of intriguing projects for themselves, for me, and for each other: a look at the teaching of writing in one high school English class to see if gendered expectations were a part of the instruction; a series of blind readings of two student essays, followed by interviews determining if the readers had thought about the gender of the writers and why; a look at writing in the various majors of some of the students in the class, determining similarities and differences in the fields of study. This collaborative work led to a second project: Two of the students from that class, John and Susan, joined with me the following semester to continue our work but to focus on their own writing as a way of coming to terms with some of the issues raised during the previous semester's work.

During our time together that term, the three of us met weekly for a few hours and spent time talking about specific pieces of their writing, about issues of gender and writing in general, and about published pieces we had read, pieces on gender and writing as well as on nontraditional kinds of research. Outside of our meetings, we each wrote a copious amount: about our reactions to our meetings, about our own writing, about how we felt about what we were reading. My initial inclination in the project was to do research as a team, write something together, and prove that this kind of collaborative research could work. As the term progressed, it became clear that composing something collaboratively (i.e., so that it sounded as if it were written in one voice) could never reflect adequately what was actually occurring in our work together. The complicated nature of that collaboration is in part what the three of us ended up writing about, a piece that began as an attempt at Tyler's "postmodern ethnography." The final piece reflects our three voices in alternating lengthy sections, voices that speak to our own particular interest in the project, that at times disagree with each other, that at times echo each other. We have voices upon voices upon voices: sections of our own writing, sections in which each of us analyzes our own and each other's writing, sections of transcribed dialogue, sections of summary and commentary.

This first attempt at evocative research, which you will find in chapter 5 of this book, was an important step for me in my development as a teacher-researcher. Although it is a lengthy chapter, I believe that laying out all three of our voices as we talk individually about our work provides a valuable lesson for other researchers even as it provided a valuable lesson for us. My temptations to summarize that work, in order to make this introductory chapter into a neat package (after all, I'm reaching the "Conclusion" part of the chapter!), is nearly irresistible. My inclination is to explicate for readers what they might see in that chapter; however, I know that by doing so, I will once again reduce the piece to a representational approach: relying on my determinations about what are the important parts, my decisions as to what sections and quotes best represent our work. And so I will avoid the temptation, and instead urge you to read it carefully in order to come to your own conclusions as to its impact.

What I can talk about here, though, is the impact such an approach to research has had upon me. I eventually came to see that the challenge of the research itself, as well as the job of the final write-up, was to recognize how the work appealed to me in dissimilar ways from how it appealed to John and Susan. Each of us made different "gains," if you will; each of us seemed to focus on a different aspect of the research and, in fact, changed in different ways, depending on our individual interests. For a while, this disparity seemed problematic to me. For too long I had been the codifier and summarizer of the research I had undertaken with students. Even as I recognized that I had to give up that role in order to see more clearly and to learn with my students, I didn't know what to do when faced with the diversity of responses that the three of us provided. I suppose I assumed that collaboration would lead to our reaching conclusions jointly—that, although each person might sacrifice a little bit, we would reach a compromise position of our understandings which might then "represent" the joint learnings we had achieved. While *I* would no longer be the representer, I had thought that our work together would reach some kind of conclusion, and our writings would show that conclusion in a public way. It didn't take me long to realize this would not be the case, and I began to panic. Did it count as collaborative research if Susan seemed to get more out of it than John? I wondered. And did it count if my interest ran in ways different from Susan's? And if Susan's ran in ways different from John's? Does collaborative research which tries to be evocative, which intends to be emancipatory, count if the growth and change for the individuals involved seem to remain at the level of the individual and not at the level of the group? Do we, in pursuing this kind of research, sacrifice the power of the "we" (to go back to the language of Rich) in our emphasis on the "I"?

My belief, as I wrote my sections of our study, is that the difference of these approaches and perspectives is ultimately the strength of this sort of research. Rather than an attempt at representing John or Susan's view through Cathy's eyes, filtered as such representation always must be, John and Susan get to speak and to show readers just how diverse this sort of collaboration can be. John's purposes in undertaking this research, his struggles and realizations, become clear, as do Susan's and Cathy's—and the fronting of the variety of purposes we took on as participants in the research becomes significant for me as it helps me to resist the temptation to force this kind of collaborative teacher-research into a mode of writing which reaches particular conclusions. The strength is that readers can see much of what we got to see: that we realized the research problem differently, that we made it our own in unique ways, and that our participation in the research process led to individual change that was only possible because of our give and take with the others in this group.

And yet, I'm not completely convinced that all teacher-research must take on the form this study took on in order to be successful. A research study that alternates voices and allows each voice to speculate rather than reaching singular conclusions is certainly appealing to me in that it moves me beyond the box into which representational research had forced me for so long. Imaginative alternatives to the genres of research as usual excite me as they help me find answers to the dilemma Geertz so eloquently posed: Is it decent? Is it possible?

But at times I wonder if this approach is merely an intellectual exercise which, while appealing at one level, is impractical at another. If one important purpose of teacher-research is to make works accessible and available to practicing teachers in ways that traditional research fails to do, does this style of writing which relies on the participating reader to draw conclusions best serve the needs of teachers in the classroom? To be quite honest, as a reader, I sometimes want the author to just reach a conclusion and tell me what I was supposed to learn.

In the epilogue to this book, I explore some of the dilemmas this kind of research raises for me, even as I suggest some ways in which alternative genres of teacher-research might be useful. In addition to summarizing some of the most informing pieces I have read recently, pieces that have helped me imagine some possibilities for teacher-research, I explain my most recent foray into teacher-research in which I am working with two colleagues to develop a collaborative case study, which has been used in a class called "Teaching College Composition." In this case study, really a work-in-progress, we are trying to create an alternative genre which is a useful one for prospective teachers.

For those of us for whom the issue of representation leads to sleepless nights and ethical angst, some of the ideas furthered by Tyler and others I talk about in the epilogue are quite provocative. Researching *with* rather than researching *on* creates a whole new set of problems for committed collaborative researchers. The solutions are not all there yet, but perhaps as we think about new genres of research, products which imply a change in our processes, we might take some steps toward truly fulfulling our emancipatory charge.

## CAN YOU HAVE CONCLUSIONS IN A POSTMODERN ETHNOGRAPHY?

The understandings about teacher-research I have come to as I have participated in these projects and have read into a wide variety of disciplines are understandings that I would never have come to by practicing teacher-research briefly or occasionally or even alone. The course I have travelled thus far has clearly been filled with bends and with barriers, with disappointments and reimaginings and encouragements and frustrations. But most of all, it has been filled with a constant hope that I might get better at this role I have chosen to take on in the classroom.

I believe teacher-researchers have much to learn from the lessons of researchers in other disciplines; we who practice it must come to see our research as grounded in the experiences of our students and ourselves, as collaborative in both conception and practice, and as emancipatory in its underlying purpose. I further believe that we have much to learn from our own practice and from the practice of our colleagues, if we take the time to reflect upon this practice in open and constructive ways. This mode of looking again at our own research attempts should become an integral part of our developing conceptions of teacher-research, I believe, as we take a necessary critical look at this movement that has transformed the lives of so many of us who have taken on its mantle as a way of life in the classroom. In order for teacher-research to grow as a movement, and in order for us as teacher-researchers to fully realize its great potential, I believe we must be vigilant as we research our own approaches. Looking critically at what we do is a sometimes painful but always necessary component for those of us who want to "do" teacher-research better and especially for those of us who instruct a whole second generation to its value.

I hope that none of what I've said here is viewed as either didactic or universal. If nothing else, I've come to learn that teacher-research relies on ever evolving sets of circumstances and that each person's experiences as a teacher-researcher should serve as the basis for her own development and change. So, while my experiences represent a personal history, I hope it is a history that may strike some chords for others as they realize moments of recognition as they read through the text. To use the terms I've come to understand as I've conducted this research, perhaps the changes I've made in my own history as a teacher-researcher might be seen as evocative rather than as representational, a reflection of the musings and adaptations of one teacher-researcher, a teacher-researcher whose understandings will expand and grow between the time I finish this (final?) draft and the time the book appears in print. Such should be the nature of teacher-research.

And so I borrow from Adrienne Rich to find the right words to close this chapter, words I think all teacher-researchers should have indelibly imprinted in their heads and hearts: "This is the end of these notes but it is not an ending" (21).

CHAPTER 2

# *Forming Literacy: Akemi's Story*

## INTRODUCTION

The case study which follows this introduction is the first of five of the case studies that make up my continuing odyssey as a teacher-researcher. Written in the spring of 1987, it records the semester I spent working with a young writer named Akemi, then a sophomore in high school. The project which led to this chapter grew out of a larger, ongoing collaborative teacher-research project between the school system in which Akemi was enrolled and the Center for Educational Improvement through Collaboration (CEIC) at The University of Michigan, a project that initially focused on the development of a local assessment of student writing.[1] In order to understand better both the system of schooling which produced particular kinds of student writing and the actual experiences of high school students within the system, I approached several of the English teachers involved in the research project and asked if I could "shadow" one of their students for a semester, hoping that such close association with one student would allow me access to the world of schools from a perspective not much seen in the research world.[2] The teachers agreed, and they suggested I work with Akemi, who was selected, in part, I think, because she was known as a "good" student, one whom they felt could participate articulately in an intensive project, one whose reflections might, in turn, reflect well on her education. And so, my short-lived career as a would-be high school student began: I attended classes with Akemi for a semester, driving the two-hour commute to Saginaw

---

[1]For more on the CEIC's work in this particular setting, work that continues to expand in a number of exciting directions, see Robinson and Stock's "The Politics of Literacy," *The Bridge* (a compilation of students' growing-up stories written out of an experimental English curriculum entitled Inquiry and Expression), and Stock's *The Dialogic Curriculum.*

[2]I was inspired to try this project by my reading of Robert Everhart's more expansive project, recounted in his book *Reading, Writing and Resistance.*

in order to be in school usually two days a week from 7:45 A.M. to 3:00 P.M.; I talked with Akemi in the halls between classes and before and after school, and occasionally I interviewed her more formally after school and at lunch time. For the most part, though, I was an observer in Akemi's school world, sitting back in class-rooms and watching her actions and reactions to her school work.

The study you will read here remains essentially as I wrote it in the months following that experience, with some minor stylistic changes for clarity's sake and some sections deleted to make the piece slightly shorter and more readable. Looking back at it now, I believe it reflects quite accurately my own understandings at that point in my project, both my ideas about literacy and literacy instruction and my ideas about research methodology. As I explain in chapter 1 of this volume, the notions of literacy within which I was working at that time were much influenced by the program of reading in which I was involved. You will see these influences in the words of Berthoff, Knoblauch and Brannon, Cook-Gumperz, and others I cite in these pages, scholars whose ideas gave me a way into explaining the phenomena Akemi and I were seeing in her approaches to writing. As I tried to explain how Akemi formed notions of her own literacy, I did so in the terms I borrowed from these authors: "muffin tin," "ceremonial discourse," and "essay-text literacy," among others. While my understanding of a form-based definition of literacy has expanded over the course of my project, I see this chapter as an attempt to depict how, at the time, I understood Akemi's literacy and her literacy instruction in both her terms and the terms of these authors I was reading at the time, an important introduction to the form-based definitions of literacy that would continue to intrigue me.

Not only were my understandings of literacy informed by both my research practice and my reading program, but my understand-ing of the research process itself was also so informed. As I worked with Akemi and read into issues of research methodology, I learned my first lessons about the telling of others' stories. The most im-portant lesson I discovered was that doing teacher-research truly is a process of discovery. Learning how to be a teacher-researcher involves not only the more theoretical concerns which I outline in chapter 1 and which I focus on in the postscript to this chapter; learning how to be a teacher-researcher also involves the more day-to-day concerns: How do I best keep a journal? Do I have to do transcripts of every recorded interview? Is it okay if my research question changes halfway through my study?

As I began my work with Akemi, *these* were the questions that concerned me. Scared as I was about beginning this kind of research, overwhelmed that if I couldn't count and label something I would be lost, I spent a lot of time reading the more "how-to" texts about teacher-research and ethnography, learning about keeping an observation journal, transcribing into text tape-recorded interviews, and arriving at themes from the information I had gathered.[3] I struggled with the question of how to know when I had found something "significant," and I panicked when my question changed several weeks into the study, a panic I carefully smoothed over as I actually wrote up the case. As you will see as you read the case, I refer quite calmly to this change of plan in the text: "As the weeks passed and I watched Akemi at work, I began to focus more closely on how she went about her writing—eventually coming to concentrate on the forms her writing took." The calm of that statement belies the terror I felt. Much as I had read about the inevitability of a teacher-researcher's question changing, I was horrified that all the information I had gathered to that point seemed to be for naught—because it had focused on a different question.

As I sat night after night surrounded by transcripts, journals, copies of Akemi's writing, and my own beginning notes on what I saw going on in her school world, I was astounded by how messy this kind of context-full research with people can be. At many points in the process I felt defeated, unable to make sense of the sheer amount of information I had, confused by what I first had thought would be an easy task: telling Akemi's story by simply recounting what I observed. As I began to learn how to elicit themes from the information in front of me, I started to feel more comfortable. Much like organizing the kind of research papers with which I was familiar, this sifting and sorting at first became a kind of search for the perfect quote to support a theme—a return for me, in many ways, to the process of research as usual. However, as I continued to read and reread my notes, I was forced to question the "reality" that I saw: a reality that was much more compli-

---

[3]Two of the books I found informative were Mohr and Maclean's *Working Together: A Guide for Teacher-Researchers* and Agar's *The Professional Stranger*. A more recent book which is an excellent introduction is Hubbard and Power's *The Art of Classroom Inquiry*.

cated than "research as usual" and which sometimes was contradictory—contradicted by my observations on other occasions, contradicted by Akemi's observations, even contradicted by Akemi's depictions from one occasion to another. Added to those complications and contradictions was my attempt to resolve the continual balancing act that is required of researchers who become close to those they're researching, something like what Geertz described as the interplay between experience-near and experience-distant concepts. As I tried to grasp the essence of Akemi's experience from my position as both insider and outsider, I searched for ways to maintain my equilibrium.

Focusing on maintaining a balance helped me in the writing of this case study; nonetheless, the study poses certain questions I have come to recognize as inherent to the kind of research I was practicing at that time. My research, as I explain in chapter 1, was caught between two worlds: that of research I knew well, the decontextualized separatist scenario, and the research world I was trying to join, context-full teacher-research. This feeling of not knowing exactly where I was situated caused me problems throughout all stages of the research process: through the gathering of information and the pulling together of the information I had, as mentioned above, but also in the actual write-up of the study. I recall quite clearly now, some six years later, my battle within myself to write this piece in a genre which would truly be representative of Akemi's school life, working hard to break out of the generic modes which I had been taught so well were acceptable for a research study. Ironically, as I wrote about Akemi's inability to break out of the "essay-text literacy" so valued by her school, I found myself nearly unable to break out of the "essay-text literacy" I knew was valued in the world of academia. Throughout this case study, as you will see, I return again and again to the voices of the experts to represent Akemi's battles, relying more heavily on their voices than I do on Akemi's. The form follows the typical form I had been taught: Akemi does or says something which makes me think; I validate the issue she raises by explaining its connection to what other "experts" have said. Much like the traditional research paper, the form of this case study conforms to a mode which relies on the succinct, well-placed quote and the organized argument reliant on the voices of others. The argument I develop in the piece oversimplifies many of the contradictions I uncovered in my research. In keeping with the form I knew a piece of research should take, I stifled the voices of disagreement which kept appearing in my notes in order to compose a logical, well-conceived argumentative essay—a genre I knew well. And although when you read the essay, you will see me occasionally mention the complicated nature of these issues for Akemi, I see those references now as rhetorical strategies: Although I admit the "emerging portrait of Akemi" is "admittedly complex and sometimes contradictory," I don't really allow the contradictions to surface for the reader. Like the good writer I had been taught to be, I smooth over the differences to make a readable piece for my audience. Even my goal of making this piece more "storylike" than my research as usual is caught firmly within the tradition of the research essay. I read now my small attempt at a narrative within the text, an attempt you will see in the section in which I describe a prototypical day in Akemi's life, and I recall the agony I went through trying to compose it: questioning its appropriateness in this piece, wrestling with the actual writing as I grappled with a writer's block caused by the split I felt about including a few descriptive words and phrases in a piece of research!

My struggle to satisfy both worlds also resulted in some inconsistencies in my telling of Akemi's story, inconsistencies centered around the issue of whose voice takes preeminence in this kind of study, an issue I will take up more fully in the postscript to this chapter. So, while I see this case study of Akemi as perhaps a less-than-ideal telling of her story, I see its value as twofold: first, as an entree for me into an understanding of the nature of literacy instruction in our schools, an understanding which led me to continue to study these issues in other settings; and second, as an introduction to the nature of teacher-research.

## FORMING LITERACY: AKEMI'S STORY (MAY 1987)

Despite an emphasis on the process of writing as discovery, writing as a heuristic, an emphasis encouraged by composition theorists from Ann Berthoff to Peter Elbow to James Britton, writing remains a form-oriented entity in many classrooms, especially at the high school and college level. As Knoblauch and Brannon see it,

> Too many teachers, like their ancient predecessors, view genres as rigid structures that must be learned precisely and then never violated if writing is to be coherent, organized, and effective. Too many believe that learning to write is equivalent to learning these

structures, that teaching writing means insisting on formal cor-
rectness, that tidying up the surface of discourse causes the matu-
ration of writers. The consequence has been to promote a ceremonial view of discourse among students, a belief that writing is
mainly a process of honoring the conventions that matter to
English teachers rather than a process of discovering personal
meanings, thinking well in language, or achieving serious intellectual purpose. (*Rhetorical Traditions* 31)

As a participant-observer this past term in one high school's
classrooms across the disciplines, I saw this phenomenon in full
force in both English classes and in other subject areas. This emphasis on form is so pervasive in most of the classes I observed that
both the teachers and students came to define writing in terms of
the form it takes (rather than in terms of the subject or the content,
for example). Thus, the questions "What are you/they writing?" is
generally answered by students and teachers alike in terms of its
form: "an essay," "a report," "a story," not "I'm writing about
Black Thursday" or "Neighbor Rosicky." As Knoblauch and Brannon have claimed it does, the formal conventions of writing tend to
overshadow any view of writing as a process of coming to know.
Through close work with one student, I've come to understand in
some speculative ways how such a "ceremonial view of discourse"
comes to affect a single writer and her approach to her own writing, seeing how she names for herself the forms in which she
writes, how her writing in school settings differs from her writing
outside school settings, and most importantly how issues of form
are tied to issues of literacy in our schools today.

Akemi's high school is known in its community by many
names: an inner-city school in a community in which the economic
conditions are worsening; a minority high school whose popula-
tion is 98 percent nonwhite, mostly African-American and some
Hispanic; an "at risk" high school, a place that is perceived to
serve mostly those who are seen locally as low-skilled students.
The namings of the counterpart high school—across the river—
serve in contrast to these perceptions: it is seen as more suburban,
more white, less a "catch-up" school. And, as one might suspect,
some blatant and some not-so-blatant examples of inequality in
these two worlds exist, apparent in the currency of textbooks and
the kinds of facilities to which students have access, for example.
Prewarned by this almost stereotyped version of a black inner-city

high school, then—in contrast to its white suburban counterpart, a world with which I was much more familiar—I brought with me a number of preconceived notions. And thus, when I first met Akemi, I was a little surprised at what I found: a fifteen-year-old sophomore in the academic track of this closely tracked school, a young black woman who not only succeeded in meeting the school's academic demands (she scored a 3.86 on a 4-point scale in her first semester in high school and made the school's honor role each marking period that sophomore year in which I worked with her), but who also excelled in the demands in the larger community of the state of Michigan (she received a perfect score on the writing component of the statewide assessment of educational progress). Although Akemi was a fairly quiet member of the bustling school world, she was indeed an active member, participating in Student Council, Drama Club, French Club, and journalism in school, and Junior Achievement outside of school. In addition, she was a practicing Jehovah's Witness, putting in the requisite three evenings a week of field service. In short, Akemi was a "good" student, one whom teachers enjoy having in class and one who was popular among her peers.

When I first entered Akemi's world, the goal I had named for myself was to look closely at the writing she practiced in her school day. Specifically, I wanted to look at the approaches she took to fulfill her work; naively, I was interested in the processes she went through in her school writing. Toward that end, I went to classes with her across her school day, scrutinizing carefully the writing she produced, watching closely as she produced that writing, and talking extensively with her about how she composed. I discovered quickly that Akemi's writing, in her words, generally came "off the top of my head." The teacher would give an assignment, and Akemi would begin writing, occasionally crossing out a word here or there, sometimes backing up and rereading a piece or a section, but generally writing from start to finish and immediately handing it in. As Akemi told me, this process for composing was the one she used to complete assignments whether they were done in school or for homework. This kind of writing, what I would term "freewriting," constituted her writing strategies. Revision for Akemi, a rarely practiced phenomenon, meant rereading to see if anything was "wrong" (that is, misspelled, mispunctuated, misquoted) and then correcting her mistakes. The "process approach" which, at the time, I was convinced was an integral part of most schools' curricula, some five years after Hairston had proclaimed that the "winds of change" were already here, seemed nonexistent in Akemi's understanding of writing. If revision was rarely practiced, prewriting never was.

How Akemi was able to practice this "non-process" approach to writing, this writing off the top of her head, and still be named as a good writer by both her school and by the wider audience of the state became fascinating to me, a devotee of the process approach. As the weeks passed and I watched Akemi at work, I began to focus more closely on how she went about her writing—eventually coming to concentrate on the forms her writing took and the almost fanatical obsession I began to see her hold with these forms.

I could see her obsession with forms and rules with some regularity since, within her school day, Akemi lived in a world in which writing, if we define it as putting pen to paper, occurred quite often. By some accounts, Akemi was writing for a huge portion of her school day; in fact, in several of her classes she seemed to be writing to the exclusion of discussing in groups or with the whole class, listening to a teacher lecture, or doing other activities. But it seemed clear to me that many of the writing tasks she was asked to perform were merely that: performances in which she simply took pen to paper, a phenomenon we can see in the following recounting of a prototypical day of school for Akemi, a composite portrait of a number of actual occurrences I observed.

At 7:45 on one particular day I attended school with her (let's call it a Wednesday), Akemi walked in the door to Geometry, her first-hour class. She strolled to the back of the class, sat at her desk, and pulled out her geometry book and homework as she got ready to listen as her teacher went over in class the answers to Tuesday night's homework problems. She also pulled out the previous night's history homework, a chart which needed to be filled out before seventh hour that day. As the class progressed, Akemi alternated looking up at the board and down at her geometry work, occasionally making a correction in the formula she'd written down and worked through (theorems and proofs are not done in this class, I was told by the teacher) and looking at her history work. Occasionally, she even volunteered to answer a question about geometry as she glanced up briefly from the history text. After assuring me in a whisper that she only needed to do about an hour of homework outside school each day to maintain her high grades, Akemi put away her nearly finished history homework and her almost perfect geometry homework and began to work on the next day's homework for Geometry in the five to ten minutes remaining in class.

The bell rang, and we headed to American Literature, where Akemi generally practiced widely varied kinds of writing: journal writing about any subject she chose; a structured two-paragraph character sketch about a fellow student; definitions of vocabulary copied from the board; one-paragraph summaries of short stories she'd read; a children's story; "ungrammatical" sentences copied from the board and corrected. This day, along with all the other students, she grabbed a piece of paper from the front of the room and, before the bell rang announcing the start of class, began to compose the required ten minutes of journal writing. At the teacher's suggestion, some students volunteered to share what they had written, and then they all moved into the next activity: a ten-minute small-group exercise in which triads decided on the three words which best described the personality of a character from a short story they'd just read. Akemi's group completed this task efficiently, seemingly effortlessly, and they soon moved back to their own seats to begin a writing assignment: a four-paragraph essay in which they wrote about each characteristic in a single paragraph, introducing the "character as a whole" in the first paragraph.

Another bell, another five minutes in the halls and we arrived at Health, in which Akemi spent the whole hour this day, as she did almost every day, constructing outlines of various chapters in her textbook and then answering questions at the end of the chapter—some multiple choice and matching, some short answer. As she read and wrote, the teacher asked a few questions aloud from the multiple choice section; Akemi kept on writing through this question-and-answer period, occasionally answering a question aloud from a section she'd already completed while she kept on writing answers to a new section. About twenty minutes later, students got back a test they had taken Tuesday, a mostly multiple-choice and true/false test with one essay, a test photocopied from the teacher's manual which accompanied the text. Looking over Akemi's shoulder, I could see that her answer to the one essay question consisted of a numbered list of responses.

From here, Akemi and I pushed our way through the crowded hall to the other end of the school, struggling to be on time for her favorite class, Biology. For most of the class, the students copied notes and diagrams from an overhead projector as the teacher explained them. While Akemi listened to the teacher's explanation, her copying of the notes was generally two to three minutes ahead of the teacher's pace; when she reached the end of a page, she patiently waited for him to catch up with her and turn to a new page on the overhead. After all the students completed copying the notes, they were given their next assignment: to read a chapter in the book, outline it, and offer short answers to the questions at the end. For the rest of the hour, students participated in a brief lab in the back of the classroom, observing and noting data for an ongoing experiment.

In the final class before lunch break, Computers, Akemi spent the first fifteen minutes playing computer games with a friend and then began to compose a program on the screen, using mostly symbols and numbers. After a few minutes of this, she attempted to run the program and found it wouldn't run correctly. She chose not to deal with the frustration of finding the errors and instead simply "borrowed" someone else's completed program, copied it onto her disk, ran it correctly this time, printed it, and handed it in with time left over to play a few more computer games.

After lunch, Akemi went to her last class of the day, U.S. History. She pulled out the chart she had worked on in geometry that morning and copied the incompleted parts from the completed facsimile the teacher had placed on the board. The class assignment that day was to read a chapter from their textbook and offer short answers to questions and fill-in-the-blank material at the end of the chapter. Akemi immediately turned to the questions, occasionally flipping back through the book to find a definition or a date, but mostly answering off the top of her head.

If we were to conduct a numerical study in which we noted how many minutes Akemi spent writing this day, or any day, we would see that Akemi indeed took pen to paper quite often; she was writing—daily—in every class she took. Most of her classes revolved around quiet seatwork in which students would write answers to questions and take notes in various ways. What we also would see, though, is that a large percentage of that writing was copying and outlining, answering multiple-choice questions: in other words, giving information back to the teacher in a form that the teacher had prescribed. In terms of "writing to discover, writing to know," Akemi actually did very little.

Carole Edelsky and Kelly Draper would suggest that much "writing" that students practice in school settings is just that: writing in quotes. They distinguish between writing and "writing" (and reading and "reading") on the basis of meaning making. "If meaning-making is not at the center of the activity, it is 'reading'/'writing' rather than reading or writing," they say. "That means that every literacy event, every activity with print, does not include an act of reading and writing" (i). In their terms, then, much of Akemi's contact with the printed word would constitute neither reading nor writing. Meaning making clearly is limited. This relationship between meaning making and writing (or lack thereof) is of interest, too, to Sharon Crowley, who adds a political dimension in terms of the issues of authority as she differentiates between writing and Writing, the latter being what Authors do. In American society, she says, "there's writing, which is the simple ordering and recording of thoughts and information and which can be done as easily by a secretary or a committee or a machine or a technical writer, since its authority is not relevant to its status as a text; and there's Writing, what Authors . . . do" (97). In her view, teachers too often create situations in classrooms in which students are allowed to write but not Write; their work is devalued and never treated in the serious fashion we treat "legitimate" Authors. Legitimate Authors, the ones whose work is canonized in the books students are assigned to read, are valued in a number of ways: students read their works, take notes on their words, answer test questions on their ideas; these Authors are presented to the students as composers who do write to discover meaning and achieve intellectual purpose. Crowley claims, and I agree, that the split between student-writers and Legitimate Authors is ever present in schools and, in fact, constitutes how most teachers design their classrooms (97–98).

For Akemi, these distinctions are appropriate ones. Many of the writing tasks she encountered within the school day seemed to leave out the element of meaning making and became "writing" tasks. Such tasks necessarily reduced her role as an author so that she rarely wrote in these school settings: she copied, she outlined, she filled in charts, she filled in forms. She did not, for the most part, have an opportunity to play with language, to become authoritative over a piece of writing, so that she might achieve what Knoblauch and Brannon see as the essential needs of student writers: "discovering personal meanings, thinking well in language, or achieving serious intellectual purpose" (*Rhetorical Traditions* 31). As I discovered in my first few weeks as a participant-observer, the pen-to-paper tasks that students like Akemi were asked to do made it easy for them to remain writers, rarely providing them the opportunity to become Authors.

Akemi's own definitions of the writing she did in school support this distinction as well. She saw writing solely in terms of its format: Pieces of writing became artifacts defined by how they were situated on a page, what rules and regulations they fulfilled. Akemi generally spoke of writing as a concept, as a noun, not a verb, with a focus on the finished product rather than on the process. She also defined writing in terms of teacher expectations: The rules for composing a piece of writing became obvious not so much because of the demands of a particular discipline (i.e., writing for English is different from writing for Biology) but rather because of Akemi's perceptions of how a particular kind of writing should exist in her various teachers' worlds (i.e., Ms. Bowling wants something different from Mr. Sampselle).

For Akemi, form existed mostly as a notion of genre. School writing fell into certain clear-cut categories, categories to which she assigned six particular names: essays, reports, summaries, evaluations, stories, and outlines. She believed each was defined in a very specific way. For example, in Akemi's terms, an essay could be seen as "writing on a given subject" with a little bit of research so that it's a mix of "one's own beliefs and someone else's." A report would be "anything other than an essay combined in a paper." It covers more than an essay; it "tells the main points" about a subject and is divisible into different parts—often including charts and graphs. But while in an essay, the writer might be permitted to ramble on a bit, a report is more succinct: "You got to do exactly what you say . . . and don't be long about it." Akemi would define a summary as "reading about something and telling about it," generally in a single paragraph. An evaluation in contrast is "reading something . . . giving the facts in the first paragraph and then telling your point of view on it [presumably in the second paragraph] . . . whether it's good, bad, what the problems they have with it." A story is "a fictitious fable. . . . You got to make it up out of your own imagination." Outlining is "taking the basic points out of the chapter and putting it into a form."

This generic sense of writing was strong for Akemi and certainly rings a familiar bell for the many English teachers who also divide writing into a set of genres, albeit a different set from Akemi's. If we look in many of the textbooks used in schools today, we can see the division of writing into separate chapters according to different forms: most commonly the separation of writing tasks into modern versions of the classical topoi (such as the definition essay, the cause–effect essay, the compare–contrast essay, for example) or into the modes of discourse (narrative, descriptive, argumentative, persuasive, for example). Knoblauch and Brannon discuss such practice at length in their chapter entitled "Ancient Rhetoric in Modern Classrooms," critiquing the tendency of teachers to adopt these schemas as set entities in the hopes that such renditions will promote better writing on their students' parts. They compare these schemas to a "painting-by-the-numbers" which, "though it guarantees a reasonably tidy product, has never yet served to make a painter" (*Rhetorical Traditions* 32). Their main concern about adopting the topoi or modes in the contemporary composition classroom, in addition to the problems inherent in focusing instruction on the distinction between such categories as persuasive and argumentative writing, for example, is that such a tendency leads teachers toward conceptualizing both an ideal text and an ideal process to achieve that text. They explain their concern in this way:

> If the modes are distinct, then so too must be the strategies for composing in each of them. This highly schematized way of thinking about discourse encouraged a dogmatic rather than speculative attitude, exaggerating boundaries of intention and therefore also boundaries of genre, boundaries of acceptable performance, and boundaries of effect. (26)

Additionally disturbing is the belief that the expressive modes (i.e., narration and description) are different from/easier than/less rigid than the expository modes and should thus be taught separately (and preferably earlier in the year), a belief that Knoblauch and Brannon see as rampant among teachers.

Perhaps not too surprisingly, what Akemi could see of form

and thus what constituted her particular taxonomy remained tied to what she saw as the expectations of her teachers. Her vision of the teacher as inexorably bound to form came through repeatedly in her explanations of how she wrote in various subject areas. For example, at the level of minutia of form, Akemi explained her reliance on the presentational form of the product in terms of those expectations. Teachers expected the product to be arranged in certain but various ways, she said: One teacher "wants only so many words per sentence, so many sentences per paragraph. . . . If he tells you to write a page and you write a page and a line, he won't accept it. He'll throw it in the trash." Another teacher focused mostly on issues of punctuation—"She wants your semicolons in place and your commas"—as a primary consideration. A third teacher concentrated on the outward appearance of the outlines he assigned without looking at content: "It's got to be in a little format," Akemi said, so that it would "*look* like it's outlined."

At times Akemi also actually defined the genre of the writing she did in terms of the teacher's expectations. When I asked her, for example, to explain what she thought a report was, Akemi responded first by talking about two different teachers and how they expected reports to be done. "A report," she began, stopped, and then continued, "like, the only person I really do a good fashioned report [for] is Mr. Brown [her Biology teacher] and Miss Stamp [her U.S. History teacher]." She explained further what constituted a report for each of them, an explanation which pushed not only the notion of genre as a changing item, dependent on the teacher, but which also reflected the form-oriented nature of such genres, as each genre became defined for her in terms of its component parts. "Mr. Brown's report consists of taking data; we make graphs out of our data, and we write our procedure and we write the basic report of it and we write the materials, list all that in there with a cover sheet, picture page and that." Miss Stamp's notion of a report was slightly different, according to Akemi: "We basically wrote the report, wrote a graph, did some political cartoons—she like political cartoons, she loves the cartoons—and then we did a slogan." Even within a single subject area, the demands of form for a particular genre varied; for example, Akemi explained that she had always been given a simple form to follow in order to write book reports in her English classes over the years, but that "every one I ever had was different." Thus, the report (or the essay or the outline) did not exist as a strictly distinct genre for Akemi, either across the disciplines or for a defined subject area, but rather a flexible genre, defined on each occasion by the teacher. Akemi, like most good students, knew well how to supply each teacher with the varying elements each asked for in a particular kind of writing in order to be successful. Thus, if Miss Stamp "loves the cartoons," Akemi was sure to make those a part of her report. If her English teacher this term wanted a different book report form from the one used last term, Akemi certainly knew which one to follow.

How Akemi came to understand how to write in each form, how she even came to make up her taxonomy of forms in this particular way, remained a complicated issue for me to understand, one that even she couldn't fully articulate, but one that seemed caught up again in teacher expectations. In many of her classes she had been told outright how her writing was to be organized. In one class, for example, she took notes on the teacher's lecture on how to outline; in another she was given an exacting form for a book report; in still another the teacher told the class as a part of the assignment the form each piece of writing should take before the student began the assignment. Thus, for example, everyone's "career report" in health class proceeded in an expected way because of the teacher's form, which stayed emblazoned on the board for over a week:

Career Report

I. Type of Work

II. Requirements
  A. Experience
  B. Training
    1. School
    2. Other . . .

Even an English class which took on some of the "write-to-know" notions fell prey to this reliance on form. As we saw in Akemi's prototypical day, after a prewriting group exercise in which student talk formed the basis for understanding a character in a short story, the students were instructed to then write up their character analyses in a highly formulaic way: four paragraphs for the essay with one paragraph of introduction, three paragraphs of development (one on each characteristic), and no concluding paragraph because, as the teacher remarked to the class, "you haven't yet learned how to write those." Such strictly devised criteria about what a piece of writing should look like certainly seem like the painting-by-numbers version of writing that Knoblauch and Brannon deplore.

How teachers evaluated student writing became another major factor, of course, in Akemi's practice of defining writing in formal terms. As Akemi said of one teacher's evaluation style, "He goes basically on his directions. If it sound good, that's good enough for him." He would look at "how many lines he want filled . . . how many paragraphs he want, how many sentences per paragraph. He go basically on that first, and then he'll come back and see what you wrote"—an emphasis on form over content. Akemi learned what to do and what not to do both from explicit teacher direction before she began writing and explicit teacher comments after she wrote. Thus, she knew that she could answer an essay test question in one class simply by listing three responses, while in another class she had to develop an answer more completely. She explained, "I know Mr. Cady [her Health teacher], he would accept that one, two, three listing; Mr. Brown [her Biology teacher], he wouldn't accept it, so I wouldn't do it like that." Thus, the form of Akemi's essays for these two classes varies greatly, as we can see by these two typical examples of essays, each of which she wrote as answers to questions on tests, one in health and one in biology, each of which received full credit:

1.  Health
    Question: In what ways can you improve your dental health and personal appearance?

Akemi's answer:

    1)  brushing three times daily
    2)  flossing 3 time daily
    3)  clean and paint my nails daily
    4)  grease hair
    5)  Flouridate my drinking water

2.  Biology
    Question: Describe the life cycle of the moss, naming the different structures of each stage.

Akemi's answer:

> Mosses have a two-part life cycle with an alternation of generations—haploid and diploid.
>
> Mosses have a mulitcellular haploid generation that reproduces sexually called gametophyte. At the tip of the gametophyte there are male organs which produce sperm antherida, Female eggs archegonia. The diploid 2nd zygote is formed after the egg is fertilized. The zygote is the first cell of the diploid generation. A long stalk grows. Both stalk and capocla make up the diploid sporophyte.
>
> Inside the diploid spores form. (h-plod) When spores germanate a green filament a protonema.

At the most simple level we can see the differences in these two essays: one uses fragments, arranged in list form; One contains mostly complete sentences, arranged in paragraph form. Still, both are clearly formulaic in nature, conform to clear expectations (we can almost hear the voice of the teacher instructing the students as to how to write these essays), and both simply give back what the teacher assigned the student to "know."

Many of these notions of a form-based approach to writing that I began to see in Akemi's practice seem consistent with the current discussion in composition circles about the promotion of an "essay-text literacy" in schools. In recent years, many researchers have talked about the existence of different communities in the classroom created in large part by the variations in the discourse of teachers and students—and the disconnections which often seem to result. Such disconnections manifest themselves most notably in the seemingly decontextualized nature of large numbers of school tasks: the in-school discourse of teachers and out-of-school discourse of students appear to be separated to many of our students, and oftentimes they can find no ties to connect the two. The in-school discourse exists for many of our students as a phenomenon quite separate from any other kind of communication they recognize from their own worlds. What counts as literate in the school world is often adherence to a set of norms, a set of values, and, most particularly, as we have seen in Akemi's case, a set of forms. If a student can fill the muffin tin—as Ann Berthoff would say—he or she is considered to be at least minimally literate. This literacy reifies the five-paragraph (or, in Akemi's case, the four-paragraph) essay, the structured research report, the rigidly designed and frigidly delivered book report—forms which are imitative of nothing in the real world and which thus conspire to make school an unreal world. These forms are artifacts of what James Paul Gee and others have seen as an essay-text literacy, what Jenny Cook-Gumperz calls a "schooled literacy," what Knoblauch and Brannon refer to as a "ceremonial view of discourse": in other words, a kind of literacy constructed by and for the schools whose demands correspond to the specific set of discourse practices required of those who will survive in the social worlds of schooling.

In the school worlds where this kind of literacy exists, forms and genres have become, for many students, as they have for Akemi, the invisible content of their language learning and the visible center of the energies they devote to writing. As students write and as teachers read their writing, form takes precedence over content, so much so that students often fail even to think about the subject matter they are writing about, so much so that students see writing as "a process of honoring the conventions that matter to English teachers," as Knoblauch and Brannon tell us, rather than a process of discovering personal meanings, thinking well in language, or achieving serious intellectual purposes" (*Rhetorical Traditions* 31). As it is practiced in schools, writing all too often becomes a game in which students strive to communicate with their teachers, but are able to communicate only in a limited sense of that word and only if they say what it is they have to say in sanctioned ways.

When literacy is viewed in this way, the structures and rules become the reality, a reality that is independent of meaning in the processes of composing. For students so caught up, in-school discourse must necessarily exist as a phenomenon quite separate from the other kinds of discourse in which they constantly engage. Because the rules for classroom discourse seem to be invented only for use in the classroom, and because they are so unlike those that regulate discourse in students' worlds outside school, they often assume a mysterious nature for student writers. Both the invented genres of classroom writing (the five-paragraph essay or the formulaic research paper) and the regulations that dictate language use ("never start a sentence with a conjunction" or "never use passive voice") leave the student at the mercy of the teacher: The genres are her genres, the rules are her rules for a language that is her language, if it is anyone's at all. Writing thus becomes, for many students, a game of choosing the right rules from a perplexing array of must-do's, never-do's, and sometimes-do's—a constantly shifting array as students move from class to class and from teacher to teacher. Caught up in the game of choosing, students have little time to think about writing as an activity of discovering personal meanings, thinking well in language, or achieving some serious intellectual purpose, by communicating discoveries and thoughts to others.

These ideas bring us back to the very basic question of how we might begin to define literacy in another, more useful way. Sociolinguists and others who view literacy from a social constructionist perspective remind us that the literacy which is most often spoken of in the public rhetoric is this school-based literacy, based in its strict notions of form. They also show us that the notions of what knowledge should be known and how knowledge should be presented, ideas which are integral to such a view of literacy, are—at least to some extent—fictions, that is, that they are socially constructed concepts and not set realities. Literacy, they tell us, should be viewed instead in its social context, as something dynamic, something defined by the particular time and place in which it is practiced, and not seen as the static entity that many would have us believe. Historians of literacy such as Geraldine Clifford can help us understand the perspective that pushes for a dynamic view of literacy. Her exhaustive historical look at perspectives on literacy over time is one of several works which reveal "how uncertain and unstable" definitions of literacy actually are ("Buch und Lesen" 474). In her study, Clifford documents how various standards of literacy have changed through the years; in the United States, for example, some of the early definitions of literacy as named; by different authorities were as varied as the ability to sign one's name, completion of the third grade (the standard for work permits by Pennsylvania law in 1897), a fourth-grade education (the 1940 census), a fifth-grade education (the United States Army).

Not only have such "authoritative" definitions of literacy shifted from time to time and place to place, but also the societal expectations of what constitutes literacy have shifted. What was considered to be the acceptable form of literacy in a social sense earlier in this country will not serve as evidence of literacy in this country today. Currently, individuals are expected not only to be able both to read unfamiliar texts with comprehension and to compose original texts but, most recently, to meet the expectations of various new competencies put forth in the recent slew of literature on the problem: According to some of these works, people are expected to meet certain standards of quantitative literacy, document literacy, critical thinking, and even "fundamental human literacy," each with some subtle (and some not-so-subtle) political implications.[4] All these additional and changing pieces of the literacy pie lead to Resnick and Resnick's conclusion and caution: "There has been a sharp shift over time in expectations concerning literacy," and we should expect a continuing shift as we move into the 1990s (370).

Despite such documentation of the changing notions of what constitutes literacy by historians of literacy, researchers such as Jenny Cook-Gumperz emphasize that today's vision of literacy, with its component parts, is, in fact, actually "*constructed* through a process of schooling" (6) [emphasis mine]. Literacy is not seen simply as acquired knowledge, but rather as knowledge "constructed through a process of tests and evaluations both standardized and informal" (7). Thus, not only does the identification of who is and who is not literate remain evaluated by the schools, but the very terms for determining what literacy entails are also constructed by the schools. What actually constitutes literacy in many people's minds, then, is still a person's ability to perform certain school-constructed tasks, tasks which we have seen rely to a large extent on formulaic measures. What these people, who are often those who implement curricula and testing in schools, forget is that these school measures imply a single view of literacy, one based in the assumption that there is one and only one kind of literate community: that which the schools construct—an assumption which has been effectively challenged not only by such historians of literacy as Resnick and Resnick and Clifford, but also by such diverse theorists of literacy acquisition and literacy use as Cook-Gumperz, Paulo Freire, Shirley Brice Heath, Jay Robinson, James Boyd White, and a host of others.[5]

---

[4]See, for example, *A Nation at Risk,* Kirsch and Jungeblut's *Literacy: Profiles of America's Young Adults,* and Kozol's *Illiterate America.*

[5]See, for example, Heath's *Ways With Words,* Freire's *The Politics of Literacy,* Robinson's *Conversations on the Written Word,* and White's *When Words Lose Their Meaning.*

If we reject those limiting and limited definitions of literacy, we can begin to imagine, with the help of these particular authors, some ways to express more accurately and in a sufficiently complex manner what literacy is really all about. I believe individual literacy is best seen in the terms James Boyd White and Jay Robinson have set forth, terms very different from those which generally comprise the literacy pie. White begins us on the path of discovery with this definition of what literacy can be:

> I start with the idea that literacy is not merely the capacity to understand the conceptual content of writings and utterances, but the ability to participate fully in a set of social and intellectual practices. It is not passive but active, not imitative but creative, for participation in the speaking and writing of language is participation in the activities it makes possible. (*Heracles' Bow* 72)

Seen in this way, literacy cannot be viewed as a list of facts to be memorized or skills to be mastered—the cornerstones of an essay-text literacy—but rather as a set of human actions which allow for full participation by an individual in a set of social and intellectual practices. Literacy seen in this way cannot be boxed into a static definition with a list of component parts, as many would have happen, nor can anyone assume that there exists one and only one limited literate community. Within this view of literacy, becoming literate must be seen as Robinson sees it, in terms of an individual's movement within the various settings in which she lives, "a movement from one range of contexts for language use in which speaking and listening predominate to other ranges of contexts in which writing and reading predominate" (101).

That notion of a range of contexts seems vital: Literacy is best understood as variously realized and as encompassing the social and intellectual practices of many different groups of people. As an individual enters into the numerous discourse communities necessary throughout her life, the demands of each community will vary as the social and intellectual practices vary, and so will the resulting definitions of literacy for that community—including, but not limited to, the movement from speaking and listening to reading and writing. Seeing literacy in terms of its local definitions in this way allows us to recognize its truly dynamic nature—a view of literacy which is clearly antithetical to the static school-constructed definitions which rely upon that single mythic literate community.

In Akemi's world, these notions of an essay-text literacy seem pertinent: She clearly had bought into the world of a school literacy, heavily based in its notions of form, and was a student who had successfully negotiated the rules and regulations so that she could be named a literate member of that school community. Despite what might have been the mysterious nature of these school forms, Akemi used them to her advantage and was quite clearly an achiever in this setting. Yet, in her case, these notions cannot be so easily categorized. Akemi maintained that, despite her movement among the many forms in response to teacher demands, she had not lost her identity—that she was, in fact, an independent writer, one who wrote for herself and not for the teacher nor in any kind of institutional way. Despite what we have seen as her clear reliance on the forms, she believed that in almost all cases, she remained the audience for a specific piece of writing. And it is true that even when she was required by a particular teacher to produce an outline which only has to "look like it's outlined," she would produce a detailed textbook kind of outline, complete with roman numerals, capital and lowercase letters, perfectly spaced and complete. Why? She explained that it was for herself, so that she had better notes and thus could study more completely for tests. Because students in that particular class were not allowed to take books home, she realized that the more detailed she made the outline, the better she would be able to study. The real audience, in other words, was herself, even as she recognized the expectations of that other audience. Again and again, this notion of writing for self arose for Akemi. Although most of the writing she produced that term seemed to an outsider to fall squarely into the traditional essay-text forms, she saw herself as exercising a certain amount of choice within those forms. Intriguingly, though, despite her insistence on writing for self, her school writing did remain within acceptable school genres—and, if anything, was even more structured than the genres assigned by the teacher.

I began to concentrate, then, on those few occasions when the demands of that other audience and the needs of self would conflict. Akemi told me a story about one such time in which she chose to use what she termed a "slang" word rather than a "proper" word in an essay for her English class. The teacher crossed out the slang term and changed it to a more "acceptable" word. Akemi chose not to change the term in the paper and further assured me that if the occasion again arose to choose between the two terms, she would still choose to use the slang. She felt the two words did say the same thing, but she liked the sound and the feel of the slang better; in other words, the slang word indicated a personal investment in her writing, even within her strong belief that she should follow the correct form. Akemi maintained, "You must have something about you that's you, and you can't change it to satisfy somebody else. If that's you, you can't be another person for nobody else; you are who you are." Despite this vehement articulation of why she felt you must write for yourself and not for others, a statement which describes this particular incident well, this type of rejection of teacher standards in favor of her own seemed to be a rare occurrence in Akemi's school writing.

We can see this distinction between writing for the teacher and writing for self as more pronounced in Akemi's differentiation between in- and out-of-school writing, two very different kinds of animals in Akemi's classification schema. Akemi, in fact, enjoyed writing, and she did a fair amount of it in contexts outside the classroom: stories, plays, poems, letters, various journalistic endeavors for an out-of-school organization's newsletter, and reactions to things she had read. These out-of-school experiences allowed her to explore "more feelings for myself," she said, while school stuff was "for a grade. It's not like a friend of mine is going to read it; it's the teacher and it's different." Out-of-school writing let her write more freely, she believed, something she valued in good writing, a quality she claimed to want to continue to develop. Out-of-school writing allowed her creativity to flourish, a major strength she recognized in her own writing: "I have originality," she said. In contrast, she recognized that in some ways her in-school writing seemed to conform to certain set forms, so that school writing in contrast was "strict." "But when I write it for my friend," she explained, "I can tell her whatever I feel and just go on and write on. . . . I just write off the top of my head." It followed, then, that Akemi's favorite kind of writing was the short story, in which she could use her originality in both form and content to the fullest. It also followed that her favorite kind of school writing in her schema was the evaluation. "I get to criticize," she said. "You can tell your point of view and otherwise you have to just give your given facts and you cannot state how you feel." In just two of her classes that term, though, was Akemi "allowed" to write in such a way. Otherwise, much of her writing existed as telling others' facts, filling others' forms, omitting her key ingredient—"originality."

Although she valued the kind of writing she practiced out of school—freely written pieces, or what she calls "freestyle writing"—she rejected its value for in-school writing. The pleasure she maintained she felt when writing "off the top of my head" in out-of-school settings, a writing which emphasized originality of form and subject, became *just* writing off the top of her head when transferred to school-type tasks. In school, she said, she would only use this freestyle writing when she was composing something at the last minute or was unsure of or dissatisfied with an assigned topic. In practice, though, it seemed as if freestyle *as a process* was fairly common in Akemi's work: When given an in-class writing task, Akemi seemed, from her outward appearance, to start writing immediately and to write straight through, spending little time either thinking about the subject or rereading parts of it as she wrote. Rarely did she cross out a word, reorder a phrase, or make any changes in the writing once it found its way to the paper. From her own recounting, her typical process in out-of-class school writing remained basically the same: She would sometimes think about the subject for a while (but only if it was going to be a long piece), then start writing and write straight through to the end, and eventually reread "to see if I made any mistakes" and, if necessary, rewrite, "changing everything I had wrong." (She explained this understanding of "wrong" in terms of fine points of grammar, spelling, and punctuation.) Finally, she would recopy her work if necessary but only if it appeared "too sloppy" for her tastes. We can see the similarities between this process and the process she described another time as freewriting: "I just sit down and start writing. And when I stop, I just stop and hand it in." The two processes of writing, which she saw as very different, come across to an outsider as very alike: writing straight through from beginning to end without prior planning and without any real revision.

Writing off the top of her head, then, whether it's termed freestyle or not, seemed a part of her everyday writing for school. I believe the difference between what she termed freestyle and thus valueless and other writing which was valued in some way lay not in the actual process itself, then, but rather in the realm of form. Those pieces written off the top of her head for school which she valued fell into expected forms: If they were essays for English class, they had the right number of paragraphs; if they were evaluations for History class, they summarized in paragraph one and expressed opinions in paragraph two; if they were reports for Science, they didn't exceed the correct number of pages and lines.

In contrast, the pieces she claimed she didn't value *looked* as if they were written off the top of her head: their forms were not recognizable ones for Akemi as valued ones in the institutional categorizations of forms she has learned as acceptable in school. Thus, what she saw as a process-oriented concern (i.e., value being equated with whether or not something was written in a freestyle manner) turned out to be more of a product-oriented problem. We can go back to Akemi's own words: "It's got to look like it's an outline" or a report or a summary in order for it to be valued—no matter how the writing process might progress to get to that product. Thus, we can see that, despite her protests of what she valued and how she wrote for herself, the form-based nature of writing tasks, conforming to teacher expectations, was more far-reaching that even she might admit.

A case in point is Akemi's reaction to the school system's first locally designed and administered writing assessment, an assessment which took place over a four-day period during my semester with Akemi. In this assessment, all students in their sophomore year were asked to write in various ways about teenage stress.[6] Her final essay, a composition in which she attempted to pull together personal illustrative incidents and some overall conclusions about the nature of teenage stress, is a piece of writing which falls into no easily categorized form. Here is what Akemi wrote:

> "Get off my case!" Stress is a fear. It is an anxiety. It will mess with a person mentally. Too much stress can lead to an early death. So you ask me to write about my stress. But I am just a child and haven't even had a little touch of stress. Why would you ask me to write about something I haven't experienced yet.
>
> So you tell me to write about someone else's stress. However you don't think about that. What if that other person doesn't

---

[6]The assessment was part of an ongoing collaborative teacher-research project between teachers from both high schools and the Center for Education Improvement through Collaboration (CEIC) at The University of Michigan. The directions for the four days were as follows: Day 1, a first freewrite; Day 2, a second freewrite; Day 3, a first try at the actual prompt; Day 4, a final try at the actual prompt.

want their problems read by a whole bunch of people they don't know.

"Just forget it!" The only stress I feel right now is the stress that you are giving me. I am upset now. You expect me to up here and right on stress, but my only stress is you. How dare you ask me about stress? All you are doing is taking a survey and you put all this stress on my back!

My teacher tells me to write well because you paper will be read by alot of different teachers at U. of M. So I try to write something good. But you give us a subject of teenage stress.

What do you want me to write some little simple things for example: "I can't talk on the phone after eleven and that pressures me so much that I want to die." People don't do that stuff today unless they are absolutely crazy.

So now I write you that stress is just a form of fear. It appears that way to me because any stressful situation that you look at has some form of fear attached to it. For example look at this stress you have on me now. It is just a fear that you will give me a (1) one on this paper. Remember reading my "first free write." I had the fear of death.

But don't let these fears get you down. You can overcome them. Just stand up to them. For instant now that I have wrote how I feel about this project, I don't care what you grade my paper. I have even overcome the fear of death. I visit my local funeral homes as often as I can to go see the dead.

So my advice to you is to stop demanding so much from your students. Stop putting unnecessary stress on them. Don't make them have to fabricate stories of stress to just satisfy some little whim you have to learn about stress. I say this to you now because they (the students) will have enough stress when they grow up so they shouldn't have to worry about it now.

Within this piece, there is no five-paragraph structure, no traditional introduction and conclusion, no inclusion of two or three examples per paragraph to develop and prove each point. It is, as Akemi described it later, a "freestyle" piece of writing, but I would argue it is so not only in the process she used to write it, but also in the finished project displayed on the page. And although the ideas and the thinking represented in this piece are far more sophisticated and engaged than many of the two-paragraph evaluations and one-paragraph summaries she regularly composed in school, Akemi intensely disliked this piece (so much so that it was the only piece of her writing that she refused almost completely to talk about with me). She did tell me she considered it valueless, hating the thought that a teacher would ever read and "grade" it (thus, the reference in the piece to her fear of receiving a "1" on the four-point scale upon which the writing was evaluated). She attributed this dislike to the fact that the content was not appealing, that it was, in fact, "boring" to her. "I have not really felt stress," she said to me again and again over the four days, adding at one point, "so I didn't have nothing stressful to write about except this paper you all gave me to write." Even the assessment's construction of four different tries at writing, designed so that students would move away from the one-try, off-the-top-of-your-head writing that typically is found in writing assessments into a more process-oriented approach, failed for Akemi. The different tries were just the same for her as a one-shot assessment, she said, so that she wrote each try as if it were off the top of her head, finding no way to relate the ideas which surfaced in her various tries. (See Appendix A for her other three stabs at writing on the three days prior to this final piece.)

I would contend that her uneasiness with the writing in this assessment is at least partly influenced by her inability to categorize each of the four pieces into recognizable forms. This inability may have occurred for a number of reasons; it might be that she truly found this topic "boring" (although she had demonstrated that she could write successfully on "boring" topics for other school tasks). More likely, though, it seemed that the invitation from her teacher-assessors to introduce personal writing into a school task—writing which fit more readily into her notions of what constituted instead out-of-school writing—seemed foreign to her. Akemi, in these pieces of writing, came up against accepting as valuable a piece of writing which clearly should be a school-like piece but which she couldn't make fit into any of her well-known school categories: essay, report, summary, story, outline, or evaluation. Her strict division of what constitutes in-school and out-of-school writing didn't work so easily in this case. Perhaps this blurring of lines so that she had to share something of herself and, in her mind, put that sharing into a school-like form led to her confusion and, in turn, dislike and even rejection of both the task and its result.

To try to answer in any complete way why Akemi feels this writing which demonstrates critical thinking is a failure and her four-paragraph character sketches a success is clearly a complicated and perhaps ultimately an unanswerable task. It seems evident, though, that one element of the answer has to do with the formally defined writing she has been asked to do—almost exclusively—in school. Such reliance on form may create a rigid set of values for how students perceive good writing, values that are hard to shake. But as Akemi has helped me to see, writing may not be so easily categorized into a formulaic versus nonformulaic dichotomy. Through such a close look at Akemi, we at least begin to see the complicated nature of what constitutes form, at least for one writer.

Perhaps a student can live in the form-based, essay-text world which our schools create while still valuing and producing other kinds of writing (of which we saw glimpses in Akemi's out-of-school writing and her choice of a slang word, for example). But we must also recognize the difficulty for most students of living in both worlds. Sadly, whatever form is valued as "good writing" in schools becomes "real writing" for most kids. Thus, in this emerging portrait of Akemi, an admittedly complex and sometimes contradictory one, we must also keep in mind Akemi's role as a successful student. As such, she has what may be a unique ability to conform and to play school games at times while retaining the confidence to break out at certain moments. Beyond the question of what these notions of form mean for Akemi, then, is the question of what happens to those less successful, less confident students—those who are less able to shift within the forms of school writing. These students are often also the ones to receive instruction in the most rigid of forms. As teachers, we need at least to recognize the constraints of such forms at the same time that we consider their complexity, if we want to move away from such rigid notions of what constitutes an essay-text literacy. Only then can we begin to use writing as "a process of discovering personal meaning, thinking well in language, or achieving serious intellectual purpose."

## POSTSCRIPT: REFLECTIONS ON AKEMI'S STORY

In my introduction to this chapter I refer to this case study of Akemi as a "less than ideal telling of her story," especially because of the inconsistencies I felt in my research stance at the time I was researching and writing. As I struggled to find a comfortable place for myself as researcher, of necessity I relied on the research world from which I came: that of the decontextualized separatist scenario. At the same time, however, I sought to join the research world about which I'd been reading, a world which seemed more in keeping with my own pedagogical stance, that of context-full teacher-research. In some ways this struggle can be seen as one of authority, of authorship: Whose story does this case study reflect—Akemi's or mine? The implications of this struggle are clearly seen in the writing of this chapter; I can see now that the scale often tipped in favor of my version of Akemi's story, in the ways to which I allude in chapter 1: As the creator of the case study, I in large part objectified Akemi, both in the researching and the writing of the case study, denying her role as a meaning maker in some important ways. My best intentions to make her feel at least comfortable with the research (if not an integral part of it—a notion that I began to understand much later) were not sufficient; she certainly recognized her role as the object of a study—*my* study. I can see this in small ways in the language I chose to talk about my role in the study; I talk of myself as "looking over her shoulder," a clear indication that I am doing the looking, and she is the one being looked at. The impact of this objectification comes across most clearly in her essay reproduced in Appendix A, to which I also refer in chapter 1, the essay written as a part of the writing assessment in response to a prompt on teenage stress. She says there, "Right now I do have a small fear. The fear is that I am sitting here and writing on stress and I have absolutely nothing to write about. Cathy from U of M is sitting here ready to read what I have wrote and yet I have written nothing." At least in this instance, Akemi feels intensely that her writing (and, I think, at some level her own self) is the subject of scrutiny by me and by the institution I represent—The University. And in this case, her response went well beyond discomfort at such objectification, probably even contributing in some way to her blocking on this stage of the writing assessment.

As I read and reread this case study, seeing it as an artifact of my own growth as a teacher-researcher, I find, too, that I am uncomfortable with some of the assumptions I seemed to make as I wrote. You will see that in the last half of this study, I contrast what Akemi thinks is going on with her writing with what I believe is *really* going on, using such phrases as "I would contend" and "Thus, we can see that despite her [Akemi's] protests . . . ," indications of an unresolved split in our perceptions with a clear privileging of my perspective over hers. Even now, I find this section difficult to reconcile. Clearly, as an outsider and an experienced teacher, someone who has seen many students' writing and who can see some of what Akemi has written in a different light, I may have some important insights to offer toward a complete understanding of Akemi's story. But at the same time, because of my worries about influencing Akemi's writing too much, a worry I raise more fully in chapter 1, I never really spoke to her about the differences I was perceiving between her recounting and mine. Such talk, at the very least, might have helped this study begin to move away from an objectification of Akemi toward a closer and more complete understanding of Akemi's world on both our parts, resulting in changes in how we might act in that world—my named goals in conducting this research.

The essence of the problem, I believe, is that despite my attempts to include Akemi's voice in this study—a big first step for me in doing this kind of research—I never really include Akemi. This problem is manifested in a number of ways. First, and most obvious, is the lack of actual talk from Akemi. Occasional quotes are included but most of those quotes are not only brief but also truncated to make them fit within my voice. A good example of this is when I explain her understanding of the genres she uses in school writing. My voice takes precedence, while her exact words fit in where they can (Akemi's words in italics here): "A report would be *'anything other than an essay combined in a paper.'* It covers more than an essay; it *'tells the main points'* about a subject and is divisible into different parts—often charts and graphs. But while in an essay, the writer might be permitted to ramble on a bit, a report is more succinct: *'you got to do exactly what you say . . . and don't be long about it.'*" At this point and at many other points in the text, I stray from my original understandings of what teacher-research should be: Although I claim to want context, I continually rip her voice from its contextual setting, relying instead on the essential quote introduced as gracefully as possible, graceful because of my own molding and shaping words. Second, Akemi's presence is reduced as the presence of experts is increased. Those who get the long cites in this text, those whose voices become familiar to readers, are Knoblauch and Brannon, Edelsky and Draper, Crowley, and others. Knoblauch and Brannon, for example, get ten lines just on the first page of the essay; Akemi's longest quote in the whole piece is perhaps two lines. And third, in my attempt to connect to the reader by using again and again the royal *we,* I create a kind of us-versus-them mentality: "*We* scholars and researchers are set above Akemi" is the message this rhetorical strategy sends; *we* understand what's going on in the school in a way she can't. "If *we* were to conduct a numerical study," I write early in the chapter, "in which we noted how many minutes Akemi spent writing this day, or any day, we would see that Akemi indeed took pen to paper quite often."

What I see now is that, despite its good intentions, this piece of research does not go nearly far enough in its attempt to include the researched as part of the research, nor is it really intended to provoke change in the life of Akemi. The idea that research might be used as an agency for change, that through the process of research I might have been able to help Akemi come to understand her own literacy differently, that research and pedagogy could be integrally connected was not an idea that had occurred to me at the time. And the notion of teachers and students as composing collaborators and the implications that term implies did not become a part of my understanding until even much later. As you read through the next three cases, you will see my attempts to move closer to these goals, as those understandings of what research could be began to emerge for me.

You will see as well my developing understanding about the so-called content of these studies, the relation of form/genre to literacy and literacy instruction. As I moved into other classes and other settings, I began to look with a variety of students at their own understandings of their writing. I found a number of students who either don't understand the forms at all and for whom such forms maintain their mysterious nature or who see and reject the forms for some reasons—both kinds of students considered illiterate in the school worlds in which they live. A student such as Akemi is able to write in these essay-text ways and is thus considered successful and literate by the schools, despite the problems which I can see in naming her as such; a student such as Sarah, as I show in the next chapter, is a successful writer in some settings, but finds it difficult to understand the formulaic methods that she thinks are demanded in other settings, and is thus considered an unsuccessful writer in these new situations; a student such as Fred, who enters into the discussion in chapter 4, is mystified by the forms and thus rejects both them and the system completely so that he is considered illiterate by the standardized measures of the world of school. Such form-based notions of literacy have become a pervasive and, I believe, a pernicious means of labeling students as either literate or not. And such labeling, as I came to see, has both ethical and political overtones. Freire believes that "illiteracy is not a strictly linguistic or exclusively pedagogical or methodological problem. It is political, as is the very literacy through which we try to overcome illiteracy" (*Politics of Education* 10). As I continued to expand my understandings of these labels, I began to ask the inevitable next question: What are the politics of a literacy through which we might overcome illiteracy in our classrooms and our schools?

# CHAPTER 3

# *Forming Literacy: Sarah's Story*

## INTRODUCTION

In a number of ways this case study of a student named Sarah can be seen as an expansion, of my ideas about form and its relation to literacy, of my ideas about conducting teacher-research, and of my ideas about the relationship of emancipatory teacher-research to emancipatory pedagogy. In one sense, the expansion results simply from the increased amount of time I was able to spend with Sarah: In contrast to the one-semester block in which I tried to learn everything about Akemi's writing, Sarah and I worked together in different ways over a span of more than three years. For two summers while Sarah was in high school, I was one of her teachers in an intensive writing program; for the next two years, when she was a first- and second-year student at The University of Michigan, I met with her regularly as a sometimes tutor, sometimes researcher, sometimes friend to talk to about a number of subjects, including her writing. In many ways, I found it easier to understand Sarah because of our similar backgrounds. We both came from rural settings and then attended what some have named elitist colleges; we came from similar economic and family situations; we both loved to write. Spending more time with Sarah and drawing upon our commonalities allowed me to compose a fuller and more detailed portrait of Sarah as a writer.

But other reasons factor into this expansion as well. Over the three years of focusing on Sarah, I increased my own reading and thinking about issues of form exponentially. As I began to study the writings of Bakhtin in particular, I came to understand many of the implications of form-based writing instruction in a new light. As a result of my time with Akemi, I had begun to understand form as "ceremonial discourse" or "schooled literacy"—in other words, as a generally limited and limiting means of teaching and learning how to write, which seemed to encourage students to think in certain preconceived ways. The complications which surfaced in my initial writing about Akemi's own perceptions of her writing had struck me as merely interesting and noteworthy complexities that would probably remain unsolvable issues. My reading of Bakhtin provided me with a frame by which I could view these complications in a new way. The interplay he sees existing between what he calls "authoritative" and "internally persuasive" discourses, a dialectic which serves as a kind of battleground for the development of an individual perspective, gave me a way to think about Sarah's writing and to reflect back on Akemi's distinction between writing for herself and writing for others. The struggle Bakhtin describes between these two kinds of discourse struck me as an exact description of what I was seeing happen to Sarah in her transition from high school to college and what I had seen happen to Akemi in her distinction between in- and out-of-school writing.

Students bring to schools the internally persuasive discourses gained from their own background and experience; teachers add to that the authoritative discourse that has been named by the schools as the "correct" kind of discourse. Bakhtin's notions of authoritative discourse could be seen as well as what I have named a *conforming literacy*, a literacy defined by the school rules and regulations, measured by students' adherence to certain forms and genres. Such literacy might be seen in contrast to an *in-forming literacy*, the literacy students bring to school settings, whose forms arise from their own language backgrounds. What I began to see happening to Sarah in her transition from high school to college was an emphasis on a conforming literacy and a deemphasis on an in-forming one. The insistence by Sarah's teachers of denying a dialectic between the two kinds of literacy—which Bakhtin insists is necessary to the development of an individual perspective on the world—led me to think about the political and ethical implications inherent in any particular pedagogy, forcing me to ask myself what it is we do to and with students when we teach.

At the same time, I began to consider just what it is we do to and with students when we conduct research on them. Just as my reading into Bakhtin and others helped me to see my work with Sarah in new ways, my reading into issues of research methodology helped me to continue to question the research program in which I was now participating. As a result of this work with Sarah, I began to think more seriously about the purposes of the kind of research I had been espousing based upon my reading. While I had begun to read quite extensively into the notion of research as emancipatory over my three years with Sarah, the full ethical and pedagogical implications of this stance escaped me until I began to evaluate the positions she and I had occupied as researched and researcher. Still caught in the traditional research world in my demarcation between these two roles, still unsure about how much I thought the researcher might legitimately influence the researched, I found my role as friend of Sarah sometimes at odds with my imagined stance as researcher. As I explain in chapter 1, I still saw my responses to Sarah as a *choice* between these two roles rather than seeing the roles as appropriately merged. It was only through the actual experience of working with Sarah that the texts I was reading about emancipatory and critical research began to make sense. Faced with what I thought were choices about what my role had to be, I had to reconsider, to REsearch my own understandings of what it means to conduct research in an emancipatory way. And, as you saw in chapter 1, the crisis of Sarah's experience as a beginning college writer pushed me to rethink this issue even more. However, it was not really until the time I was ending my work with her that I was ready to call myself even a neophyte emancipatory teacher-researcher.

Although my role as a more emancipatory teacher-researcher, then, rarely emerges in the reading of this text (never does the reader see that moment of crisis with Sarah which I lay out in chapter 1, for example; as you'll see, I reduced it to "Sarah had become completely disillusioned with her writing and had lost confidence in her ability to write," a watered down version of the tears which were shed by Sarah and the resulting crisis of understanding for me), I now can see in my rereading the seeds of my movement toward such a stance. Most critically, Sarah's voice takes on a more important role here than Akemi's did in her case study. A number of factors combined in making this so: As a researcher more comfortable with my role, I began to view talking with Sarah as a conversation rather than as a typical interview with me searching for the perfect question and sifting through her responses for the ideal, "quotable" answer. Our talks, as reflected in the pages and pages of transcriptions that sit next to me now on my desk, began to take on the tenor that actual conversations do, with me posing real questions and, as I learned to listen better, with Sarah answering in growing detail. And, as Sarah furthered these conversations by asking me questions about my experiences, I began to feel more at ease in responding in kind. As a result, we were able to delve into the issues at hand both in more depth and in a more natural way. Sarah's responses became fuller over the course of our time together, eventually heading off in directions unforseen by me and, almost always, leading us into intriguing new territory. The resulting text, then, is able to feature Sarah's voice in some prominent ways: Her words and her understandings take the lead here, and her quotes are more sustained tellings of her perspective. No longer was I searching for the perfect insightful quote to prove a point that I or others might make; while the voices of experts certainly are present, you will see Sarah speaking more and thus maintaining some authority over her own understandings, a beginning toward a more emancipatory moment.

This fuller portrait of Sarah also emerges as I felt increasingly comfortable in another way: shifting my own understanding of what the genre of research might be. By including more details of Sarah's life ("her writer's portfolio: a box in her closet" with the details of its contents, for example), I was able to present Sarah in a more context-full way. While in part this was because I had known Sarah for much longer than I had known Akemi, I recall a self-awareness on my part in this writing, as I tried to shape this portrait more like the ethnographic and phenomenological studies I had been reading, in which attention to atmosphere and setting took on importance. As I had learned in my reading of a number of cases, the more detailed the portrait of the person or setting being researched, the closer the reader can come to that "aha!" experience. When those who are researched can become real people rather than flattened characters, readers are more likely to make associations with those described, granting more weight to the portrait and thus to the conclusions that are reached. For the researcher, a fuller portrait helps in getting across the subtleties of the research experience that are located between the words: the nuances and atmosphere so necessary for a more complete understanding. As you read, you will see my shift toward this more descriptive genre as just a beginning movement away from the mode of research-as-usual, but for me it represented an important, self-conscious shift. You will see as well that I remain mired in one of the mainstays of that traditional research genre: the hypothesis/proof model in which loose ends get tied up and conclusions are reached seemingly without effort. Later in my research journey, I began to be intrigued by the notions inherent in the postmodern stance (as I describe in chapter 1) with multiple voices contributing to a heteroglossic understanding, but at this point the lesson Bakhtin was teaching me about form in Sarah's writing didn't transfer to my own composing style. While, in this text, I had moved away from the pattern of idea gleaned from expert—leading to insightful quote from researched—leading to my summary (in part due to the increasingly complicated positions I found Sarah espousing when I learned to listen), the general form of the research as argument leading to inevitable conclusion (inevitable, of course, because as writer you've set up the argument in that way) is still present. The piece makes some moves toward a *re-forming* mode of research, but remains pretty firmly a *conforming* model.

Once more, then, from the perspective that only hindsight can bring, I now view my portrayal of Sarah's story in mixed ways. I recall the pleasure I felt at the time at my movement forward as a researcher. Certainly I was becoming more comfortable in the role of a teacher-researcher, and the seeds of emancipatory research were becoming planted. Now I am most aware that Sarah's participation in this study still placed her quite firmly as an object of the research and not as a researching subject, a distinction that has come to take on increased importance to me as my own understanding of research has progressed. In the postscript that closes this study, I will explore in more detail my positioning of Sarah in this role and how I came to understand the contradictions inherent between this assignment of roles and the positions I began to see as more appropriate for both the researchers and researched.

## FORMING LITERACY: SARAH'S STORY (DECEMBER 1988)

I first came to know Sarah in the summer of 1986 when she had just finished her junior year in high school and was participating in a summer writing program for high school students from the northeastern part of Michigan. Sarah was one of the "stars" of the program, at least from a teacher's vantage point: She loved to write and spent hours composing, revising, critiquing both her own and her peers' writing. So involved was she with her writing that even when the summer program came to an end and all the students' various writings were handed in (to be published in a book), Sarah was still writing: "I'm going to keep working on [my piece]. I have a copy of it. I'm going to revise it," she told us.

Sarah had been writing on her own since she was about twelve, prolifically composing poetry and short stories in out-of-school settings and keeping them in her own writer's portfolio—a box in her closet. She cared passionately about her writing; even as she talked of becoming a professional writer at some point in the future, she already saw herself as an author. By the end of her high school career, she was confident and compassionate about her writing, always receiving high grades on her writing assignments, while still striking out on her own, both in and out of school, to try new ideas and new ways of composing. At one point she revealed to those of us who were her teachers that she prefers this kind of writing, because she often feels "a little rebellious when people tell me what to do." She instead seeks to write what and how she wants, "not according to someone else's structures."

The Sarah I know now, a sophomore at The University of Michigan, is in many ways the same person I met four years ago: She is bubbly, enthusiastic, friendly, and intelligent; but in other ways, she is quite different. After a year and a half of college, she's lost confidence in her writing, rarely writes on her own, and lacks much of the passion for the written word that once consumed her. She says that now, "even when I'm writing, I don't feel like I'm writing." Instead she feels as if she's "fulfilling a require-ment . . . doing something I don't want to do. It's really strange because I've never not wanted to write—*never*—and now, with every paper, I just want to cringe." She goes on, "I think it's because I've discovered there are types of writing that I'm not good at, and I'd never entertained that possibility before. . . . I've learned how to be defeatist since I've been here."

What happened to Sarah is a story about how students struggle to acquire the kinds of literacies they need in order to survive in college settings and a story of what the discourses of various aca-demic disciplines demand from their students. For Sarah, like Akemi, the notion of "what counts" in these settings has a lot to do with how the writing is formed, with the rules of a game she hasn't yet learned to master and which she now doubts she ever will. In Bakhtin's terms, the college forms of literacy are, for Sarah, a kind of authoritative discourse which remains quite separate from any kind of discourse she knows or understands, what he terms "the word of a father, of adults and of teachers." He continues, "The authoritative word demands that we acknowledge it, that we make it our own; it binds us, quite independent of any power it might have to persuade us internally; we encounter it with its authority already fused to it" (*Dialogic Imagination* 342). Bakhtin sees the authoritative word as a discourse unto itself in which no play is allowed, no heteroglossia is possible. He believes, "It enters our verbal consciousness as a compact and indivisible mass; one must either totally affirm it or totally reject it" (343).

For Bakhtin, the struggle between an authoritative discourse and its dialogical opposite, what he calls an internally persuasive discourse, is an important struggle. Internally persuasive discourse, that which is "backed up by no authority at all and is frequently not even acknowledged in society" (342), enters our consciousness not in the rigid and unchanging manner of authoritative discourse, but rather as "intense interaction, a *struggle* with other internally persuasive discourses" (346). If authoritative discourse denies heteroglossia, internally persuasive discourse celebrates it.[1]

The struggle between authoritative and internally persuasive discourse is, for Bakhtin, a struggle that is central to one's formation of an individual ideology. He argues that as we begin the "process of assimilating the words of others," an assimilation that is based in a constant dialogue with these various discourses, we begin to formulate our own ideologies (341). Only then can our own voice begin to emerge from this cacophony of voices to which we are exposed, and only then "can one's own discourse and one's own voice . . . begin to liberate themselves from the authority of the other's discourse" (348).

In many ways, Bakhtin's notions of individual ideology and its formation relates to the ideas laid out in my case study of Akemi about literacy acquisition, ideas informed by such diverse scholars as Paulo Freire, Jay Robinson, and James Boyd White. Adolescents in particular continue the forming of their literacy on a battle-

---

[1]In *The Dialogic Imagination* Bakhtin defines heteroglossia as "another's speech in another's language, serving to express authorial intentions but in a refracted way" (324). Michael Holquist, in his introduction to that book, sees heteroglossia as celebrating "the immense plurality of experience" (xx).

ground similar to Bakhtin's struggle: The school notions of literacy, the essay-text formulations, stand as authoritative discourse, what I want to call a conforming literacy. The out-of-school, everyday talk of our students, gleaned from their own backgrounds, exists as internally persuasive discourses, what I want to call an informing literacy. The consistent dialectical interplay between these two, in its most positive moments, helps constantly to re-form student literacy and is thus important to student growth in reading and writing. But more often, this interaction is played out in a less positive way in schools, and the interaction truly becomes a battle in which students, I believe, are often the losers.

I will argue in this essay that Bakhtin's depiction of this struggle and its correlation to issues of literacy can help us understand in some ways what has happened to Sarah. Prior to her college experience, Sarah was a writer for whom the struggle between authoritative discourse and internally persuasive discourse—as well as among various internally persuasive discourses—was a constantly vitalizing presence in the formation of her own literacy. Sarah's individual ideology has been formed in many ways by that continuous and active interplay between the two. In college, however, authoritative discourse has triumphed, looming large in her psyche and reducing her confidence in any kind of discourse she sees as her own. And, I would argue, this intense and almost blinding focus on Sarah's part toward authoritative discourse has begun to limit her continuing literacy growth.

*Sarah in High School: The Struggle between Authoritative and Internally Persuasive Discourse*

The summer of 1986 was in many ways a turning point for Sarah in the formation of her own literacy. Participation in a summer writing program allowed her to be around numerous other student-writers who shared her enthusiasm for and commitment to writing. Prior to this time, high school writing for Sarah was divided for the most part into two types: writing in-school and writing out-of-school, each defined by certain characteristics which helped her to maintain their separate states.

In-school discourse had become defined for Sarah by its authoritative nature, as it had for Akemi, and as it has become defined for a host of other students. It seems that all too often, the in-school discourse of teachers is situated in a separate discourse community from that of the students, and thus, students see many of their school writing tasks as decontextualized tasks, separate from their own discourse communities. In these cases, writing often takes on the dimensions of a game between teachers and students, with students trying to follow the rules in order to win the grade. When this happens, the school ways will generally win out—at least for those students who are willing to play the game and who are then able to match the expectations of the essay-text literacy. Such schooled literacy seems to be what Bakhtin has in mind when he speaks of an authoritative discourse, a discourse which maintains its status, not because its form is constitutive of outside authority, but rather because of the authoritative manner in which it is handed down to students. As Bakhtin would say, such discourse comes to us whole, "with its authority already fused to it." Authoritative discourse, then, with its conforming literacy, sits on a plane quite removed from (usually "above") any sort of internally persuasive discourse, any in-forming literacy.

Conforming literacy, as we saw in Akemi's story, is based in the structures and rules which surround it, rules which seem actually to constitute the writing, rules which appear to be handed down from teachers. Rules become the central focus of the students' writing and maintain an identity independent of any meaning in that writing. As such, in-school discourse, conforming literacy, has the potential to remain separate from other kinds of discourse our students know and understand.

Much of this description of conforming literacy certainly matches Sarah's experience in school up until 1986. Control over the form of the discourse rested quite comfortably in the teachers' hands, and Sarah responded to in-school writing by following the rules and regulations that had been set up for her, rules pertaining mostly to a range of notions about form: from what Sarah sees as "picky things," such as width of margins to larger issues such as the format or mode the writing would take. Sarah, for example, told us, just as Akemi did, that the most important characteristic of high school writing was that "it had to look good. You had to have the right margins, you couldn't have eraser marks, really picky things like that." "Looking good" also included such aspects as punctuation, spelling, and grammar. For one teacher, she told us,

"I have to write certain kinds of sentences, my commas have to be placed correctly, my spelling has to be correct, I can't start a sentence with *there is* or *there was,* I can't use *be* verbs."

The most important aspect of school rules for Sarah, though, dealt with issues of the overall format or mode the writing took. For Sarah, this focus on *how* the writing had to be formulated rather than on *what* the writing actually said seemed curious even to her, which she articulated for us in this way:

> For school they say write a descriptive piece and you have to choose what you want to describe, but you still have to write descriptively. . . . You have to rack your brain to think of something to describe. When you do it that way, it's a completely different pattern that you follow because you start off thinking descriptive instead of being struck by something and saying, "I want to describe that, I want to capture that."

Sarah herself recognized a kind of cart-before-the-horse mentality about this approach to writing, an approach which forces students to see form as the substance of their writing, with substance coming in a distant second—or third or fourth. Despite her recognition of the problems of this version of school literacy, Sarah nevertheless succumbed to its authority. "Teachers say 'this is what I want' and they make it abundantly clear," she explained. "I have to stick to the set rules which will get me the grade that I want, which is an A."

This authoritative discourse was clearly associated for Sarah with her teachers and their expectations. And as long as she was writing in school she did her best to adapt to the rules and to write in the sanctioned ways—and, as her high grades in writing courses reflect, she certainly learned to master the expectations of their world. In this way, Sarah and Akemi had much in common. But Sarah, unlike Akemi, also understood that not all writing is like that, and for her the real writing, the writing in which she was the Author and not merely a writer, took place outside of school settings.[2] Sarah's bulging portfolio of her writing, hidden in the deep recesses of her closet, came to symbolize the nature of her out-of-school writing: myriad pieces of varying styles (letters not sent, descriptions of people and places, journal entries, poetry) but pieces that remained private and not to be shared with other

---

[2]I am using the language of Sharon Crowley in her distinction between writing and Writing and authors and Authors.

people. In these writings there was no external authority, no voice of the teacher telling her what she had to do, only the authority she possessed within herself, an in-formed literacy created through her encounters with the many discourses of her family, friends, and community. Such writing was truly an internally persuasive discourse as Bakhtin describes it, a personally convincing, self-satisfying approach. And, not surprisingly, this was the writing which in Sarah's view truly mattered.

Thus, Sarah—a writer for whom authoritative discourse and internally persuasive discourse were completely separated into an in-school/out-of-school dichotomy—was ripe for the experience a summer writing program could provide. Housed in a school building and taught by University of Michigan and area high school teachers, the Huron Shores Summer Writing Institute might have had all the trappings that school writing seemed to evoke for Sarah. However, the philosophy of this program closely resembled that of Bakhtin's heteroglossic leanings. The Huron Shores Summer Writing Institute, especially in its first two summers of existence (1986–87), served the purpose of uniting secondary-school students from several schools across rural northeastern Michigan in a common goal: to research the heritage of their communities and to retell the stories of their families, neighbors, and friends in a written form. Students relied on their own sensory impressions of their surroundings by trying to look with fresh eyes at their very familiar environment; on the words of their community by interviewing mostly older people about their recollections of various experiences of their youth; and on the words of more distant researchers by reading historical documents from newspapers, magazines, books, letters—all found in the area's historical museum. Students then tried—some more successfully than others—to find a way for these various voices to come together with their own authorial voice, in order to recount a particular occasion, a movement, or a person. Their writings were finally collected in a book, entitled *Breakwall* by the students, with the following explanation included on the title page: "A breakwall prevents erosion of the earth. We hope that our Breakwall will prevent the erosion of our Northern Michigan Heritage. This book is dedicated to the people of Northern Michigan: past, present and future."

For Sarah, as for other students, the focus on a content which she helped to design and about which she soon recognized herself as the expert (after all, those of us from Ann Arbor were separated from the culture of the area by more than the two hundred miles of gorgeous Michigan countryside) provided a change from what she had come to know as typical school writing. For the first time in a school-like setting, form emerged from content and the variety of forms and styles which came to characterize *Breakwall* were as vast and varied as the content itself: personal reflections on small town prejudice, character sketches of older people in the community, narratives of the stories of local Vietnam veterans, poems about the surrounding environment, reports on the wives of sailors in the town, satire on the state of women today, letters between women from the World War II era.

Sarah excelled in this environment, penning a piece garnered from her own imagination and a series of interviews with five older women who had lived their entire lives in the area. Sarah's piece is entitled "Diery: Katy," and she characterizes it as "an excerpt from the fictional diary of a six-year-old girl" in the year 1916. Sarah in this piece aptly mimics the voice of a six-year-old, a voice well-known to her as someone with a family of younger brothers at home; at the same time, she brings out incidents and factual information told to her by those she interviewed. For example, here is the entry she created for September 30, 1916 [see Appendix B for the entire piece]:

September 30, 1916

Deer diery

    To-morrow is my first day of skool. I will walk to skool with Willie and Jacob after we milk the cows and do are chors. I am verry ecksited to go to skool and to meet the teecher. Mama uste to be a teecher and I can reed and rite letters. Mama teeched me to reed and rite when I was sik of the smal poks and had to be in my bed all the times. The dikter told Mama I wuld die but I am not ded. yesterday papa hiched up the teem after we pult up the weeks in the potatos and he tuk Willie and Jacob and me to get new shews at the stor for us to go to skool in. My new shoes are verry nice and hav buttons all the way up the side.

With fond admurashen<br>Katy

P.S. I got a new dres to but Gussie my sister who is three dint get a new dres or new shews becauz she isnt going to skool. Gussie wares my old close.

The bout of smallpox, the new school clothes, the chores are all ideas gleaned from her interviews but pulled together in a voice she created based on her own background and imagination. The language itself is a mix of voices: that of Sarah's re-creations of how a six-year-old might write, complete with misspellings; short, choppy sentences; simple vocabulary and syntax, but also that of a six-year-old who herself has pulled together her own language from various sources as well. In the entry of June 16, for example, when "Katy" first signs "with fond admurashen, Katy," she puts an explanatory note, "This is how Omi uste to sine her letters. Omi is my Grandmother." Thus, we see mixed voices heaped upon mixed voices: Katy's heteroglossic language comprised of her own six-year-old voice influenced by the more adult voices of her family; Sarah's heteroglossic language comprised of her own voice and that of her interviewees.

This sophisticated amalgamation of style and voices is reminiscent of Bakhtin's notion of conscious hybridization, what he calls *"an artistically organized system for bringing different languages in contact with one another"* (*Dialogic Imagination* 361). Bakhtin considers such hybridization as distinct from the simple diversity of voices found any time sources outside one's own experience are incorporated into one's speech or writing. (For example when a student writes a research paper and merely cites certain sources, the two voices remain distinct and separate.) While the roots of such "double-voicedness" are *merely* separate and distinct voices, the roots of hybridization are an internal mixture—a "collision," Bakhtin calls it. He distinguishes hybridization in this way: "a mixture of two social languages within the limits of a single utterance, an encounter, within the arena of an utterance, between two different linguistic consciousnesses, separated from one another by an epoch, by social differentiation or by some other factor" (358).[3]

Sarah's diary entries start her on a move toward hybridization, a move which allows several differing voices—voices which speak from various discourse communities, which come from different

---

[3]Bakhtin uses the terms hybridization, double-voicedness, authoritative discourse, and internally persuasive discourses in his explanations of the form of the novel. While I am adapting his terms for my use and imposing certain value judgments on these terms, his use of them is quite neutral in nature.

linguistic consciousnesses—to "collide," to "struggle," to "interact" as various internally persuasive discourses. We hear traces of the voice she recollects from her own childhood, a voice made more immediate by her dealings with several younger brothers, that is, the voice of a contemporary six-year-old. We also hear traces of the eclectic voices of the five women she interviewed specifically for this piece, voices which, in adult fashion, recollect their own growing-up experiences. These various voices collide in Sarah's consciousness and become a hybridization, but remain a hybridization over which she takes control, over which she takes authority—as she becomes an Author. Thus, these are not the stories of those whom she interviewed transferred *en masse,* nor do they become the language of her younger siblings alone; either of these would, of course, be a kind of authoritative discourse, where the authority of the word rests in hands other than Sarah's. Instead, the discourse of this piece serves as a perfect example of heteroglossia, a heteroglossia gained by the confrontation of varying internally persuasive and authoritative discourses, a heteroglossia resulting in a conscious hybridization.

Sarah ended her first summer at the Writing Institute with a different attitude toward public writing, writing that would be shared with others. She told us that in the Institute, it was "the content and the style and everything that mattered; and that's never mattered before. And I like having those matter." Sarah returned to her senior year of high school with this new feeling toward what school writing could be and found herself stretching, breaking some rules, moving beyond what previously had been authoritative discourse for her. And she discovered that, as long as she met the basic rules and regulations of school writing, she could do some stretching. As she explained, as long as "you had your punctuation correct and your spelling correct and all the structural things, then you could basically say anything you wanted . . . in any *way* you wanted to. And anything above and beyond the spelling and punctuation and grammar was incredible." Sarah began to excel even more than before as she found a new kind of fit between her private, out-of-school writing and the characteristics she had previously reserved for that, and the more public in-school writing with the restrictions she associated with it. She began to find some common ground between the in-school conforming literacy and the out-of-school in-forming literacy.

Sarah returned to the Writing Institute in the summer of 1987 ready to roll. The experience of the previous summer, coupled with an encouraging senior year, led to her seeing herself even more as an author than she had the previous summer, and thus she began the two weeks in a ferociously productive mood: writing up a storm, helping others with their writing, listening hard to others' critiques of her writing. She finished up one piece, a sensory description of the shore of Lake Huron, a piece that was eventually selected by her peers to open *Breakwall II*. Sarah did this piece as an alternative to one we teachers had suggested on a field trip to a nearby waterfall on the first day of the summer session. Rather than writing an impression of that scene, she chose to close her eyes and imagine another familiar scene, one that she later described as more inspirational to her. Immediately, then, Sarah began the summer as her own writer, choosing her own subject and form.

As the two weeks progressed and Sarah finished this piece, the Author Sarah began to disintegrate before our very eyes. During the previous winter, Sarah had decided to interview her grandmother as an entree into one of her summer pieces. She explained what happened next:

> When I started out I sort of wanted to do something historical and I wanted to do something about teachers and I thought of her [my grandmother] . . . she had some really neat stories. I thought it would be kind of neat if I could just take one of those stories and could just write it—or rewrite it. The more I got talking to her the more it got to be a story about her.

Before the institute even got under way, Sarah had begun to feel pressure from family members, other than her grandmother, about writing this piece. Sarah's "neat" idea had suddenly turned into a family project. Sarah recalls, at one point, her father even telling her, "This is your grandmother and she's not going to be around that much longer and if you don't write about her now, you might never get the chance."

She continued, "It got to the point where I didn't even want to write it anymore, because I had to write it. I wasn't writing it for me and it was because they wanted it and I didn't know what they wanted. I didn't know what they expected . . . but I knew that I had to meet their expectations." The expectations coming from outside sources that Sarah felt about this writing are again reminiscent of Bakhtin's authoritative discourse. Unlike the authoritative discourse Sarah found in school settings, though, this kind of authoritative discourse became terrifying in a new way—because she didn't know what the rules of the game were. She had a vision that "they" wanted something out of this piece—a content, a form, something—but had no idea what it was. Sarah later described this feeling as "playing piano in the dark. . . . There's no room for mistakes, but you can't *not* make mistakes."

For Sarah, this experience was a crippling one; she found herself unable to take pen to paper. Amid tears and self-recriminations, she finally let her fears out, and then decided to go ahead and write the piece—not for the book nor for any other public audience, but rather to her grandmother, the only person she felt had no expectations of how or what the piece should be.

Although Sarah ultimately felt unsatisfied with this piece, it again serves as an example of Sarah's increasingly sophisticated stabs at a kind of heteroglossic writing. In the piece, entitled "Cronk School," Sarah took on the voice of her grandmother, narrating in a carefully crafted first-person stream of consciousness the story of Mae Busby's long three-mile trek through the snow on her way to teach in a one-room schoolhouse, reflecting on the scenery, the school, and the students along the way. Again, Sarah put together a mix of voices: the immediacy of her own language as a young woman with feelings about cold weather and the welfare of children (two issues I've heard Sarah mention time and again) and the voice of her grandmother who reflected for Sarah on various incidents of the three years she actually taught at the Cronk School in the 1920s. Sarah encapsulated the stories of those three years into a single day and made the details lively through her own imaginings and consciousness. Sarah began her piece in this way:

> Three miles. I have three more miles to go. Somehow it never seemed to take this long to get to school before. I walked this distance every weekday all fall. Now that it has snowed, the distance seems so much longer. Brrr! It is so cold! I'll probably be a solid block of ice before I get there. I wonder how my students would like having to thaw their teacher before they could have lessons? But, they can't thaw me without heat, and I'm the one who has to build the fire in that great big floor furnace every day. I couldn't ask one of the children to take on such a big respon-

sibility. I do wish there were some way to bank the fire for the night, because I hate going into the school when it's as cold as an ice house. I can't risk leaving it all night and burning the school down, though. How would I explain it to my supervisor, Mrs. Robinson?

Again we see Bakhtin's hybridization, albeit more subtly expressed. The mesh of voices this time does not take us so far from Sarah's own voice as "Diery: Katy" did; still, this piece does not represent a mere transcription of her grandmother's story, but rather blends in both the concerns which touch Sarah as a person and some linguistic forms common to her own voice. We see heteroglossia, and not an authoritative discourse, as Sarah remains the Author of this piece.

Sarah was quite aware that this piece and many others written in the preceding year placed her in the position of Author. Her comments on writing in general at this time showed her clear control of her own writing, especially in terms of this issue of voice and its relation to style. She reflected, "All my pieces are really different. I have a lot of different styles. I never write the same all the time, and I use different voices a lot." She characterized the significance of voice as well in terms of the rhythm of her prose. "There are certain words I can and can't use because they don't fit the rhythm of the piece that I'm writing." Such self-conscious recognition of her own voice and style also prompted Sarah to explain an important difference she now noticed in her own writing: "I'm not as afraid to meddle with my writing, because before if it sounded OK, I was afraid to do anything to it because it might not sound OK anymore. Whereas now, I know that there are a lot of different ways to say the same thing."

Sarah now knew that there were "different ways to write the same thing," an important step for her in coming to see authoritative discourse as a false and inappropriate way to think about her writing. Clearly, at this point, Sarah's own in-forming literacy, a literacy that continued to be shaped by the various discourses she encountered and incorporated into her own discourse, was winning the battle.

*Sarah in College: Authoritative Discourse Wins Out*

Accepted into the Honors College at The University of Michigan, Sarah moved to Ann Arbor in the fall of 1987 to begin her studies.

Although she was nervous about starting college, about being in a university so large, she was nonetheless still confident about her writing and looked forward to the challenges of writing in college. Sarah knew she was a good writer—and clearly the English Composition Board (ECB) agreed, as Sarah was one of only a small number of incoming students exempted from Introductory Composition based on her response to the fifty-minute writing assessment the ECB gave at that time to place new students into appropriate writing classes. Sarah was pleased, and opted for a schedule which included many writing-based courses: Great Books (a course required of Honors College students), an introductory philosophy course, cultural anthropology, and French.

I spoke with Sarah only a few times that first term and so was quite unprepared for the tenor of the talk we had in the middle of December, just before finals began. Sarah had become completely disillusioned with her writing and had lost confidence in her ability to write. She told me, "I've always thought that writing was the one thing I could do. In senior writing [in high school] I got *A*'s and *A*+'s. So now the one thing I can do isn't doing me any good." In her philosophy and Great Books classes she was consistently receiving *C*'s and *B*'s on her writing and admitted to "not knowing what to do; I'm just trying and it's sort of like a shot in the dark. Every paper I write, I feel like I'm groping in the dark." Sarah also had stopped writing on her own, and so the bulging portfolio she imagined would get even bigger in her college years remained closed.

What happened to the Author Sarah? In many ways, the problems she found in writing for these courses and for the courses she took in the second term seemed similar to the problems she had had in writing the *Breakwall* piece about her grandmother. Once more, Sarah had become paralyzed by what she saw as the expectations of others, expectations she felt she couldn't meet. Just as Sarah had said at that time that "I didn't know what they expected, but I knew I had to meet their expectations," she now explained that she didn't know exactly what her present teachers wanted: "I don't know exactly what they want and I can't say I know what would make a good paper, because I don't. I have no idea, I'm guessing." She went even further, "I don't think I can write the way he [her Great Books teaching assistant] wants me to write. . . . I think he wants [me to write] the way *he* would write."

Authoritative discourse once more took over, so much so that Sarah regressed to earlier days when she believed that there was a right and a wrong way to write. And increasingly now she began to feel that the single right way would be determined by the teacher and was, for some reason, beyond her understanding. As Sarah, explained, this was a new experience: "I think . . . before [in high school] I knew what it was they wanted and I could do that but I wanted to do something else. Now, I just feel as if I'm missing something, because I don't know what they want."

For Sarah, this renewed focus on authoritative discourse seemed to fall into two related areas: the authority of the voices of the texts she was struggling to understand in Great Books and philosophy (the two courses which demanded the most writing) and the authority of the forms that her teaching assistants seemed to her to demand for that content. Although she recognized there were elements of both in each of the classes and, in fact, that the issues of content and form were closely allied, she generalized the problem in this way: "My philosophy papers are bad because I haven't got the content; I'm not saying what she wants me to say. With Great Books I think it's because I'm not saying it the way he wants me to."

First, the content of both her Great Books and philosophy courses provided real struggles for Sarah. Both courses looked closely at the works of such thinkers as Aristotle, Plato, Thucydides, Descartes, and others. According to Sarah, many of the students in her classes had received basic introductions to these works when they were in high school, but for Sarah, all was new. Sarah found herself entering a completely new discourse, one in which the words were a mystery. Not only were the words of the original authors outside of her experience, but also the words of the class members who seemed to be already well versed in such matters failed to take on much meaning for her. She explained, "A lot of times when people were saying things, I didn't know what the words meant, and it's really hard when you're hearing a lot of terms for the first time and you're supposed to apply them. . . . The concepts were brand new to me."

James Boyd White reminds us that the only way to participate in a discourse is to engage in the conversation of that community and, in so doing, to come to understand "the invisible discourse" surrounding the conventions of that community. Bakhtin specifically speaks to this issue as he sees inherent in every utterance a response or potential response; "every word is directed toward an *answer*," he says. "The word is born in a dialogue as a living rejoinder within it; the word is shaped in dialogic interaction with an alien word that is already in the object. A word forms a concept of its own object in a dialogic way" (*Dialogic Imagination* 279). For Bakhtin and others then, the word is dialogical, conversational, born in the realm of the social.

But when the word fails, as it did for Sarah, to enter one's consciousness in a dialogical way, when the word remains authoritatively "the word of a father, of adults, and of teachers," conversation does not result. The word remains objectified and alien, separated from one's own internally persuasive discourse. Sarah felt herself situated on the outside of the community of philosophers, and the cycle seemed to get worse and worse. She didn't understand the content of the readings, so she didn't understand the content of class discussions, and when it came time to write papers for her courses, she believed she didn't grasp enough content to write decent papers, a belief she felt was verified by the comments and grades she received. While she thought she could fairly adequately summarize and express the basic meanings of these texts (a task that was admittedly quite difficult for her), she believed that her teachers wanted something more than that in the content of her papers. She admitted, "There's some other step that I don't know. I really have no idea what the other step is that I'm supposed to take." She went on, "I feel like I'm over my head. It's beyond me and I keep trying and I keep stretching to find something and I'm trying so hard and I don't know what it is that I'm trying to find."

Not only were the content of the readings themselves and the imagined content of the assigned writings a mystery, but also the form that her teachers seemed to require eluded Sarah as well. She explained the relation she saw between form and content:

> I didn't fully understand *what* I was saying, so it was really hard to say it well; and I didn't really *want* to say what I was saying because I knew I wasn't saying it well, and I didn't like the *way* I had to say it because I knew it wasn't right. . . . I'm never really sure if I'm saying the right thing. . . . If I'm not saying the right thing why should I bother saying it the right way?

For Sarah, what constituted "saying it the right way" was multifaceted. At one level, she characterized the form of her writing in terms of "mistakes," mistakes that could be corrected, in many ways reminiscent of her earlier focus on issues of the rules and regulations of grammar, punctuation, and spelling. Form as a notion of correctable errors was complicated for her, though, by the responses of her T.A.'s. In the beginning of the year, Sarah, the eager learner, waited impatiently for her teachers to hand back papers with the mistakes marked, so that she could then "correct" them and learn from those mistakes for future papers. But these teachers waited weeks to hand back papers; in one class, Sarah was writing her fifth paper while she had still not received back her third and fourth papers. For someone who had begun to define right and wrong in her papers in terms of teacher markings, this was disastrous: "I don't know what mistakes I've made in the past and so I don't know how to correct them."

Sarah also characterized form in terms of the general format of the papers, how the various parts were to fit together, and it was this facet which proved to be the most difficult for her. Once Sarah began to feel unsuccessful in her writing, she began to resurface the notion learned in early high school—that if only she could discover the form that the teachers expected, she could perhaps make the content somehow fit and thus write more successful papers. Sarah's experience in her philosophy class exemplifies this problem well. After receiving a *B-* on her first paper, Sarah decided to talk with her teacher to figure out what she was doing "wrong." The T.A. spoke to her in terms of form, suggesting that Sarah write her next paper in a way that might allow her to include both the author's ideas and her own. Sarah interpreted her teacher's suggestion as a two-part paper: exposition in the first half and original thought in the second. Although at other times this suggestion may have seemed a bit too formulaic for Sarah, at this point she willingly tried anything: "I tried to do all the things she said to do. . . . I worked a lot on it." Despite this effort to understand and produce what she saw as the "right form," Sarah received an even lower grade on this paper. Sarah attributed this, in part, to her continued lack of understanding of the form, based on the T.A.'s inability to explain exactly what she wanted.

Sarah came to believe that there are rules for the various academic discourses to which she was now being exposed and that she must understand these rules and their implied forms in order to write successfully in college. Although she recognized that there are different forms for different academic disciplines, she saw these forms purely in terms of the authority of the teacher and not in terms of the discourse itself. Case in point was Sarah's experience in Great Books, a two-semester class, taught by a different T.A. each term. She believed that by the end of the first semester she had begun to regain some of her lost confidence, "because I started understanding. . . . I understood the approach I was supposed to take to the books a little better and I guess I started knowing what the T.A. wanted." This all fell apart during the second semester when Sarah started all over again with a new teacher whose expectations she was never able to understand. Because she could not learn what this new T.A. "wanted," Sarah received lower grades and more negative comments on each of her papers.

Thus, by the end of her first year in college, Sarah believed that the sole authority for the form of her writing rested in the hands of the teacher. And for her, this form remained in those hands, separate from her experience and her understanding, and defined in terms of right and wrong. She summarized her experience with form in this first year of college in this way:

> I guess I really didn't understand the form. . . . I don't know how people expect papers to be written. I don't know all the steps. The form was really obscure; I didn't know what it was and so that affected me because I couldn't take it [my writing] where I wanted it to go because I knew it wasn't going in the right directions.

She still knew that for the discourse to become her own, for it to become internally persuasive and informing, she had to have her own voice struggle with the authoritative voices, but admitted, "you have to know the rules before you can bend them. You have to find them. . . . Never before have I not known the rules."

By looking at a paper Sarah wrote for Great Books first semester, we can clearly see how her preoccupation with correct content and correct form affected her writing. Here, in part, is what Sarah wrote [see Appendix C for the entire paper]:

> In the world of Thucydides' *The Peloponnesian War*, the    1
> Ancient Greek world in which Athens and Sparta were the battling superpowers, there arose in smaller countries the need to form alliances. Some countries managed to stand alone for some time, yet eventually even they had cause to ally themselves. In this

tumultuous time of wars, debates, conventions, and treaties, alliances were frequently being made and dissolved. Why did these countries join together, what made them remain obedient to central authorities, and what made them break these alliances and treaties?

Many decisions of this sort were based upon considerations 2
of utility. Especially just before the onset of a war, countries become aware of their weaknesses and vulnerabilities. They feel the need to strengthen their position in preparation for the war, and the most efficient way to do this is to secure allies. Not long before the beginning of the Peloponnesian War, "The Athenians tightened their hold on their existing allies and sent embassies to places in the neighborhood of the Peloponnese, realizing that they could carry on the war all round the Peloponnese if they could establish firm and friendly relations with these places." (II, 7 p. 128)

After listing the member countries of both the Spartan and 3
the Athenian alliance, Thucydides says, "These were the allies on each side and these their resources for the war." (II, 9 p.129).

Without these other countries as their allies, the strength of 4
the Spartans and the Athenians would be greatly lessened.

Another of primary motivating forces behind all political 5
and diplomatic decisions is goodwill. When Corcyra wishes to leave alliance with Corinth and place itself under Athens, one of the arguments it uses to sway Athens is that "if you (Athens) welcome our alliance at this time, you will win our undying gratitude." (I, 33, p.55)

They argue that "an act of kindness done at the right mo- 6
ment has a power to dispel old grievances quite out of proportion to the act itself" (I, 42 p. 61) and try to convince Athens that "to have us coming over voluntarily into your camp, giving ourselves up to you without involving you in any dangers or any expense," (I, 33 p.55) will promote among the allies of Athens a feeling of good will and will make them more willing to remain subjugated to central authority.

When the Mytilenians entered an alliance with Athens follow- 7
ing the Persian War, it was with the understanding that "the object of the alliance was the liberation of the Hellenes from Persia, not the subjugation of the Hellenes to Athens." (III, 10 p. 198)

A feeling of goodwill between the Mytilenians and Athens 8
caused them to remain content within their alliance. "So long as the Athenians in their leadership respected our independence, we followed them with enthusiasm." (III, 10 p.198).

> Not until Athens began their attempt to take them over did    9
> the goodwill dissipate. Then, the Mytilenians turned to the Spar-
> tans in hopes that they would act in goodwill. "You should take
> us into your alliance and send us help quickly, thus revealing
> yourselves as people capable of helping those that should be
> helped and at the same time hurting your enemies." (III, 13
> p. 200)

We can see how such issues as heteroglossia and multilanguaged-
ness have disappeared for Sarah. The only interaction between
voices in this paper becomes an interaction between the voices of
the teacher and the text of Thucydides, two alternate versions of
the same authoritative discourse, and thus not even a real interaction. Sarah takes her subject matter from a topic her teacher suggested from a written list of topics: "In Thucydides' world, how do
fear and goodwill compare as bases for a) international alliances,
b) obedience to central authority." By choosing this topic, Sarah
already has agreed to a given content and a given structure: The
paper will deal with fear, goodwill, alliances and obedience; and
the form will be a compare/contrast essay. Within the paper, we
can see how the voices of the teacher (through the suggested topic)
and the text interact, but we see nothing of Sarah's voice. For
example, the internal structure of paragraphs 5–9 (and later 10–
17) takes on a specific pattern: first, a clause or phrase which
refers back to the words of the suggested topic, with an occasional
summary line from the text, and second, a citation from the text
which supports the clause. Paragraph 8 is a perfect example of
such form:

> A feeling of *goodwill* between the Mytilenians and Athens
> caused them to remain content within their *alliance* [reference to
> content of topic]. "So long as the Athenians in their leadership
> respected our independence, we followed them with enthusi-
> asm." [proof of statement from text]

Over and over this pattern continues; the voice of the teacher-
authority supported by the voice of the author-authority. Paragraphs don't seem to build strongly and logically, one from each
other; instead, the logic of the paper seems to arise from the quotations, rather than the quotations supporting a well-conceived argument. Sarah told me that she wrote this "one paragraph at a time"
and her planning notes for the paper seem to support this; her first

step in writing the paper was to come up with a list of quotes in outline form on fear and goodwill, as we can see in this section from her outline which corresponds to paragraphs 5, 6, 7, and 9:

II. goodwill
    a. international alliances?

* (I 33, p.55) If you welcome our alliance at this time, you will win our undying gratitude (aka goodwill) [corresponding to paragraph 5]

* (I, 42 p.61) You will find that an act of kindness done at the right moment has a power to dispel old grievances quite out of proportion to the act itself. [corresponding to paragraph 6]
    Mytelena-Athens alliance after Persian war

* (III, 10 p 198) the object of the alliance was the liberation of the Hellenes from Persia, not the subjugation of the Hellenes to Athens. [corresponding to paragraph 7]

* (III, 13 p 200) You should take us into your alliance and send us help quickly, thus revealing yourselves as people capable of helping those who should be helped and at the same time hurting your enemies. [corresponding to paragraph 9]

We can see the transition from these notes to her final paper: each quotation has become, in order, a separate paragraph.

Sarah's way of composing seems quite clearly to be the opposite of Bakhtin's notion of hybridization in which voices collide in order to create a new linguistic consciousness. Instead, Sarah here merely layers the voices of her teacher and the text she's read and produces a discourse in which she is truly not the author. This piece—and the others she wrote in her first year of college—remain, for the most part, attempts to mimic authoritative discourse, both in content and form. We don't hear Sarah's voice, and we don't see her thought in this paper as we did in her earlier work. Granted, this writing and the other pieces from her first year are early attempts on Sarah's part to enter into a new discourse community. In such early attempts, we might expect this kind of hybridization. But this layered writing, devoid of Sarah's voice, coupled with Sarah's disappointment in her writing at that point in time, gave me pause. Sarah believes that writing papers like this has negatively affected both her writing and her feelings about writing in general: "I've lost any style I once had. I don't find that I have any style because I'm so worried about the content that I forget about the style. . . . I just write it, type it, and hand it in and I'm not at all happy with it." Sarah's discouragement led her to limit her involvement with the writing tasks she was asked to do. The worry becomes that this rejection may lead her to remain within authoritative discourse, closing off the various internally persuasive discourses, which, as Bakhtin argues, may limit the growth of one's individual ideology. If literacy involves, as I believe it does, this development of an individual stance on the world, such rejection may limit her growth even further.

*The Separation of Internally Persuasive and
Authoritative Discourses*

I wish I could start this section by writing that the story of Sarah has a happy ending . . . but it doesn't. It does have some glimmers of hope, though: Perhaps there will yet be a happier ending.

Sarah today, three terms into her college career, is able to be a bit more distanced and reflective about her writing than she was in the midst of that disastrous first term. Since that time, she's continued to have more than her share of discouraging moments of writing for her various classes, but she's had some positive experiences as well, experiences which have allowed her to once again think of herself as an author—at least in some situations.

Sarah spent the summer after her first year of college employed by her hometown newspaper as a writer for a new summer feature magazine: She wrote stories, edited them, and laid out the pages for publication. The glowing Sarah who told me about this experience was reminiscent of the Sarah I remembered from three years earlier telling me about her interviews with the elderly women and turning those interviews into "Diery: Katy." Among other pieces, Sarah wrote such stories as "The Lure of Thunder Bay Country Lighthouses"; "Star Light, Star Bright," a piece about the local planetarium; and "The Complete Angler for the Complete Novice," stories which required her to research into the words of others by reading primary and secondary materials and interviewing people before she mixed these words with her own voice.

In part because of the experience of that summer, Sarah decided to take a creative writing class in the fall semester and was pleased by her experience in the class. She found it a difficult but stimulating course. In this class, students received written and oral critiques from every colleague, teacher and peers—a scary but worthwhile experience for Sarah, who began to look carefully once more at the negative as well as the positive critiques she was given in order to rewrite her papers. Sarah's writing reflects the close attention she paid to the critiques of her colleagues, again a kind of mixing of her own voice with the voices of her critiquers. In at least these two situations, then, Sarah was once more an author, one who took control of her own discourse, while she listened to the various discourses of others interact with her own.

When we talked at the end of the fall term, though, Sarah recalled with almost terror the experiences of the previous year and maintained that "college writing" was still something she was incapable of doing. She remained fearful of doing that kind of writing, telling me she still approached it with "dread." The experience of the previous year "still affects me a lot," she said. "I have a psychology term paper . . . and I'm terrified. I don't want to write it. I keep procrastinating. I have absolutely no confidence in my writing—in that style of writing—right now."

What is it for Sarah that keeps "that style of writing" separate from other kinds? At first I believed the distinction lay in a kind of creative/expository split, a distinction based purely in genre, genre seen in some traditional ways. But Sarah took exception to that characterization, explaining that the pieces she wrote for the magazine in particular really were a kind of blurred genre, a mix of creative and analytical. Sarah posited that the distinction might instead lie in what she called inspiration—specifically, whether or not she had reason to become invested in a particular piece. "The thing about writing," she explained, "is that I've got to care" either about the subject matter or the person she is writing for. She explained this further in terms of an article she wrote for the magazine in which she interviewed people and really "wrote the article for them." "It was me, it was something I cared about and it was about people. I guess that's the difference; it was about people and they cared about what I was writing. *It mattered,* whereas a lot of times when I'm writing papers [for school], I don't really care about what I have to say."

Such inspiration needn't be only in out-of-school settings for Sarah. In her philosophy class of the preceding year, she found herself surprisingly invested in one of her papers, a paper on Descartes, a paper she "wanted to write." She talked about this paper in terms of really coming to know Descartes and coming to like him; thus, it became important to her to represent his words and his ideas well, in a theme that she discovered herself. "I was really trying to understand Descartes and I really thought I had a grasp on it and so it was important to me to say it, whereas in the others I really didn't care, but I had to write a paper about it." Even though Sarah did not receive a particularly high grade on this paper, she still speaks of it with pleasure, as a paper which truly "inspired" her. It seems that when Sarah was able to allow her own developing voice to struggle with the words of Descartes, as she was able to do in this case, she was able to understand the words better and to find a place for herself within those words. Sarah seemed to be practicing what Bakhtin sees as a hybridization within the two kinds of discourse. Despite feedback from the teacher that indicated this was not a great paper, Sarah still felt confident in her writing of it.

For Sarah, though, this kind of occurrence is a rarity in her college classes. She parallels her problems of writing for college with the problems she saw in writing for high school when her teachers would assign the form of the paper to be written:

> It goes back to the thing about when you're assigned a description and you have to write a description whether you care about it or not. . . . It's like being assigned this theme for this book because the T.A. says "this is a good theme; do this." You can do it, but you can hear the gears moving  . . . it doesn't have anything except what it's supposed to have.

Sarah is convinced from her experiences that for most writing at the university, the kind she terms "college writing," the subject matter and the forms that the teachers present are predesignated; as Bakhtin might say, they remain in the realm of authoritative discourse, the entity that "enters our verbal consciousness as a compact and indivisible mass" that "one must either totally affirm . . . or totally reject" (*Dialogic Imagination* 343). And although a complete understanding of the precise form and full content often eludes her, she still thinks that she must try to meet those expectations in order to be a successful student. Sarah speaks about an upcoming psychology paper as a good case in point, a paper for which she has, in fact, chosen the topic because it is one in which she is interested: dream interpretation. Still, she says, "I don't really care about my psych. paper." Why not, I asked? And Sarah responded from the heart:

> I'm going to write about dreams and I'm going to take the psychoanalytic approach because my T.A. sees everything from the psychoanalytic approach to dreams—but, oh well, I'm going to write it that way. . . . I'm really interested in dreams, but the kinds of things I'd want to say are not the things I'm supposed to say in a psych. paper.

So what can we conclude about Sarah and her notions of literacy acquisition from this portrait of her writing experiences over the last few years? If, as Bakhtin tells us, "the ideology of becoming a human being . . . is the process of selectively assimilating the words of others" (*Dialogic Imagination* 341), we can recognize some of the implications of the problems that Sarah is discovering as she tries to find a space for herself and for her words in what she sees as an unyielding authoritative discourse. For Sarah, who at one time believed in, if not a struggle, then at least an interaction between her own words and the words of her teachers in whom both she and the system had invested authority, it is in a way surprising that, at this point, she fails to resist the authoritative words of her college teachers and college texts. Sarah is someone who understands that "real writing," writing in which she truly becomes Author, is writing in which she brings to bear her own discourse upon the words of others; at the same time as the collision of those discourses takes place, an increasingly literate and more ideologically certain Sarah emerges.

But Sarah also increasingly believes that such "real writing" must be a rare occurrence in college settings in which the form and content of her reading and writing force her into a subservient position—in which one choice and one choice only exists: to learn the discourse of the particular teacher in the particular subject area. For Sarah, who was willing to meet this demand but who found herself unable to discover the rules of the game, such a single option must result in what she sees as failure. And increasing numbers of failures logically lead to what they have for her: an opting out of trying. Sarah will continue to write papers such as her recent psychology paper on dream interpretation—not what and how she wants to write but rather what and how she believes the teacher-authority wants her to write.

Such a system also causes Sarah to separate writing into two types: college writing and real writing. Fortunately, Sarah has discovered some spaces in which real writing can take place—in her creative writing class; for her magazine; even occasionally in school, when she is inspired and cares more about the subject than she does the grade—spaces she thought were nonexistent during her first year in college.

It is unfortunate, though, for Sarah and for a host of other students, that these two types of writing must remain separated, separated into what I call a conforming and an in-forming literacy. The task for teachers and for students is, I believe, to discover spaces, to find places where the two can interact, so that a truly re-forming literacy can take place.

## POSTSCRIPT: REFLECTIONS ON SARAH'S STORY

My writing of Sarah's story reflects in many ways the reading and thinking I was doing about research methodology at that time. The influences of other teacher-researchers and phenomenological researchers, in particular, are clear: I rely heavily on her voice to tell the story, and I question my ability as an individual researcher to understand fully what I was seeing. Her voice immediately becomes important in this portrait; not only are the first words of the case about Sarah (as opposed to the quote about literacy which opens Akemi's piece), but her words fill its pages through not only more quotes but more sustained quotes. As I reread now, I see that, for the first time, I included quotes from someone I researched of more than four lines! Less often in this text did I try to cut and paste words of Sarah's into my own words, bending and shaping her words to fit the conclusion I had already reached. Instead, Sarah is allowed to have her say in a more complete context. For example, I introduce a six-line quote from Sarah with the words "she articulated for us in this way," a movement toward allowing *her* to be the one articulating the sentiment. Such longer quotes allow Sarah to be a presence in the text; I believe as a result she emerges as a three-dimensional person rather than a cardboard cutout, clearly a goal of this kind of research.

This fuller portrait of Sarah also seems to arise from the perspective I took as author. In addition to giving Sarah more lines in which to speak, I attempted to write more from her perspective.

Rather than my approach in Akemi's story, in which my beliefs or the beliefs of experts commanded the reader's attention by coming first and occupying more space, Sarah's perspective dominates in many parts here. "Sarah came to believe," I wrote at one point; "Sarah explained." While this attempt to understand from her perspective falters at times, there are many occasions of this shift of authority. Although subtle in its place in the text, this shift represents a big change in my understanding of how research might work. Sarah's understandings were the lead in my coming to understand the issues of literacy which emerged here; my concurrent reading of Bakhtin and others helped me find words to express what she was telling me. This serves as quite a contrast to my work with Akemi in which Knoblauch and Brannon and others served as my major informants; I then became intrigued at how well her understandings fit into what they had suggested.

Also important in this emerging portrait of Sarah is my willingness to question the understandings I was able to reach as sole researcher, the beginning of my redefinition of what it might mean to be a researcher, of what the relationship between the researcher and the researched might ideally become. Whereas in my research and writing of Akemi's story I quite easily distinguished between the separate duties inherent in the roles of the researcher and the researched, in my work with Sarah the roles were not always quite so clear-cut. In my attempt to reduce the research hierarchy in which the researcher and her perspective take star billing and the researched—whose story supposedly is being told—takes the supporting role, I self-consciously searched for the ways in which this might become research *with* rather than research *on*. Such a stance implies not only a change in text (i.e., including more of her words), but also a change of heart. When I began to think of Sarah as a participant in creating the meaning of her story, I adapted the roles I had assigned in my own mind. Sarah, in contrast to Akemi, participated in this study by reading and critiquing everything I wrote. In this start toward collaboration, the definitions of our roles became less clear-cut. Like Freire's notion of teacher-students and student-teachers, in which all those collaborating in the educational process learn from each other, I began to think of my work as teacher-student/student-teacher-research. As I saw our roles becoming more equal, then, I learned to listen and revise my understandings. Thus, when at one point "Sarah took exception to [my] characterization," I listened to her voice and reflected that revision in the text. Listening to Sarah and accepting her understandings of her own literacy helped me make a start toward granting her ownership of the research. No longer is the research merely *about* her; it *is* her story. Working in this mindset, I was able to help shift Sarah's role from being an object of the research to being a researching subject.

As I discuss in chapter 1, though, I see now that this small start did not go far enough. The resulting text still remains mostly my creation and not the creation of Sarah or truly even a collaboratively composed work. While it is true that I treat Sarah with more respect, featuring her words more prominently than I had with Akemi, Sarah still is objectified in ways quite similar to the ways in which Akemi was objectified. Even though we both make our presence known, our roles still remain quite traditional: *I* am the one who is able to "treat Sarah with more respect" and "feature her words more prominently"; I am still the one with the star billing. Who gets to establish the research question? Who selects the transcripts, writes the piece, chooses the structure, the tone, the voice, the metaphors? Who is it who cared about Bakhtin's relationship to the text or who even found that connection valuable? Clearly it was still my work: I initiated the study, I did the research, I wrote up the findings, even though Sarah served as a critical reader of the text. Hiding behind my author voice (represented still in the royal *we*), I pulled the strings and controlled the text. As I identify in chapter 1, certain phrases jump out at me now that indicate the stance of researcher in control: "Thus, Sarah . . . was ripe for [this] experience," I wrote, or even "By looking at a paper Sarah wrote . . . we can clearly see how her preoccupation with correct content and correct form affected her writing." I continually worked to establish a connection with my imagined readers, an audience of teacher-researchers, again and again using the term "we can see" to help maintain this connectedness. I believe now my aligning myself with these teacher-researchers in conjunction with my objectification of Sarah separates me in many ways from the more important "we" of this study: Sarah and me.

My recent reading of Michelle Fine's provocative article, "Passions, Politics and Power: Feminist Research Possibilities," gives me another way to think about my work with both Sarah and

Akemi. Fine speaks of the various stances that some feminist researchers take. First, she explains, is ventriloquy: "The author tells Truth, has no gender, race, class or stance." Ventriloquy, she continues, citing the work of Clark (1990), means "never having to say 'I' in the text—treating subjects as objects, while calling them subjects" (212–14). The second stance is when researchers use voices "to accomplish a subtler form of ventriloquism . . . while researchers appear to let the Other speak . . . we hide, unproblematical" (215). My work with Sarah, I see now, places me firmly in the second stance. Convinced it was important to include her voice, I failed to consider fully my own presence. Appearing to let her speak, I still managed to take a great measure of control, hiding, as Fine would say, behind the words I chose. This subtler form of ventriloquy still had me treating Sarah as an object at times, though at the time I wrote this text I would have argued vehemently that she was indeed a subject.

Fine suggests a third stance for feminist researchers, one in which the research "commits to the study of change, the move toward change, and/or is provocative of change" (220), research in which we articulate how and why we include voices in our method. The implications of this stance take on an immediacy for me in this story of Sarah, more so than in my writing of Akemi's experience, perhaps because Sarah's story is that of a struggling student, one who was uneasy with the writing she was asked to do in the college setting. If I had taken on the role of true emancipatory researcher and collaborator with Sarah, accepting my role to help her through her struggle, working with her to find ways out of the corners into which she was writing herself, she might have been able to find a voice in the school world where she instead felt quite voiceless. While Akemi's voice as represented in her case study remained muted by my telling of her story in even more obvious ways than Sarah's has been, Akemi's position as a successful student helps to free this muting of some of its ethical overtones: Because Akemi was a good student, the concerns I felt about whether or not to try to change her understanding of literacy were less immediate. No matter what I thought about her writing and her literacy, she was succeeding in the worlds in which she was participating. For Sarah, these concerns were at a very practical level: A formerly successful and excited writer, Sarah, upon entering college, found herself almost unable to write because of her fears about writing correctly. I now believe a more emancipatory approach to my work with Sarah, an approach which saw as its main concern helping Sarah out of her dilemma, would have been more honest.

And so, despite my small but important moves toward making this piece a more emancipatory study for both Sarah and me, I believe it remains a study which maintains the traditional roles for the researcher and the researched—a subject/object pairing with the researcher-subject controlling the research and ultimately limiting its liberatory potential for the researched object. Perhaps because of the ethical dilemmas this portrait began to pose for me, the study helped me learn a great deal about the kind of research I was committed to practice. As I entered into subsequent classrooms, I was able to put these new understandings to work; I began to try to practice a kind of research in which the goal would include a more emancipatory approach to my students even as it attempted to depict their worlds as fully and accurately as possible, an approach intent upon making connections between the research and the pedagogy.

Recognizing the inherent connection between emancipatory research and emancipatory pedagogy helped me to define my joint roles as literacy worker and teacher-researcher. As someone who had learned a great deal about the formation of literacy through my work with Akemi and Sarah, I felt ready to put some of that knowledge into practice in my literacy instruction. Sarah and Akemi had taught me about forming literacy; I now wanted to think about how to re-form it with the students in my own classrooms.

CHAPTER 4

# Re-forming Literacy: High School Students Become Researchers

## INTRODUCTION

As a teacher-researcher, I began to learn with Akemi and Sarah when I opened my eyes and my mind enough to let them tell me what they knew about their own writing and their own learning. What I learned manifested itself for me in two ways: first, they helped me to see the complex relationship of form to issues of literacy (and their inevitable counterpart—issues of illiteracy) and that a new look at form's relationship to literacy might change the way we teachers and students view our teaching and learning; second, they helped me look at the research process in new ways and think about how collaborative student–teacher research might change the way we teacher-researchers see the worlds we inhabit. My search for new ways to unite these issues of pedagogy and research—as well as to continue viewing them in all their complexity—led to the substance of the next two chapters, chapters which lay out the attempts I have made with my students over the past few years to try our hands at a different approach to teaching and learning. Such an approach not only incorporates many of the beliefs I began to hold about literacy and research, but also seeks to understand the interconnections that, as a teacher-researcher, I can make between literacy instruction and research in my classroom.

I had thought about literacy in terms of the implications of a ceremonial view of discourse, an essay-text view of literacy, in my work with Akemi; I had expanded upon these ideas to think about Bakhtin's version of authoritative and internally persuasive discourses in order to inform my work with Sarah—both helpful notions which center around the formation of literacy in schools

131

today. When I began the teaching recounted in this chapter, however, I was ready to think about re-forming those definitions of literacy, and I turned to the work of Paulo Freire and other critical theorists to help frame the ideas underlying emancipatory renditions of these understandings in light of the power relationships inherent in the formal definitions of literacy I had seen at work among students in classrooms.

Paulo Freire reminds us, in a quotation that introduces the case study in this chapter, that what we do in the classroom has political overtones: not only what we teach but how we teach it. The political world in which we live often sees illiteracy and literacy as separate states, as dialogic opposites: illiteracy as a disease which needs to be eradicated and literacy as a panacea to the world's ills. As we've seen, there exists a certain reality created by outsiders to the worlds of schools who name literacy solely in terms of one's conformity to a specific means of expression: an essay-text literacy, perhaps, or, as I have called it, a literacy of conformity. New definitions of literacy—definitions offered by Heath, Robinson, White, and others—help us see literacy instead as situated action, as the ability to speak and act and communicate in specific situations, certainly a more complicated and complete view of literacy, one which seems to reflect more accurately the life-worlds of people like Akemi and Sarah. What is seen as literate in their worlds is a shifting definition, one that depends on the time and place, the situation, the occasion. Akemi and Sarah are both literate. They exercise that literacy at school and at home in different ways, and they explain those differences primarily in formal terms.

As we've seen with Sarah and Akemi, students hold a wide-ranging understanding of form in their writing: from the minutiae of presentation to the rules and regulations of a five-paragraph essay to the constitutive make-up of various genres. Forms, especially in their more generic terms, are not negative entities. As Bakhtin has told us, forms are indeed inevitable necessities that allow for communication among people. Sarah, for example, as she enters a new discourse community, needs to uncover certain forms of expression in order to get started in that community; Akemi finds herself foundering when she can't find a form in which to place her ideas. Forms are, in fact, potentially enabling structures, especially for those who enter a new discourse community in this way and thus come up against new definitions of what is literate. However, forms can at the same time be constraining, limited and limiting means of expression. If forms remain authoritative, to use Bakhtin's terms once more, resulting in a strictly conforming literacy, and are not in constant dialogue with the internally persuasive discourse of an in-forming literacy, students (and others) cannot—will not—form their own ideologies, but will remain in the struggle for literacy in someone else's terms, in someone else's world. "Good" students, students such as Akemi and Sarah, represent one kind of problem associated with this view of literacy. Named by the system as literate, they can usually survive within such institutional constraints, although, as I have tried to show, they often opt out of certain kinds of challenges because of the split between the two kinds of literacy. Other students, though, the students we'll see in this chapter, find the struggle more difficult. For those students for whom the forms and thus the intended literacy remain hidden, any struggle between in-forming and conforming literacies is really a nonstruggle: Students resist, refuse, and thus remain labeled as slow learners, as reluctant learners, as illiterate. Thus, as Freire tells us, not only is the naming of students as literate or illiterate a political act, but the means by which we teach our students to become literate is equally political.

I came to believe, through the work detailed in this chapter, that all of these students would be better served by a kind of pedagogy quite different from what I had seen or what I had practiced previously, an approach toward reading and writing which recognizes the necessary dialogue between the various discourses one possesses and which in turn promotes a kind of literacy which places such dialogic interaction at its center. In this chapter, I look at an attempt to enact just this kind of literacy, an enactment which tried to draw on the students' own notions of forms by celebrating their own in-forming literacy, that placed as prominent a social view of literacy, that most of all attempted to re-form the reality of the conforming literacy present in school worlds. The attempt is, as Freire would say, political in its very nature as we teachers and students together tried to define in these classrooms the kind of literacy by which we could overcome what others have named illiteracy. In the work recounted here, I was a co-teacher in a high school classroom, a classroom of thirty-two juniors named by the school system as "lower track," students who, for the most part, seemed to be both uninterested in writing and unable to meet their school's expectations for their writing. I spent one to two days per week in the class for a semester, teaching with their regular teacher, an excellent and dedicated teacher with over twenty years' experience in public school teaching; together, we introduced to students some new ways to think about their own literacy. In our work, we had in mind the kind of instruction James Slevin speaks of in his essay "Genre Theory, Academic Discourse, and Writing within Disciplines":

> If students are to understand and control their writing, and not just *adapt* it to the signifying system we call "academic discourse," they will need to do more than successfully imitate its surface form or receive instruction in its conventions. That is, they need to do more than simply manipulate this discourse. Rather, they need to engage fully in its production, to question it, perhaps even to challenge its purposes—in effect, they need to become involved in the kind of analysis which composition scholars and teachers themselves often undertake. (14)

In our case, students began to look carefully at themselves as writers and as producers of certain kinds of discourse in order to begin to ask the same kinds of questions we teachers were asking about why such discourse exists and how much (or how little) resistance one might show to the accepted forms and still be considered literate. By doing so, students became collaborative researchers with their teachers, looking together with us at issues to which neither group had predetermined answers and learning together—from each other—about how the search for answers might inform and ultimately improve both their writing and their visions of themselves as literate Authors in the worlds in which they had too often been denied such naming. Such denial of being named *by* and such insistence instead on being named *with* is, again, a political act, in Freire's terms. Thus, the very notions we chose to place as central as well as the ways we chose to explore those notions represented a change in "teaching as usual" for us, and began a new awareness on all of our parts (both teachers and students) as to how we might better teach a re-formed pedagogy.

This collaborative approach to teaching and research was based in a number of ideas explored more fully in chapter 1. I had come to believe with the phenomenologists and critical theorists that striving toward emancipatory goals should be the motivating force in the classroom. Like Freire, I saw the folly of teaching in a way that reduced students to object status, recognizing that although students can never be truly empowered by other people, in order for them to take on subject status themselves, we as teachers must create a space in the classroom where empowerment can flourish. A setting that allows for—in fact, encourages—student experience and student understanding by placing these at the center of the curriculum can end the "many modes of mystification" which, as Maxine Greene has noted, often surround the classroom curriculum (*Landscapes* 53). In naming this mystification, Greene looks to schools as primary sites which mystify both students and teachers as they allow their inhabitants to feel at home in "an unexamined surface reality," a setting which may seem natural but which may cover up underlying repression and alienation, a setting in which people uncritically accept the version of the world they have been given (54). Greene, Freire, and a host of other critical theorists look to these notions of a liberatory pedagogy in order to demystify this unexamined surface reality, freeing its participants from what Freire has called "the culture of silence" present in so many schools.

The goals of emancipatory pedagogy became integral to the issues of research which also inform this book. An emancipatory approach to teaching in the classroom must be equally informing to the research we conduct; we cannot espouse liberatory principles in our teaching while we continue to conduct research on students by treating them as the objects of that research. The dilemmas which surrounded the research I had conducted *on* Sarah and Akemi seem even more egregious in light of the emancipatory ideals toward which I was moving in my own teaching. By treating Sarah and Akemi as the research objects, I was not only denying their status as subjects in the search (after all, whose worlds and whose lives would such research rightfully affect?), but I was limiting their ability to participate fully in their own change. I seemed to be sending a mixed message to them: that it was appropriate for them to become empowered and to rename their worlds, but that I would hold the reins on that empowerment by withholding certain understandings from them, reserving those understandings for others whom I considered more able to appreciate them, that is, my own professors, other classroom teachers, my fellow graduate students. The very essence of the research remained out of their control; I made the judgments about what was significant in their stories by what I chose to include in the telling, and I decided who should be the recipients of that information by selecting the audiences with whom I would share the case studies. Student growth and change, if it occurred, was coincidental to the research process. Reviewing carefully my work with Akemi and Sarah as I read into the work of the phenomenological theorists and pedagogues, I began to understand that if we had looked *together* at our shared world in order first to understand what was problematic in it and then to change it for our mutual benefit, Sarah, Akemi, and I might have achieved, as Langeveld and others told us, a praxis-oriented research, integrally tied to a praxis-oriented pedagogy. I started to understand that a freeing of horizons, as Freire names it, depends in large part on Gadamer's notion of a fusion of horizons.

As I describe it in chapter 1, Gadamer's fusion of horizons depends on a conception of understanding not as a simple reconstruction of events, a recreation of a given reality, but rather as a mediation between subjects. He believes each person's creation of meaning is necessarily limited by the background and incumbent prejudices she brings to a situation, just as my background experience with basic students and my students' backgrounds in writing create, even as they limit, certain meanings for each of us. When I see a class designated, for example, as a basic class, and when I see in their faces the same things I've seen before, my own prejudices allow for certain meanings to be created: They'll be nice but unmotivated, or they won't write very well if they write at all. In a like manner, the students' prejudices will only allow for certain meanings: English teacher equals lots of stupid writing assignments, those same old grammar exercises I've seen before, and so on. It is only when these individuals' meanings come together to form a kind of fused horizon that understanding can result. In this way, we can see that understanding is dialogical in nature, social in practice.

A methodology which looks to include students as co-inquirers with their teachers—so that together they may ask the questions and together they may look at the answers—became the first level of the praxis-oriented, emancipatory research I attempted with my students in this chapter. The work that led me to write this case study showed me that when students themselves name the problems and search together with their teachers and their peers for the solutions to those problems, they conduct research which moves closer to reflecting a shared understanding of pertinent issues. If students who participate as co-inquirers then reflect about the experience, they can begin to think about how they learned. The result is that these students start to talk about ways of learning and ways of knowing. Such an approach constitutes praxis in the Freirean sense, and is the necessary end of this kind of phenomenological research: Students and teachers critically reflect through the dialogue about their own lived worlds and take action through a reformulation of how individuals come to learn. In other words, researching together with students might serve at least two related purposes: Students who look with their teachers for workable answers to vexing questions about their schooling not only can help their instructors toward new ways of understanding how their own literacy manifests itself but also can help themselves toward a better understanding of how to rename their own literacy—resulting both in research that comes closer to representing the students' lived worlds and in teaching and learning that serves an emancipatory function.

In the pages that follow, you will see the attempts of two teachers and one class to put these ideas about research and about teaching and learning into practice. As students worked with teachers to name the problems about writing which were important to them, they became researchers into the forming of their own literacy. And as student-researchers and teacher-researchers together sought answers to problems, we all were re-forming the kinds of literacy instruction practiced in that classroom.

## RE-FORMING LITERACY: HIGH SCHOOL STUDENTS BECOME RESEARCHERS (JULY 1988)[1]

> Critically speaking, illiteracy is neither an "ulcer" nor a "poison herb" to be eradicated, nor a "disease." Illiteracy is one of the concrete expressions of an unjust social reality. Illiteracy is not a strictly linguistic or exclusively pedagogical or methodological problem. It is political, as is the very literacy through which we try to overcome illiteracy.
>
> —Paulo Freire

---

[1]Sections of this case study have appeared in two other venues: a paper I presented at the 1988 Right to Literacy Conference sponsored by the MLA and as "Re-forming Literacy: A Collaborative Teacher–Student Research Project" in Jay L. Robinson's book *Conversations on the Written Word*.

If we believe with students of literacy such as James Boyd White and Jay Robinson that literacy is always socially constructed, we must inevitably turn to the question implicit in Paulo Freire's words. What are the politics of a literacy through which we might overcome illiteracy? For our students today, as we saw with Akemi and Sarah, such politics are firmly situated in the world of schools. In the Spring of 1988, as I cotaught in a high school English class, I began to look seriously at the implicit definition of the literacy valued and taught in schools, a normative definition of what I have called a literacy of conformity.

The English class in which I cotaught this past term, the class which produced the collaborative research described in these pages, taught me a great deal about a world of literacy conceived as conformity, and taught me to think hard about how this politics of literacy impinges upon various groups of students in schools. The students with whom I worked that semester live in a classroom world labeled "discover level"; in other communities in other schools that classroom might be labeled "basic," "at risk," "skills"—whatever euphemism is currently in vogue as the means to separate out and name groups of high school students whose literacy does not meet the standards set by the institution. These particular high school juniors, like others so labeled, are typically asked to do very little writing during their school day—maybe fill in a form; write a structured two-paragraph summary (including what the chapter said and what you think); define a list of words from the textbook—and they are generally assumed to resist or to be unable to manage any other kind of writing tasks. Not only can't they do it, the story goes, but because they don't know how to do it, they hate it so much that they'll *never* do it, and they probably won't need it to get a job anyway, so it's not worth it, right?

As I looked around this class the first day of my teaching, a class carefully chosen by my coteacher and their regular teacher, Sheila Smith, as the one whose members would be "most willing" to participate in this research (although she assured me that even this group wouldn't be easy), I saw bored faces—definitely polite, but nonetheless bored. In those faces I saw the look of the basic students I had taught over the years, and I assigned to that look the meaning I remembered assigning to other students in other places: boredom in school, resistance to creative work, general good-natured willingness to please the teacher by following forms and directions to the hilt, but not moving beyond that: the litany of complaints that I, and a host of other teachers I knew, had about these basic students.

Sheila and I decided to push against the expectations that attach themselves to labels that have been applied to these students. We decided to ask questions that might instead form new expectations. We chose to base at least part of the classroom agenda for the term on the notion that these students probably were the best sources of knowledge about their own writing and that by calling upon their own understandings formulated in their own language, we could all learn something about these students' literacy. When we asked our students to join us as co-researchers in this project, we discovered to our initial surprise that they knew a lot about writing and were willing to share that knowledge with us: They were aware of the demands various teachers of various subjects made upon them; they had intuitions about the differences between in-school and out-of-school discourse; they understood some important things about their own processes of writing. Even more to our surprise, we discovered that many of them enjoyed various kinds of writing, a notion which seemed antithetical to all expectations called up by the labels they brought with them to class.

With themes of emancipatory research and emancipatory education uppermost in mind, Sheila and I attempted to implement a pedagogy with the students in fourth-hour English which would be based in a student-designed research program. Students would research their own and their peers' writing; whatever it was we would discover together would serve as a starting point for talking together about pertinent issues of school writing. Critical reflection could lead then to action: Students (and teachers) who looked in critical ways at the constraints of school writing might be moved to change their conceptions of how they go about these tasks of learning and teaching writing. And, we told ourselves, if we were able to effect such "emancipation of the imagination," as Giroux has called it, could other kinds of emancipation—i.e., changes in their actual writing and in our teaching of writing—be far behind?[2]

---

[2]While this teaching approach relies heavily on Freire's philosophy, readers of his work will see that it is not strictly Freirean in its rendition. In *Pedagogy of the Oppressed* and *Education for Critical Consciousness,* Freire indicates that within his literacy projects, students are responsible for, among other things, selecting their own themes for study. This is something we clearly did not have our students do. We took as our model instead an adaptation of Freire's work, some aspects of which are discussed in Ira Shor's *Freire for the Classroom: A Sourcebook for Liberatory Teaching.*

Good plan, we thought, prematurely patting ourselves on the backs, but, as you might imagine, one easier planned than implemented. The first constraint on my part came out of my own horizons and the prejudices which I brought to this teacher-research—and, more importantly, my failure to recognize these biases. My background told me that basic students like these didn't write, hated writing, refused writing. I had tons of evidence to support this: years of teaching such students, seeing their puzzlement about the written word, their attempts and failures to write in the ways I wanted them to, and their eventual refusals to write the assignments I had created, assignments designed to coax them out of the shells they inevitably retreated into whenever it was time to write. My own hypothesis about these students, a hypothesis that gained more credibility for me as I saw what had happened especially to Sarah in her school worlds, was that when students either hated or feared writing, they necessarily turned to the forms teachers had taught them to use all through school: the five-paragraph essay, the structured research report, the rigid two-paragraph summary. Form took precedence over content, so much so that students failed even to think anymore about the subject matter of their writing; rather, they immediately fit *any* subject matter into one of the prepackaged forms they recognized.

As a learning teacher-researcher, though, I began to put aside my own notions of what was "really" going on in the classroom, as much as I could, in order to try to learn with my students, a process of learning which now seems to me best described as a journey. My journey in this collaborative classroom began that first weekend of the semester as I sat at home, half-heartedly flipping through the pages of their first journal entries: We had asked them to write about how they feel when they write, expecting to read their equally half-hearted attempts to explain their notions of writing. Instead, I found myself increasingly intrigued by what these students were telling me. I read Scott's entry early on, an entry that got my interest rolling. He wrote, "When I am writing I never think about what I am writing. Then I read it over to see if I made any mistakes and if I should add something to it. When I am writing I block out everything. And I have to be comfortable." Pretty interesting, I thought; he shows some self-analysis, some understanding of the process he uses to compose. I was encouraged to continue reading, this time a bit more carefully, when I came to Stephanie's:

> When I write I like to be at the kitchen table where it is usually quiet, at night. With one light on to make it relaxing. Our kitchen is furnished in earth-tone colors; it makes it very relaxing. Then I pull out paper that is colorful (red, green, yellow, blue) and write on and on without stopping. When I make a mistake I scribble it out just to make the letter more laid back. Not real neat because the way you write your words and letters brings out your personality to other people, I think. I like to make my letters funny, full of jokes and scribbled out words, because that's my personality. And I make it a point *not* to copy the letter over.

I began to wonder why this student had been placed in a basic class. Sure, there were some problems with sentence structure and punctuation, but I was impressed by her understanding of some very complicated issues that surround the connection of authorial voice and style. "The way you write your words and letters," she said, "brings out your personality to other people"—a fairly sophisticated notion of intentionality in one's writing, a notion I had failed to think of as an informing one for "these students." I began to sit up and take note now as I read on and on, surprised at how many students articulated a similar understanding of their own writing, bolting upright when I came to Andrea's:

> When I am writing a story, I usually find myself on a beach and fill my lungs with ocean air. In the background I hear no seagulls, not even the ocean. Just the sensation I get from that very first breath, I guess it's similar to the feeling you get when you're being hugged or when you yawn. It relaxes my imagination as the blank wall that sits in front of my typewriter fills with the images of the people, places, and situations my mind creates.

A short story writer, I told myself. Look at the metaphors, the rhythms. Not only does she understand a lot about her own writing, but she writes artfully about her understanding. Again, I asked myself why a student who writes like this would be labeled "at risk"?

As I continued to read the other journals, more carefully now, I recognized that while not all the students were this articulate about their own writing, they all showed a greater understanding of their own composing processes than I had expected. While these students were resisting the writing they were assigned to do in school classes (a resistance that manifested itself in a variety of ways, from being absent on days when writing was due to simply refusing to write in class to writing the bare minimum expected, often on the way into class as the bell rang), they were writing up a storm at home: Fully one half of this class admitted their interest in and practice of writing outside the bounds of school. While these students were vehemently denying any interest in writing when we had class discussions in school, they were penning journals, poems, short stories, and plays at home. Melvin, for example, the self-appointed class poet, maintained an initial silence about his composing when we tried to elicit talk in class about their writing selves, but then wrote in his journal about why he writes what he does:

> I feel that journals help me
>     realize things,
> Stories make me think what
>     I lack,
> Poems help me chill, you know,
>     lay back and relax.

His choices for writing, if not his reasons, seemed typical for those who slowly began to admit to not only writing on their own, but enjoying that writing. Marty, an almost nonwriter of school assignments, said, "Sometimes I sit down and write short stories" when there's nothing else to do; Jenny, a well-mannered but fairly nonproductive school writer, writes poems because "they give me a great feeling"; Traci, a good student who always fulfills assignments but generally doesn't go beyond her teacher's expectations, likes journals because they "bring back a lot of memories." How could these be the same kids who moaned, complained, even refused to write when asked to do so in class? The same kids who would say in unison during a class discussion on the subject that they hated writing? The same kids who were labeled at risk or illiterate or preliterate or semiliterate, labels of which they were well aware? Clearly these students weren't illiterate, but they did fail to measure up to the standards of a conforming literacy, the only kind their school—and a host of other schools—seemed to recognize and value. Maybe, Sheila and I began to think, these students possessed that other kind of literacy I had seen in Sarah and Akemi, an in-forming literacy in which students formulate literacy from within themselves, using their own forms which emerge from their own backgrounds and experiences, forms which seem to be disparate from the school forms.

Calling upon our inclinations about these two literacies, Sheila and I decided to explore their implications for student-writers by asking the students in this class to search with us for answers to the dilemma of what constitutes literacy, beginning with the questions their journals had raised for us and for them. We asked them: Why don't the schools recognize and value your words, your language, your forms? What are the differences between your kind of literacy and the literacy expected by the school? What's wrong with the school forms? Why can't you seem to meet the expectations for literacy demanded by schools when you can clearly use written language so effectively in other settings? When it comes to school writing, why do so many of you not only fail to meet the expectations but simply refuse to take the challenge, a resistance to school literacy which results in your designation as preliterate or illiterate or just plain at risk? Why is it that you who show us both pleasure and interest in out-of-school writing seem to have little or no interest in in-school writing? Our search for answers took the students in a number of directions: interviews with their peers in the classroom and out, analysis as a class of specific pieces of their writing, and surveys and other information gathered to research specific projects about literacy which they designed.

More specifically, we designed a flexible curriculum whose major goals were twofold: first, to help students think of themselves even more as writers—as Authors, in fact, who were capable of making decisions about how and what they wrote—and second, to help them see themselves as researchers, so that what they learned about composing by looking at themselves and at their peers might begin to counter the form-centered composing models put forth by many of their teachers. We believed that if these related goals could be achieved, then these students might be more open to writing, might practice more writing, and, in fact, might start to celebrate a new-found literacy—a re-formed literacy which, as Bakhtin tells us, finds its basis in the interplay between their own in-forming internally persuasive discourses and the conforming, authoritative discourse of their school worlds.

Sheila and I had already begun the hard task of trying to

engender in the students a feeling of their own authorship by that first writing assignment in which they wrote about how they "are" when they write (described above). We decided to start at the same time the push for students to see themselves as researchers, but researchers in the qualitative sense that our own experience with teacher-research told us was important. Like the models of research most teachers know from their forays into educational psychology the traditional research model that these students knew from their science classes focused on numbers, percentages, and objective analysis as the name of the game. We told them instead that their own observations, their own perceptions, were valuable research tools and that, by relying on these tools, we could all learn a lot. We took to heart the notions of phenomenological research put forth by Barritt et al., in their monograph *Researching Educational Practice,* instructing students in "the phenomenological way." For phenomenological philosophers and researchers (a category into which Freire and Gadamer certainly fit in many ways), an individual's examination of the ordinary experiences of her life and her relating of those to experiences of others around her is the only way for us to understand meaningfully our world.[3] Barritt and his co-authors place this central belief into a context of how to actually do research: They advise researchers first to think and write an individual experience of the everyday world; then to analyze several people's experiences as a group, searching for the individual themes that stand out; and finally to determine common themes from that analysis, always keeping an eye out for the variations as well.

We took on this approach, with some variations. Our students began by trying out what we called exercises in observation that helped them trust their own observing selves as they looked at the ordinary world around them in new ways: Eric attempted to use all of his senses in observing and describing the flag in front of the room, even walking up to it and burying his nose in the material to try to glean its scent; Andrea used her imagination as she anticipated what it would be like to chomp into the juicy orange she had brought into class to observe: like a "dam bursting," she wrote.

---

[3]There are wide variations within the philosophy of phenomenology, seen in the works of Husserl, Heidegger, Merleau-Ponty, Sartre, and Gadamer, for example. For my purposes here, I refer mostly to existential and hermeneutic renditions of phenomenology.

After students completed their most in-depth observation assignment in which they observed people and events in a public place for an hour, we introduced the notions of analyzing and thematizing. Students in groups analyzed and named individual themes in the information they uncovered in a variety of different places, eventually coming to categorize these themes into common categories. They started with the more obvious categories of smells, sounds, and sights, but soon moved to such categories as "mushy stuff," "horseplay," fighting, and talk—categories that remained a constant across the various places in which they observed: a dance, the mall, a hockey game, the halls between classes. Students began to see themselves as researchers as they came up with some hypotheses based on their observations. When we later asked them what they had learned about observation, their responses covered a range of ideas: "Observation is to observe something with your eyes and your mind" (Stephanie); "You can do whatever you want to absorb the atmosphere" (Margie): "I think it is the study of something like a book or a person" (Satara); "While observing you are suddenly aware of what's happening around you" (anonymous); "I think when you observe you look at things around you, you are aware of what is happening in almost every direction. It's like when you drive a car you can't just look straight forward. You have to look around and see what is happening" (Fred).

We next tried to transfer the skills they had learned as researchers to their own and their peers' writing, asking them to start gathering information by a number of means about the writing of students like themselves. We started with a talk-write in which each student paired with another to relate a past negative school experience (one student told a story while the other noted exactly what had been said). After we had all read the various experiences and talked about the individual themes, together we began to categorize and thematize, asking ourselves what we could find as common to all the school experiences of this particular class. We next switched specifically to looking at their own writing backgrounds and experiences: Each student interviewed another student in the class about her writing self, asking about past experience, interests in writing, how/what/when she writes, how she feels about writing. Students wrote up their findings and shared with one another in small groups; one group (which included twin sisters Charlene and Catherine Payne) penned the following:

"Charlene and Catherine are lots of fun—they hate to write but they get the job done. But Melvin, Tracy and Satara, they use their brains. They love to write, opposite of the Paynes."

We then introduced another factor into their research—the actual writing students in this class had done. Students brought in samples of writing from both in-school and out-of-school; we photocopied these writings and together analyzed the pieces, trying to ascertain the conventions and rules for the various kinds of writing (see Appendices D and E). This aspect proved particularly fruitful. Students looked at examples of their peers' writing, such things as notes taken in class, stories, summaries, journals, definitions, reports, and poems, analyzing and thematizing what they found just as they had done in their sensory observations and talk-writes. As students began to argue about what makes a summary a summary, for example, they began to see that the basis for such definitions lay in the hands of their various teachers and to understand that what they had originally seen as strict categories of genres really varied according to individual preferences.

We hoped all these approaches to research would pay off in the final projects for the class, an assignment which involved small student groups actually researching on their own some theme about writing which had arisen over the course of the term. Groups formed around three issues they raised as interesting to pursue: the role of mood in writing, the differences and similarities between in- and out-of-school writing, and gender differences in writing. Groups came up with both interview and survey questions, and gathered information from both the class itself and outsiders (other students in the school, family members, teachers), and then put together their reports in any way they chose. On my last day with the class, students presented their findings in a variety of ways: skits, oral reports, written reports, and one rap.

One of the first things we discovered through this approach was, as mentioned above, the students' acknowledged interest in writing, at least in certain kinds of writing. We began to ask each other, through the talk-writes and interviews, why students seemed to care more about some kinds of writing than others. Many students were eager to tell us about school writing, which they saw as different from most other writing—although at one time in their pasts the two seemed more closely tied. Despite some of their memories of early school writing as often a plethora of rules (use your thumb to indent, write on the big lines, don't have messy handwriting), writing for most was pleasurable in early grades. Many remember stories they wrote, stories published as little books which other students then read.

For whatever reasons—whether it was the kind of writing, the approach to writing, or the teacher responses to writing—writing in elementary grades was enjoyable, even for those whom we would consider the most negative toward writing now. What happened to those happy memories? Most of the class spoke about the change in their feelings toward writing in terms of its increasingly rule-bound nature.

Marty's story is a perfect example of the shift from enjoying school writing early on to disliking it to the point of refusing to do it in many classes now. As he told me in an interview:

> MARTY: I like to write, I like thinking about it. One year in elementary school, I wrote a little story. Got sent (mumble). I guess it won a prize or something. I never got it back. It was about, it was about some underwater thing. I don't really remember—boat creatures, like a little family.
> CATHY: Did you like writing then?
> M: Sort of, cause then everybody had messy handwriting . . .
> C: Have you had teachers who criticized it cause your writing hasn't been good? Is that—
> M: Uh, all through. In elementary you used to get the penmanship grade and when we were there in first to fifth it used to be pluses and minuses, I used to get minuses. And then—
> C: Yea.
> M: Like sixth on up through, they were doing, they were *A* and *B* and *C* and *D* and all that. I always got *D*'s and *E*'s in penmanship. Just never been good, teachers (mumble) cause they couldn't understand it, so they didn't want to correct it.
> C: Yea.
> M: Which is, "it's messy, take it back and do it over," and I'd get exasperated and say no, I did it once, I'm not gonna do it over.

For Marty, the presentational issues of form were important, as they were for Akemi and, to a lesser extent, for Sarah. In Marty's case, the issue of his own handwriting and what he perceives as increasing teacher severity has turned him off to writing. Yet, despite the difficulty, he still writes outside school:

MARTY: A friend of mine wanted me to write a testimony for him and that was, like that was like three pages long. And that was just the beginning of it.
CATHY: Wow!
M: And, uh, it was all—I tried, I tried writing it out—it wouldn't write out good so I tried printing it out. It came out OK. But like it was still all, all messed up, you know, cause I'll keep writing and then I'll know where the sentence ends but I won't end it there keep going so in my mind, it, you know, it's OK, but when it goes on paper and other people read it—
C: Yea . . . That's great, so that sounds like it's the longest thing you've ever written.
M: Yea, true, just about. It was, like three pages. Sometimes I sit down and write short stories (mumble).
C: You do? Just on your own or in school?
M: Just on my own.
C: Like, what kinds of things do you write about?
M: Everything, just stuff that crosses my mind.

The themes revealed in Marty's responses became fairly standard renditions of students' experiences, we began to see. Stephanie, for example, told us this after conducting an interview with one of her peers:

> Megan likes to write about herself but doesn't like English or poetry. She likes to write in her kitchen or out under a tree. When learning how to write she had to do introductory paragraphs and had to be neat. In elementary she never wrote anything very long. In junior high and high school, she said it was a different story. Rough drafts, outlines, brainstorming, essays, etc. She said it got harder for her to write. Rules teachers told her to remember were writing in blue or black ink or typed, very neat, no mistakes and put things in specific order.

This interview and others led interviewer Stephanie to conclude, "Most students don't really do much free writing [in school]. They seem to write to communicate with others and that is all. As for writing in school we have to and write enough to answer the question or get the job done."

This contrasts sharply with the image of writing many of these students remember from elementary school. Many remember enjoying writing, being praised for their writing, and writing lots of different kinds of pieces in lots of different ways. Writing in high school for these students clearly has lost whatever appeal it once had; it's now seen in the businesslike context into which Stephanie placed it: They have to do it, and they have to do enough of it to get the assignment done. Writing in school to fulfill teachers' preordained notions of communication serves the function of a commodity, its trade value seen in terms of a grade. As such, school writing has come to lose most of the value or meaning that these students themselves at one time assigned to it, as a means to come to understand something, a way to discover something new, to help remember your past or come to grips with your present or even to give you pleasure. We all began to ask ourselves why this had happened.

As we teacher- and student-researchers looked carefully together at students' writing practices, the way our students understood form informed our understanding of their failure to master the literacy of conformity. As teachers, we first began to see this as we listened to the student-researchers try to describe certain pieces of writing that various class members had done—again and again, the only descriptive words they could come up with would be the "name" of the particular form or genre the writing took. For example, on one occasion a group of students was looking at a list of definitions one student had written in a consumer economics class, taken from a unit on the stock market. The group decided the subject matter, the actual content of the writing was "definition." When I suggested that "definition" might not describe the subject matter, but might instead be the form, an argument ensued. I asked the students, "If you read a story about animals, would the subject matter be 'story'?" Although these students acknowledged the distinction I was making in my example, they insisted that the content of their classmate's written list was, nevertheless, definition. "We don't have any idea what this is about," they told me. And the implication followed: If you don't know what it's about, how can you possibly see a content? We could begin to see that an emphasis on form had become so ingrained for these students that it completely overshadowed content for them. We began to see why the question "What are you writing?" inevitably would be answered, " a report," "a research paper," "a paragraph," "a summary"— not "I'm writing about one of the characters in this short story" or "the effect of AIDS testing on the workplace" or "a film we saw in class."

This seems to be a confused approach to writing in which students see form as the substance of their writing, with content, if it follows at all, coming in a distant second. Such an approach is reminiscent of Sarah's telling comment about descriptive writing:

> For school, they say, "Write a descriptive piece," and you can choose what you want to describe, but you still have to write descriptively. . . . You have to rack your brain to think of something to describe. . . . You start off thinking descriptive instead of being struck by something and saying "I want to describe that, I want to capture that."

There seems to be, for all these students, a world of difference between writing because you have something to say and finding a form in which to say it and writing in a form whether or not you have anything to say. In schools, where students are often placed in situations in which they have nothing much to say or in which they don't want to say much, they seem to revert to the sanctioned forms, the safe structures which allow them to get by without composing their own informed selves into the writing.

The students with whom we worked in this class in particular seem to have at least one clear belief about form: They know not only that such structures are safe but that they need the structures if they are to survive in their school worlds. They acknowledge, at least implicitly, a split between form and content, and accept the preeminence of form. Despite this knowledge, however, they often still choose to reject and resist such forms.

Fred comes to mind immediately as I think back to how and what we teachers learned with our students about resistance to the school forms. His "theme" about writing—the notion that kept coming up for him again and again throughout the term—was one of subject matter, or the lack of subject matter in most of the writing he knows about. Fred is a student who told us from the start that he hated writing. Why? we wondered, and as the term progressed we began to piece together a few clues to answer that question. Early on in the semester, when he interviewed a peer about *his* writing, Fred came up with this conclusion: "He thinks his writing could be good if he could have a subject matter to write on, otherwise he doesn't like it." He went on, "People can write if they feel like it. When they do write they do a good job of it." Occasionally in class, Fred would mention this belief that he can write but that he doesn't because he has nothing to write about. By March he was able to articulate this a bit more, as an entry in my teaching journal reflects:

> It was an interesting class today—I handed out notebooks as some of the students came in and tried to comment specifically on what some of the kids wrote. I told Fred especially that I liked his imagery about the car a lot. [Fred had written a nice response in his notebook to the question "What is observation?"; he wrote, "I think when you observe you look at things around you, you are aware of what is happening in almost every direction. It's like when you drive a car you can't just look straight forward. You have to look around and see what is happening."]. . . .
>
> We brainstormed questions about personal background and about writing together and then they went at it alone. . . . Fred was particularly interesting. He talked about how little he cared about writing—how he hated it, wouldn't do it. Started by talking about how he'd get letters from girls and wouldn't write them back. Why not? He didn't know; he just didn't know what to say. Moved later into talking about history class—he wouldn't outline chapters, so he kept failing. Why not? "I don't know much about history," he said, "so how do I know what's important and what isn't?"

Fred, clearly capable of important insights as you can see by his creative use of the car metaphor, explains here that he can't do outlines because he doesn't know or understand the subject matter—and if he doesn't know the subject matter, he can't know what's important and what isn't, and thus he can't possibly conform to the genre of the regimented outline with its Roman numerals and capital letters. While this does seem a serious concern to Fred, at first I wasn't sure how seriously to take his resistance to the task of outlining chapters in history. Is it true that Fred's lack of understanding of content kept him from filling the forms, or is it just Fred's way of avoiding the task? I later recalled Akemi's comments about how she did outlines: She clearly pointed to the lack of subject matter she needs in order to write outlines, a view almost opposite to Fred's. What an outline says—its content—isn't what's important, she believes. It only has to "*look* like it's outlined," she told me; "it's got to be in a little format."

For both students, the form's the thing. For Akemi, whose academic success means that she has learned how to conform to the school rules, an understanding of the subject matter isn't important; she knows how to take any subject matter and make it fit into a preordained format. For Fred, who doesn't conform, who either hasn't learned to or who has chosen not to negotiate the rules that govern school discourse successfully, subject matter is closely tied to the form—so much so that finding the right form without knowing the content is either an impossibility or a meaningless task he refuses to undertake. His lack of understanding of the subject matter, and thus his inability to fit into a form, leads to his failure to conform, a failure which is costly in this setting: Fred eventually failed the history course a second time.

For Andrea, another student in Fred's class, it isn't the lack of subject matter which causes resistance but rather the limitations placed on what the subject matter can be. In her view, when students are limited to certain kinds of contents, they are necessarily limited to certain kinds of forms. Students in school thus write both in prescribed ways and with prescribed opinions. She says, "School writers are sometimes phony. Instead of writing what they feel they write what's expected of them without expressing what their opinions really and truly are." For her, this leads to the following conclusion: "I don't like writing assignments but I love writing on my own." In other words, the limited contents and the limited forms that define school writing for her result in her resistance to school assignments; when she can write what she wants and how she wants, she does, and she does so copiously, outside of school. When she has to write in the school ways, ways which she thinks force her to limit her own ideas, she opts out. Stephanie seems to agree with this characterization. Her perception about school writing is that "when it comes to school work we really don't have a lot of choices in writing. Because of our homework 'rules': most teachers have an answer key in their books and we have to have that answer in order to get it right." This emphasis on "correct" structure and form leads Stephanie, like Andrea, to a rejection of school writing, but she, too, stresses, "I love to free write and be different in every way possible." Again, the distinction these academically unsuccessful students make about freewriting, which rejects the school forms and which they value, and school writing, which is based in specific forms and which they don't value, brings to mind the academically successful Akemi. She values what she calls "freestyle writing" in out-of-school settings;

but when, for whatever reasons (lack of time, interest, etc.), she writes an in-school piece in that freestyle format, she ends up rejecting that writing. The great pleasure she finds in writing "off the top of my head" outside school becomes *just* writing off the top of her head when transferred to school-type tasks. Like her notions of outlines, her school writing has to look like an essay, a report, a summary, in order for it to "count" in her world.

For Akemi and for Stephanie, Andrea, and many others in their class, the preference for writing on their own or freewriting carries with it an element of resisting the school rules, the school forms. Students described for us writing outside the bounds of school assignments as less rule-bound, freer, with more of an element of themselves involved.

Case in point was Dennis—a very unenthusiastic member of the class, the student all of us who have taught recognize as the complainer, the one who says over and over, "This is boring; why do we have to do this?" When we asked him to write about what (if any) kinds of writing he enjoyed, he surprised us by responding that he likes to write things that he can put himself into. "Journals are fun because you can tell someone what happened to you," he began. "Stories are fun to write because you can make a true story or a fake story. You put in your own words and you can make it interesting or boring. But that's your opinion." He continued in a way that further surprised us, "Notes [taken in class] are fun to write because you can put your own words into it." Notes are fun to write? Although we were a little shocked at first by this seeming contradiction to our experience with students over the years, Dennis's tying together of notes to stories and journals makes sense. All are kinds of writing which allow the author's voice to control the other voices speaking in his or her text, as the writer interacts with the subject matter to shape and mold the content in a way he or she wants.

For all these students, though, their resistance doesn't go so far as to allow them to write in school settings in the ways they know and, in many cases, value—that is, to reject the conforming literacy in favor of their in-forming one within the structured setting of the institution of school. Instead, Fred refuses to write at all; Andrea and Stephanie resist school writing strongly (although they do it at times), while they write furiously outside of school; Akemi keeps the two kinds of writing separate and writes copiously in both ways; Sarah, too, keeps them separate, to the point of abandoning school writing in favor of other kinds. The two kinds of writing, reflective of the two kinds of literacy, remain separated for many students, particularly for those called illiterate by the schools.

As our students began to raise questions with us teachers about the limited and form-based notions of literacy put forth by the schools and we teachers consciously strove to create a place in our classroom where both a literacy of conformity and a literacy of informity might be explored, we all participated in a constitutive pedagogy. We took Bakhtin's words to heart as we searched for a space within the confines of the classroom in which the two forms of discourse might struggle with each other, resulting, we believed, in a positive dialogue, a dialogue which might help students to think and to act more critically as they began to forge, in Bakhtin's words, "an individual ideology." Perhaps not surprisingly, we found our students showing less resistance to writing and, in fact, writing more effectively. By the end of the term, many students who initially had refused to write and to talk about their writing began to join with us to research the issues and to write up the results they had uncovered.

Such participation in their own critical literacy brings us back to the words of Paulo Freire which opened this chapter and the implications of his work for all of us literacy workers. As Freire explores the politics of the literacy by which we might overcome illiteracy, he stresses the basis of such a literacy: People must learn to be critical, participating members of the literacy club they join; people must name these worlds for themselves as they first critically reflect on the world at present and then act to change it. In our classroom, our students' continually expanding literacy depended on just these elements, elements which seem to me central for an expanded constitutive pedagogy: Students learned first to reflect critically on the literate worlds they inhabit by naming the forms that surround their school and home discourses and then to act upon that new knowledge by trying to bridge the gap between the two. As students began to name these forms, we all began the long process of expanding our critical consciousness about why such forms exist and what limitations they have, while at the same time recognizing what benefits forms—when more openly defined—might offer readers and writers. Such critical questions challenge the literacy of conformity put forth by our schools as the only literacy students need to know—a notion of literacy that results in labels for students who do not conform, labels that are inaccurate and harmful as characterizations of capacity and interest. As a result of their reflection on such issues, students and teachers in this classroom began to take action: We began to push toward establishing an environment in which we all could reformulate the definitions of what might be called literate, allowing the struggle between the two literacies to surface and interact. If we agree, as we came to do, that the literacy of conformity so common in schools is limiting because it does not allow students to bring their contextualized literacy practices to bear upon it, then we had to conclude first that the nature of literacy instruction in schools is unsatisfactory and second that a literacy of in-formity, while personally satisfying, needs to make meaning in more publicly shared ways. By implication, we concluded that new space must be created where students and teachers can re-form literacy instruction and perhaps the definition of literacy itself.

One group of students in our class chose to define that re-formed notion of literacy in their final report, the culmination of the short research project in which students looked into questions about literacy they chose to explore: in this case, the question was "Do boys and girls write differently?" After surveying, interviewing, and analyzing their own and their peers' writing, these students chose to share their information with the class, in part, in an oral rap:

> Wrote this rhyme last night
> Trying to help our group pass
> Trying to scrape up a grade
> for a literature class
>
> Explaining the female whole life style
> Story of lyrics
> When they write a letter
> It's long, neat and serious.
> This rhyme is far from over or done
> Cause they express their feelings like a slow song.
> This is not a person, place or thing
> Like a pronoun, fraction
> This is strictly a verb
> Cause they show nothing but action . . .

> Boys are in the other direction
> If they make mistakes they don't make corrections
> If you don't assign to type it
> You won't understand their handwriting
> They destroy your brain, mess with your red blood cells
> If it was a crime for writing
> Boys would be under the jail.
> This is a rhyme about the triple S
> Sloppy, short and serious.

Here is a piece that clearly does not conform to the genres of school writing but is instead situated in another genre brought to bear upon the task from the students' lived worlds outside school. It is a genre students chose to exercise as they worked to shape their in-formed literacy. In using this form, the students were able to meet some of the desires we teachers have for all our students. The students who wrote this show me critical thinking and a sense of play with language. These are students who were writing to discover personal meaning, who were thinking well in language, and who were achieving serious intellectual purpose. Writing such as this piece can only be viewed as a beginning for our students, but for me it seems like a great place to begin. Could the rap be better? Of course. But for the students who wrote this, students who had refused to participate in the reading and writing of most of their classes, students who continue to be labeled illiterate, this rap, a start toward a mix of their own form of literacy with that of the school's, is a significant step toward achievement of a meaningful, workable literacy.

And for me, this kind of action, action based in critical reflection, is a significant achievement as well. For me, it's the way we who are teachers can join with those who are our students in order to make real and attainable for them and for ourselves the implications of Freire's notion. It seems to me that these are the politics of the literacy through which we can and we will overcome illiteracy.

## POSTSCRIPT: REFLECTIONS ON "HIGH SCHOOL STUDENTS BECOME RESEARCHERS"

The experience about which you read in this chapter reflected my growing understanding of issues of literacy instruction and of research methodology—and of the connections I was starting to make between the two. I see now that many of the goals I had set for myself as a result of my work with Sarah were becoming fulfilled. First, I see this work as a greater movement away from the traditionally separated roles of researcher and researched, with teachers occupying the former and students occupying the latter. As you recall from the case study of Sarah, I continued to be concerned that despite my attempt to include her in the research, our roles retained their traditional flavor in terms of authority. As the person who both set the research question and determined the audience for its dissemination, I was the sole definer of what constituted the research. In this case study, these roles shifted dramatically. Students, with their teachers' guidance, named some of the issues about their writing which seemed problematic to them. Students became researchers: They used talk and writing to recall their own experiences as writers, to interview each other and us teachers, and to analyze their own writing and that of their peers. As students took the lead here and defined their classroom roles as researchers, we teachers took on the role of learners: As the research served as the content of the class, Sheila and I constantly redefined what we thought we knew. For example, my initial surprise when I discovered these students actually had something to say about themselves as writers forced me to rethink my own prejudices about students labeled as these kids were. As we allowed ourselves to learn more from the students, Sheila and I shifted gears time and again to try to create a classroom setting which let their emerging knowledge set the direction for the curriculum. A curriculum emerging from the students' knowledge naturally resulted in changes in my research stance. The wavering line I was beginning to feel between those terms *researcher* and *researched* followed naturally from the wavering line I was admitting between teachers and students. As we came closer to Freire's notion of teacher-students and student-teachers, I began to give the students' perspectives real weight as the fodder for both curricular change and research, evidenced by both the honest questions I asked in interviews (as I did in Marty's: "You do [write short stories]? Just on your own or in school?) and by the assumptions I made that students did understand their own findings (as I did with Dennis when I sought to make sense out of what at first seemed to me a contradiction: "Notes are fun to write?") . I can see my new sense of collaborative research reflected in the actual writing of the case study, as I was more comfortable making our joint discoveries a prominent part of the text.

The related goal I had set for myself was to see research in its full emancipatory sense, to emphasize the power of research to provoke change. The set-up of this course assured that to a certain extent. By having the students' research serve as the major content, Sheila and I experienced a need for a continual refiguring of emphases. As the curriculum emerged from the students' findings, then, we kept revising the curriculum in the true sense of the word: seeing anew what was in front of us. The most obvious occasion of this occurred when the students came up with their own research questions for the final part of the course. Despite our setting the terms for the overarching theme of their research (i.e., their own writing), students arrived at their own questions and their own approaches to that research. As they saw their own research setting the direction for the class, these students began to see themselves differently: as Authors whose words were important. Because many of the students felt an increased understanding of themselves as writers, they experienced growing feelings of confidence in their own abilities to be named as Authors. And as students' confidence rose, they felt more able to branch out and take the risks that real Authors take.

In true reciprocal manner, the work also created long-lasting changes in me as a teacher and researcher. Not only did I learn specifics about literacy from these students, specifics which have helped me develop my own understandings about form and its function in writing pedagogy; I also learned about the benefits of a pedagogy in which student research serves as the focal point of curriculum. Both lessons continue to inform my teaching as I constantly strive to develop an emancipatory approach to my pedagogy.

The lessons I've learned about research from this experience continue to evolve. All the case studies show me that practicing teacher-researchers will never be—and should never be—satisfied with the results of their work. Understandably, I now see problems in this, my first, foray into emancipatory student–teacher-research. Although my coteacher, students, and I achieved much of what I see as important for a praxis-oriented approach, a couple of nagging questions still remain.

The first seems an issue of genre and form. When I made the

shift to treat this experience as the study of a class rather than of an individual, I made a number of sacrifices. Lost are the more in-depth portraits that emerged in the studies of Akemi and Sarah. The issues that so consumed me in my hindsight look at those cases largely disappear then from this study: concerns that I included enough quotes or that the quotes were of sufficient length to really portray Sarah and Akemi. As I look at this study again, the questions instead become these: If the focus becomes a whole class and course structure, as it has here, as opposed to the development of a single individual, is it inevitable that we lose some of the depth? In sacrificing the three-dimensional look at an individual in order to talk about a class with a number of different personalities whose individual understandings add to the whole, do I achieve something that is equally important? As I reimagine this case study, I wonder if there are ways to combine the two approaches that may result in a fuller look, while not making each case a book-length portrait.

The second question arises from my current rereading of this case study. Despite the increased awareness that reflecting on my work with Sarah provided, I find myself in this case still relying on a *we* to describe and explain what happened in the class. At times this *we* seems to refer to Sheila and me; at times it seems to refer to the students and teachers together. The confusion I feel from this pronoun as I read the case now seems to me to arise from my zealousness in attempting a collaborative research project. Using the *we* to express what was happening in the classroom seems, at first glance, a way to set the tone that this experience really did involve teachers and students together; at second glance, though, it seems to imply a group mind-set that doesn't allow for individual difference, a problem I take up more fully in the next chapter. As well, I still am caught at times in the trap of trying to represent for the reader what I think a student "really" means; for example, when I follow up Andrea's conclusion about the phoniness of school writers with my own explanation, an explanation that defines her understanding in terms that carry significance for me: "In other words, the limited contents and the limited forms that define school writing for her result in her resistance to school assignments."

The third question, posed to me by a former university student and prospective teacher who read an abridged version of this chapter, seems integral to this kind of research and related to the issue of voice and audience raised above. As I mention in chapter 1, she asked about how far-reaching this kind of teaching and research really can be. Despite all our hopes that this praxis-oriented approach results in real changes for students (as it appears to do within the classroom setting here), she wondered if these students would be prepared to take the new understandings about issues of form they had gained from this experience and apply them to the more traditional settings they would encounter in the rest of their high school experience. "Do you think that they would react differently to [the rules] this time, and be able to apply their heightened interest and ability in writing to the structured, rule-oriented high school writing that they would probably be asked to do?" I think her question gets at the heart of this work: Was this project a one-time undertaking, something that seemed important merely within the confines of a particular classroom, or a start toward students truly expanding their own notions of literacy? I fear the former is true in large part, and I ask myself the implications of this occurrence. Why, for example, didn't Fred hand in the written assignments for social studies, thus failing the course, despite our discussions about those writings? How has Fred survived in his classes since that semester? How has he been empowered?

My recent reading of Patti Lather's book *Getting Smart* helps me point to some of the contradictions that I recognize in this particular case study—a study committed to emancipatory action but which I now see as having still fallen short of its goal. Lather believes that truly praxis-oriented research, what she calls "advocacy research," relies on two occurrences: reciprocity and dialectical theory building. Reciprocity between the researcher and the researched, in her view, is essential to negotiate meaning and to empower the researched. In other words, in order to continue to diminish the line between researcher and researched, both parties must talk and exchange ideas, revealing something of themselves, as a way of creating shared understandings. As both parties participate, the "researched" become a more integral part of the process, resulting both in a stronger interest in the subject at hand but also in more confidence in understanding the implications of that subject. The result of this, according to Lather, is dialectical theory building, theory which is built in response to critical inquiry by all participants at all stages of the inquiry. Thus, as participants negotiate meaning at all stages in a "fundamentally dialogic and mutually educative enterprise" (63), theory becomes part of the lives of the researcher and the researched rather than being imposed by only the researcher. The implications of this are profound, calling into question assumptions of authorship, and speak to the problems I saw with my own research, not only in this instance but also with Akemi and Sarah. If research can be seen as theory building for both parties, then the definitions of theory must change.[4] If theory is to be useful for all participants, (the only way change resulting from the research really can be long-lasting), Lather believes "it must speak to the felt needs of a specific group in ordinary language." (65) Thus, if Fred is to reap the benefits of his integral particpation in the research of the class, he must be involved even more fully in it—from start to finish. The theory building that emerges from the research findings must emerge *with* Fred and others rather than *from* them, in language which is understandable and important to them. By naming their new understandings, to paraphrase Freire, they should be able to rename the rest of their worlds.

Lather suggests some approaches to research which begin to shift emphases toward these goals of reciprocity and dialectical theory building. One shift she advocates is toward an understanding of "the social relations of the research act." She explains,

> Who speaks for whom becomes a central question. Such a question decenters what Dreyfus and Rabinow (1983) term the "Great Interpreter" and what Foucault calls the "master of truth and justice" (1977:12) whose self appointed task is to uphold reason and reveal the truth to those unable to see or speak it. Conversely, a reciprocally educative focus breaks down the distinctions between emancipatory research and pedagogy by producing a collaborative analysis that doesn't impose the resarcher's understanding of reality, that doesn't say what things mean via a privileged position and theoretical presuppositions (Gitlin et al. 1988:18). (91–92)

In other words, focusing on dialogue that allows more participants in the research to speak and be heard begins the move toward a more emancipatory stance. Like other feminist researchers, Lather

---

[4]For more on the connection of theory to teacher-research, see Ruth Ray's *The Practice of Theory.*

suggests that true advocacy research rejects the traditional interview for gathering information, substituting instead a reciprocal conversation in which all parties to the research contribute ideas. When researchers participate in this way, inserting some of their own experiences, the dynamics of the relationship between researcher and researched shifts. As the line between the two diminishes, a number of results occur: At an ethical level, those who are researched are less likely to feel like guinea pigs whose words are important only for how they further the research of some outsider; at a research level, a fuller conversation may result in deeper understandings about the subject at hand; at an advocacy level, such participation is more likely to bring about long-lasting change. When participants take ownership of the research by talking about it in their own words, Lather suggests, the research will become more meaningful for them—a part of their lives, a reason to make change.

Interestingly, my recent reading of this work by Lather reflects some of the intricacies about teacher-research that, at the time I wrote the case study, I was just beginning to think about. As I continued to ask myself how we as teacher-researchers can join with student-researchers in more significant ways, resulting in research studies that retain their empowering nature beyond the scope of a semester or a year, many of the notions she raises cropped up in my own approaches, a shift you will see in the next two chapters. My own thinking at the time I began my next case study was strongly influenced by Stephen Tyler's call for a "postmodern ethnography," one that reverberates with the voices of both the researcher and the researched in its making. The essay you will see as chapter 5 is an essay written by two students and myself, and reflects our attempt to put his ideas into practice.

# CHAPTER 5

# *Re-forming Literacy:*
# *Researchers Write Together*

## INTRODUCTION

The study you will read in this chapter lays out the next progression in my thinking about what teacher-research can be in its most imaginative sense. The genre and the method which are shown here evolved out of my years of thinking through my own theory and practice and reading about the theories and practices of others. While some gaps still exist between the theories which drove my understandings as I worked with these particular students and the actualities of the resulting study (as I will point out again in the epilogue which follows this chapter), it does begin to deal with some of the most important questions I have come to recognize as integral to research in general and teacher-research in particular: Practically, how can we represent the experiences of others; ethically, is it acceptable even to try to do so, and, if it is, how can we guarantee that such research will benefit those who are participating in ways important to them? How might the research we practice integrally tie in to the pedagogical stances we espouse?

These questions heighten the stakes of what I saw as the issues underlying teacher-research when I began my work. They look to a deeper understanding of the nature of collaboration between teachers and students in an effort to increase our understanding of the classroom. All research is, of course, in some sense collaborative. Even researchers who enter schools as outsiders cannot function without that researched Other: a teacher, an administrator, a student. However, collaborative research, as I now understand it, implies a different way of thinking about an Other as the research process unfolds. Researching *with* students implies a different kind of mind-set about the nature of knowledge, about the role of research, about the relationship between teachers and students, than does conducting research *on* students. Researching *with* students, I

163

have found, implies the kind of collaboration between the researcher and the researched in which a search for shared meaning between the self and other becomes of primary importance. However, as my work with Akemi and Sarah and the students of that English classroom have taught me, the issue is more than just research *with* versus research *on*. Even when we do research *with* our students, the nature of that collaboration is a complex and challenging proposition.

As you can see from the pages which precede this chapter, some understandings about collaboration did become clear to me over the course of my studies. I learned that collaborative researchers believe that knowledge is socially constructed among participants and within particular cultures. Following the work of hermeneutic philosophers such as Gadamer, I came to understand how collaborative researchers see knowledge as an active—in fact, an interactive—experience: Knowledge is not the reflection of some preexistent truth awaiting a single person to uncover it, but instead is an entity actually constructed by those who experience events together. Thus, if we truly want to understand how and what students write, for example, we have to learn with them without making prior assumptions about which questions are the important research questions or by answering those questions based merely in our own observations. In order to get at those shared constructions, the lines between researcher and researched must blur so that true dialogue occurs, each participant talking, listening, and reflecting on this new knowledge.

As I began to share knowledge and experience, I found the research itself had to be owned differently. When I connected with my students in these ways, no longer could I hold onto the research question or the method of coming to answers as my own. The students' questions became my questions; the students' discoveries about ways to create answers became my methods—and vice versa. And when we created new ways of understanding gleaned from our local experiences, the next step seemed to result naturally: research as praxis; research as an agency for change; research as the basis of pedagogy. Change for the collaborative team occurred in some ways for all those involved in my studies: for the student-researchers as well as for me. When I researched with my students about their writing, I tried to celebrate the changes that occurred in all of us. As I learned with them, I reflected on my own approaches to teaching, often altering quite radically how I approached a particular issue. Students, too, changed in various ways, based on what we learned from each other: As you saw, particularly in chapter 4, students often began to play with their writing, ultimately composing pieces that showed a different kind of investment on their part. Students tended to become involved in the subject of their research—their own writing—and, in most cases, became, if not better writers in any measurable way, at least more interested writers, more aware writers, people who defined themselves more often as authors.

The ethics of this kind of collaborative research become complicated, however, as we begin to consider how this connection between Self and Other really plays out. In many ways, teacher-research is a political struggle, a movement toward teachers controlling the discourse which exists about their own classrooms, discourse which has traditionally belonged to outsiders to those classrooms. Teacher-researchers look to give voice to those who traditionally have been rendered voiceless, calling for teachers and students to tell the stories of their own lived worlds and to reject the ready categorizations created by those who don't occupy those worlds. As I began the work you see in this chapter, though, I was beginning to wonder if these efforts at collaboration really had gone far enough to give voice to the voiceless. Surely, teacher-researchers working with students come closer than traditional researchers in being able to represent their students' stories. The question for me became immersed in that word *represent*. Like Geertz, I began to wonder whether or not representation of an Other is even possible. And even if it is possible, is it ethical?

As conscientious researchers, we often rest on the assumption that if we connect with those we're researching by searching hard to understand their life-worlds, to really grasp what Geertz calls the "winks upon winks upon winks," we will be able to express those worlds to others. As committed collaborators who have shared our selves with those we're researching, who have created a dialogue with those Others so that the lines between researcher and researched have diminished as much as possible, we generally take on authorship in order to represent the shared understandings we've gained. And yet, as we've seen in these many pages, when I as teacher-researcher have written about my collaborative ventures with students, I often do so from my position of authority, either self-consciously in the text itself or more subtly in the persona I've created for myself as author. This assumption of authority from those with whom I'm researching happens time and time again in these case studies: As the author of the texts, I have written such statements as "By looking at a paper Sarah wrote . . . we can clearly see how her preoccupation with correct content and correct form affected her writing" or "For Marty, the presentational issues of form were important, as they were for Akemi and, to a lesser extent, for Sarah." Even when I have included the voices of the student-researchers who have joined me, as I have tried to do increasingly over time, as final composer of the written piece my voice has shaped the product—and it has been my voice that has shaped much of the process leading to such a piece. Because I have worked hard in all the ways I mentioned previously to establish a situation in which shared understandings emerge, I have made certain assumptions as to my ability to represent that shared and constructed knowledge. My continued thinking about this work, particularly at the time I began this next study, led me to question what I really mean when I take on this role of representer. Does my close association with the students with whom I research give me permission to represent their perspectives? Do I truly achieve the shared understandings that I imply when I use *we* in these texts? Or does my use of a *we*—metaphorical, I think, in its implication of a shared process to achieve such understanding—contradict the multivocal nature that defines true collaboration?

This contradiction seems the inherent paradox of much of teacher-research. As I explain more fully in chapter 1, Adrienne Rich captures the spirit of this dilemma as she speaks of the political implications of using the pronouns *I* and *we*. As she says, "The problem was that we did not know what we meant when we said 'we'" (11). Saying *we* results in a kind of authority in a text, a rhetorical strategy which goes far toward convincing a reader of the "truth" of the findings. As a writer, I find the metaphor of the *we* a satisfying device: It allows me to reach conclusions, clean up contradictions, create a style and a content which seem consistent and aesthetically pleasing. Yet using the metaphorical *we* reduces the presence of the individual contributors in favor of that sustained unitary voice. I began to wonder if, as I intentionally attempted to blur those lines between the researcher and researched, as I had come to believe was essential for this kind of research to be the praxis-oriented dialogue I sought, I created a kind of collaboration which blurred individual perspectives. I knew that traditional research was guilty of masking the voices of individual participants. Was the work I was attempting masking the voices in merely another way?

Yet, I asked myself, what else can I do? Opening up a piece of writing to the individuals who created it seemed to me a kind of Pandora's box: Who knows what gremlins might emerge! Contradictions, differences in perception, variations in understandings and style would necessarily abound. The necessary end of a research study, even the most collaborative teacher-research—as I understood it—was to reach some kind of conclusion; sacrificing the solidarity of a *we* for the individuality of a bunch of *I*'s seemed not only scary but contradictory to the very purpose of such research. Yet the paradox remained: What did we teacher-researchers mean when we talked about a kind of collaboration which relies on the representation of others' voices? What becomes the purpose of such research? If our purpose is to create a kind of dialogue between the Self and Other, what possibilities exist for how we might represent this dialogue?

I've come to believe that, in large part, the problem inherent in representation in teacher-research is a problem of audience and form. When I ask myself for whom most of the research I do is intended, I come up again and again with a complicated answer. Even the most emancipatory research I've conducted with students seems to have a dual audience. While it is intended initially for the students and me, so that we can effect change in attitudes, in classroom procedures, in curriculum, and so forth, it is also intended quite clearly for an audience of *my* peers. For the most part, the products are composed in a form that fits the norms and expectations of those audiences and that speaks in a language appropriate for those norms and expectations: the research journal, the academic essay, the conference paper, the dissertation. This focus on dual audience now seems as problematic for me in my writing as it is for my composition students when they write papers for "real" audiences, even as they know that I—and not that real audience—will ultimately evaluate it. When we see teacher-research, as we rightly should I believe, as a process emancipatory for both our students and our colleagues, we've expanded the Self–Other dichotomy beyond the ken of just the teacher and students/the researcher and researched. We bring in yet another Other—a reader-colleague.

And so, the Self–Other notion becomes more complicated. As a researcher, I begin with the researcher as Self and the researched as Other. In a collaborative venture, the lines between those two often become blurred in good ways as the two collaborators seek a common language in order to come closer to an understanding of what makes the other tick. Enter the notion of publication and the anticipation of a new Other in the form of the reader, and the blurring of perspectives and created common language often fall by the wayside to make way for the creation of some common ground betweeen the researcher/researched team and this new audience— a way of speaking and writing which, in appealing to the new Other, loses much of what made it vibrant in the first place. The form and language conform to that which we associate with teachers or with researchers (as I continue to do in my writing of this book or as I do depending on whether or not I seek publication in *Research in the Teaching of English, English Journal,* or *English Education*) but remain for the most part outside the experience and interest of our students. Do I, as teacher-researcher, take on the language of representation because of my need to appeal to this other audience? Do I present this unitary front, this assumption of *we,* in order to speak in the collegial forum I believe is essential to the continued growth of the teacher-research movement? As I tried to work through these issues, I began to ask myself if there were alternatives to this kind of representation?

It was at this point in my questioning that I encountered the work of Stephen Tyler and other postmodern ethnographers. Tyler's work in particular became important to me as he spoke of *evocation* as opposed to representation and the changes in approach that renaming implies. Tyler believes that the whole point of ethnographic discourse should not be "how to make a better representation" but rather "how to avoid representation" altogether (128). For Tyler, "The whole ideology of representational signification is an ideology of power" (131). In other words, teachers who attempt to represent the experiences of their students for even the most emancipatory purposes run the risk of contributing to the students remaining in the position of objects. Whenever one person represents another person, the representer necessarily comes to take on a position of power, leaving the represented, at least in some ways, powerless. Representation, as well, conjures up images more appropriate to a scientific rather than a hermeneutic way of seeing the world, a rhetoric Tyler explains as entailing such terms as " 'objects,' 'facts,' 'descriptions,' 'inductions,' 'generalizations,' 'verification,' 'experiment,' 'truth' " (130). One way out of this representational trap, he believes, is for the ethnographer to think in terms of evocation rather than representation. For him, this difference is more than a mere changing of terms. Evocation implies a different kind of mind-set than that of representation: less of a belief that there is a "truth" that the researcher can discover and then depict for others and more of a focus on the participatory function of both the reader of the text and the makers of the text. Research based on evocation, then, focuses on laying out the stances of the researched as fully as possible rather than representing to the reader some limited version of what those stances mean. Evocation, in other words, looks to be a different kind of product evolved through a different kind of process: a product whose main intention is to "make available" the stories of the participants in their fullness, in a form which cannot be predetermined (123). The form of the product, Tyler suggests, "should emerge out of the joint work of the ethnographer . . . and [his/her] partners" (127).

My reading of Tyler conjured up for me an intriguing connection between the process and product of a research study. I began to see my past work as making moves toward a more collaborative process, a process in which I worked hard to collaborate with students to set the question and discover answers, drawing upon my understandings of phenomenological and feminist research principles to achieve a praxis-oriented situation. But what I had failed to see was how collaborative processes might result in a different kind of product, a genre which might allow for all those involved in the research to draw attention to differences of interpretation as it strayed away from the tidy form I had found myself tied to.

Tyler's notion of a postmodern ethnography, then, seemed to speak in some ways to the paradox I had felt: By creating a text with student-researchers which allowed for multiple interpretations—in fact, demanded multiple interpretations because of its multivocal nature—the text might perhaps reach its true potential for advocacy for both the participants in its composition and the participants who would later read it. Tyler's vision of a postmodern ethnography, then, began to inform my developing vision of what teacher-research might be: a praxis-oriented view of teaching and research which might evoke for both the readers of a text and the makers of that text an increased understanding of the world that has been depicted, as well as provoke all participants (both the readers and the makers of the text) toward some kind of action in their own worlds. Again, as Tyler explains it:

> A post-modern ethnography is a cooperatively evolved text consisting of fragments of discourse intended to evoke in the minds of both reader and writer an emergent fantasy of a possible world of commonsense reality, and thus to provoke an aesthetic integration that will have a therapeutic effect. . . . The hermeneutic process is not restricted to the reader's relationship to the text, but includes as well the interpretive practices of the parties to the originating dialogue. (125)

Tyler impresses on me here the importance of "the interpretive practices of the parties to the originating dialogue." A cooperative venture between the researcher and the researched, a postmodern ethnography in Tyler's terms demands a blurring of the lines between the positions of these participants. Like Freire's understanding of teacher-students and student-teachers, Tyler's position encourages us as researchers to find ways in which we might work with those we research in order to intentionally erase the lines that exist and to give voice to those others who have traditionally remained voiceless: to be collaborative researchers.

Having tried out the collaborative-emancipatory version of teacher-research in the classroom as I had in the last chapter helped me to realize the powerful implications in Tyler's approach. As I bemoan in the postscript to that chapter, we were unable to realize all the possible implications of such an approach in that particular setting for a number of reasons, from the brevity of the actual experience to the fact that Sheila and I were still learning what we might do and how we might help push successful collaborative research. Perhaps most important, though, I now believe, is an inablity on my part still to actually visualize this research in its most imaginative and empowering sense. Yes, in my work with Sheila and her class, students themselves took on the roles of co-researchers and co-teachers, while we teachers became co-learners as we came to conceptualize with the students the demands of a conforming literacy they were striving to understand. But we teachers, particularly this teacher as the university collaborator, retained control as the primary analyst for the writing which would eventually be distributed about our students' stories; in essence, I remained the representer of these others' experiences. Despite my leanings in this direction, the actual process of putting together a completely collaborative research project seemed just beyond my grasp of understanding. Although I had begun to read in these areas (and subsequently have read even more), I was still caught in the web that McDermott and Hood describe (and that I explain in chapter 1): Because I was still so much a part of a particular language and perception of research—even in my new perception of collaborative research with its emphasis on reducing the distance, sharing my own stories with those with whom I was researching, trying to include everyone's stories in prominent ways—I had difficulty imagining what a new genre might actually look like, what this new relationship with the researched might actually feel like, what this process of researching together might actually entail. In language I now can begin to understand, I was stuck in what Fine calls the ventriloquy mode, albeit the "subtler form of ventriloquism" (215). As I read into Tyler and others, I began to wonder what might happen if I could break down the walls of my perception of what even collaborative research might be, if the control of a research project could become a truly collaborative venture from start to finish: in other words, if students and teachers who researched together furthered their collaboration so that the analysis and writing of their findings as well as distribution of those findings would be in the hands and the voices of all those participating. What kind of impact would that have—both on the findings themselves and on the students' relationships to their own learning about their own literacy?

Tyler's work took me that final step in my imagining the possibilities for teacher-research. For him, such work is "intended to evoke in the minds of both reader and writer an emergent fantasy of a possible world of commonsense reality, and thus to provoke an aesthetic integration that will have a therapeutic effect" (125). Like Stenhouse's call for research which provokes an "aha!" experience in the reader, Tyler's notion recognizes the inclusion and even participation of a reader in any research study. Tyler would argue, and

I would agree, that the impact of any research should go beyond praxis for its immediate participants—one of the necessary components for collaborative research—to potentially reach praxis for those other participants, the readers of the text who recognize in it some thread which speaks to their own lived situations.

This seemingly obvious truism—that the reader of the research text becomes an integral participant in its creation—helped me to rethink some of the problems I had been experiencing in my own composing of collaborative studies. And as I continue to read into others' work, I see some examples and analyses of products that have served as provocative models for me, embracing not only the complications of the polycharacter Self/Other relationship, but also the implications for research which self-consciously draws on the participation of the reader. Among the many influences are these: dialogues presented as real conversations and which explore issues from two or more points of view, such as Shor and Freire do in *A Pedagogy for Liberation* and the many author-participants do in *Composition and Resistance;* narratives which weave together a number of seemingly contradictory stories about shared classroom experiences such as David Schaafsma does in *Eating on the Street;* fragmented tellings of one person's understanding over time and space, tellings and retellings which reflect a change of mind such as Jenifer Smith does in "Setting the Cat among the Pigeons: A Not So Sentimental Journey to the Heart of Teaching"; multiple readings of a particular classroom by the same researcher, such as Patti Lather does in *Getting Smart: Feminist Research and Pedoagogy with/in the Postmodern,* resulting in what she calls "tales" grounded in the journals and interviews of students in her classroom; increasingly complicated versions of a classroom anecdote made fuller by the contributions of the various teachers who hear about it and add their unique perspectives, as Patricia Stock does in "The Function of the Anecdote in Teacher Research"; even tellings of a particular instance from different perspectives, tellings which may be seemingly contradictory because of the individual stances, such as Magda Lewis and Roger Simon do in "A Discourse Not Intended for Her: Learning and Teaching within Patriarchy."

What all these forms have in common is the lack of a single theme or lesson set forth succinctly in an easily isolable thesis or summary statement. What all these forms require in order to be successful is the entry into the research team of a self-conscious Other, the reader who participates in the conversation evoked by the researcher and researched in order to make sense of the piece of writing in terms of her own lived experience. This more self-conscious extension of reader response seems to me one of the foundations of collaborative student–teacher-research: various voices responding to an issue, inviting readers (be they students or teachers) to be conversant at whatever level seems appropriate to trigger that "aha!" experience so essential to making the reading of a text part of one's own developing knowledge and understanding.

When Stenhouse spoke of this need for the "aha!" experience years ago, he explained the necessity for teacher-researchers to publish, so that the lessons of teacher-research become part of "a community of critical discourse" (Ruddock and Hopkins 17). As various teacher-researchers read each other's works, they all gain new perspectives that they may in turn apply to their own situations: You see someone writing in real ways about a situation you've encountered or a practice you've been contemplating or a student who sounds just like Jennifer in fourth hour—and the writing hits home, makes you rethink your own experience in light of the experience the author has painted for you.

What Tyler's postmodern ethnography adds to Stenhouse, I believe, has to do with authorship. In Tyler's version, authorship becomes shared by researcher and researched, in any of the ways I've just mentioned: through dialogues, by different authors responding to the same issues in separated sections of text, in narratives written from individual perspectives. Rather than reducing the authorship to a *we,* this postmodern ethnography seems to celebrate the *I*—but an *I* that exists within a context of others, both those others within the text itself who share authorship and those others outside the text who share readership. The language employed by the writer-participants then may speak differently to different audiences, resulting in those "aha!" moments for various readers at various occasions in the text.

With these thoughts floating through my mind, I returned to college teaching during the two years following my work with Sheila Smith and her students, intent on applying these themes as I continued to be a teacher-researcher in my various classrooms. The work that comprises this chapter is my first attempt to participate in evocative research, research in which I tried to rethink the genre as I continued to develop methodologies which centered around the need to include those with whom I was researching at every step of the research process. The write-up here draws upon three related sources: some research conducted with the twenty students enrolled in an Argumentative Writing class I taught in the Fall of 1989; research conducted with a subset of that class, ten students who met outside of class time over that same semester; research conducted with a further subset, two students who continued working on some of the same issues with me over the Winter 1990 semester. The original case study that emerged from these interrelated studies is a lengthy piece in which I spend a lot of time laying out the parameters of the research projects in a reportorial mode.[1] For the purposes of the argument of this book, however, I have cut much of the reporting of the first two in order to allow more space to talk about the third, especially as the lessons I learned from that work helped inform my growing inclinations toward what teacher-research could, and perhaps should, be.

## RE-FORMING LITERACY: RESEARCHERS WRITE TOGETHER (JUNE 1990)

In the Fall of 1989, I taught a course in Argumentative Writing. Twenty sophomores, juniors, and seniors participated in the class that term, an elective course designed for those who had already completed the semester-long introductory composition course required of most students in the University. I had designed the course to revolve around issues of the languages of racism and sexism, at the same time emphasizing the ways in which I had come to think about form and genre from my work with Akemi, Sarah, and Sheila Smith's students. I described the class to the students this way in the first-day handout:

> What makes a good piece of argumentative writing? Many
> times textbooks and teachers represent it as following certain
> forms and structures: an Aristotelian argument or a Rogerian

---

[1]One complete version of this study can be found in my dissertation, "Re-forming Literacy: Informing Teacher-Research."

argument, for example. In this course, we will look at argumentative writing somewhat differently: as writing which may be sometimes more narrative, sometimes more analytical, which may in fact mix forms and styles. We will develop our own criteria for good argumentative writing, based (I hope) in the criteria used by the noted anthropologist Clifford Geertz in describing good anthropological writing: is it persuasive? believable? does it give you as a reader a sense of "being there"?

At the same time we will look at the complex relationship of language to issues of power, especially in terms of the language of racism and sexism. I believe, along with a host of linguists and philosophers, that language influences how we view the world around us, in fact that the world around us is constructed through language. My hope for the course is that through some close analysis, we will all become more aware of some of the subtleties of language use that surround us—both in our immediate community and the larger world—and more conscious of the effects of language on us and others.

In order to achieve both ends, we will, in this course, be reading and writing a lot. We will read and analyze many examples of arguments on the subjects of racist and sexist language written by professional writers in communities other than our own immediate ones, and you will be asked to write often in response to these arguments. As we read and analyze together the argumentative styles of these others (both the professional writers and your peers in this class), we will use the criteria we develop to help both in analysis and in development of effective argumentative styles, styles that will make your own writing work for the various audiences and purposes you will be exposed to both in your writing in college and beyond. Later in the course, you will be asked to shift from analyzing how others view racist and sexist language in their communities to look closely at racist and sexist language in our own shared community: The University of Michigan. In groups or on your own, you will be responsible for investigating specific occasions of racist and sexist language in some area of the university you choose, and to write a kind of position paper on your original research. We will collect and reproduce these papers in the hopes that they might be useful teaching and learning devices in other settings.

In describing the course in this way, I had hoped to lay the groundwork for several understandings: that in contrast to most courses in Argumentative Writing taught at least at this university, the focus of this course would not be on learning isolated forms that one might attach to any subject; that together, as a community, this particular class would develop the criteria for what makes good argumentative writing; that the notion of community always implies shared understandings that may shift as one shifts membership in communities (and that likewise the understanding of what effective writing might be would most likely shift in various communities as well); that the research and writing that we would do in this class would result in the creation of new knowledge that none of us held at this point; and finally that their research would be directed to other students so that their peers in this class and outside this class might learn from what they had learned—namely, in the production of a book of their position papers which would be made available to their peers and to other teachers of composition through the auspices of the composition program.[2]

In addition to this approach which the whole class would be asked to take, I inquired early on in the term if any students might be interested in conducting research with me in which we would investigate some issue concerning form and literacy based in their own experience (the specific topic to be decided upon together) and write up our findings as a group. Hoping for the participation of maybe one or two students, I was stunned when over half the students decided to stay after class that day to talk about this project with me. Eventually, ten students regularly joined with me outside of class hours each week to pursue a topic that we decided upon together; we began a study of their original college entrance essays to The University of Michigan, doing blind readings and attempting to characterize the essays in various ways, ultimately looking at two·issues: how difference in the students' gender and intended major related to the form or genre in which the students chose to write that essay. For weeks we read these essays as a group, using phenomenological analysis to discuss the essays, a method based in our group readings of Margaret Himley's "Deep

---

[2]The students produced a number of interesting papers for this book, entitled by them *Discoveries in Argumentative Writing: Essays on Sexist and Racist Language*. The subjects they researched and wrote about ranged from sexist language in the teaching and learning of law to sexist language in the fraternity/sorority system to the discourse spoken by young black students and how it differs in some ways from the Black English Vernacular that is reported in linguistic texts.

Talk" and Loren Barritt et al.'s "Researching Educational Practice." After the fashion of these researchers, the students and I took turns reading their entrance essays aloud. We listed our impressions about the papers with reference to our issue of concern: What could we say about the form or style of the writing? After each of us listed our ideas, we attempted to categorize the papers, for the moment ignoring issues of gender or curriculum interest. Eventually, working from our descriptions of each piece and our then best guesses about the gender and major of the essay's writer, we searched for commonalities among our responses across papers. Students then expanded upon this activity with various group projects they designed to help them learn more about the writing of students and its relation to gender. Some students interviewed professors in the various disciplines to learn what they believed writing should look like in their fields and if they noted differences among male and female writers; some students looked at writing by high school students to see if issues of gender might be present in students' approaches to writing at that time in their academic courses; one student proposed a "metalevel" study of our group, looking at how what we did together might change our perceptions of teaching and learning. Throughout this research project, our intent was to write a collaborative paper at the end, but as the term drew to a close in December, we found ourselves only halfway to where we wanted to go. We settled for group papers from the participants on their particular segment of the research, and most of the students expressed interest in continuing the work the following semester.

The papers that the students produced that term, as well as the discussions that accompanied the production of those papers, were an interesting beginning to a study of the relation of gender to students' literacy. For the most part, our discussion and writing seemed to evolve almost exclusively into those issues of gender (rather than around intended major of the writer) as students increasingly became concerned with the stereotypes surrounding some of the standard depictions of men's and women's writing, stereotypes which seemed second nature to them in their discussion of their peers' writing and which seemed to find a basis in some of the published pieces many of them read about men's and women's writing.

In our Argumentative Writing class, the stereotypes associated with men's and women's writing seemed a pervasive part of our readings of other's writings. Each week after we would discuss together an anonymous piece of student writing, I would ask the students if they thought the piece was composed by a male or a female. Students overwhelmingly guessed correctly at this game, basing their guesses on many of the same perceptions that other authors we had read identified: to the students the women's writing seemed more "flowery," while the men's was more "concrete"; the women seemed to wander around the subject weaving many different strands into the piece, while the men seemed to write more straightforwardly, more logically, more assuredly. When we discussed this issue in our research group, Susan raised her concerns about our work contributing to what she saw as the dangerously simplistic depictions of women's thinking to which stereotypes contribute.

> SUSAN: All right, this all comes down to—say that I were to do a study and find that females do write more passively than men and don't drive their point home enough, or whatever. That kind of hurts me.
> CATHY: But you're seeing it all in terms of kind of negative associations.
> LEN: Yea, it doesn't have to be negative. 'Cause they write differently doesn't mean it's a bad thing.
> CATHY: Or maybe they write differently, but it's not in stereotypical ways.
> SUSAN: But if it's not going to get them as far or something?
> LEN: Who said that?
> SUSAN: Let's say you did a study on women's success versus men's success and how each of them write . . .
> LEN: In our class so far, one thing we have said about differences in men's and women's writing was a compliment to women. We said men tend to be real dry and they just state the facts and women got more creative. . . . I thought that was a compliment, cause I am definitely guilty of writing drily, factually. And I would like to be more creative.
> SUSAN: That's true. Then, if we could prove that, then it wouldn't be detrimental.

Despite Len's insistence that he saw such moves by women as positive, much of the language brought forth in class seemed reflective of Susan's concerns: women's writing was perceived as less able to fulfill the forms and styles privileged in school than men's writing, and was described predominantly in terms of its deviation from those forms.

The concern raised here by Susan became one focus of the research that the individuals in this group of ten pursued over the semester. They looked at such issues as the socialization of women to a particular form and process of writing, at how such socialization affects the readers of texts as well, at how this socialization leads to privileging certain ways of reading texts based in our perceptions of the gender of the author. By the end of the term, our work had progressed to a point in which we began to recognize that these differences were more complicated than we had originally suspected. While we noticed that the men and women whose work we read did seem to write in some identifiable ways, we realized that our own readings of the texts were at least somewhat influenced by our gender. We tended to find what we expected to find. We began to wonder about the effects of socialization on writers. How could we as student- and teacher-researchers ever determine what was "natural ability" in someone's writing style as opposed to "socialized skills"? As some of us agreed to continue the work we had begun into the next term, we agreed to think of ways we could continue to delve deeper into these issues.

## The Project Continues

As second semester began, the academic and personal commitments of various group members took over and our group of ten students dwindled down to two enthusiastic students, John and Susan, and me. We decided to continue our work of the previous term but to focus on our own writing as a way of coming to terms with some of the issues raised during the previous semester's work. In other words, we opted for a research method and style that would emphasize the personal, the experiential, the local. In the next pages you will read a rendition from each of us about both the research itself and the method we used to conduct that research. I begin with a discussion of the specifics of the methodology we used and its relation to a gendered look at student writing, connecting both to other notions of literacy that concern me. John and Susan follow this section with their own discussions in which each analyzes his or her own writing in relation to the other, reflecting as they go on their own understandings of the research we conducted.

### Cathy's Turn

As John, Susan, and I began our work together, I introduced them to some of the current thinking informing feminist research methods. Such methodologies seemed to arise naturally from the readings we were doing about gender and writing and, further, seemed to me an appropriate extension of the phenomenological methods we had read about and utilized in our earlier work together. Three interrelated elements in particular from feminist methodologies became key parts of our approach to research: First, we looked to see research as grounded in our individual experiences, made concrete by our use of everyday language and stories; second, we looked to see research as a shared interactive experience, made real as we continually redefined our understandings of the roles of *researcher* and *researched* through our sharing of stories and analyses; third, we looked to see research with its full emancipatory potential, made significant through the changes we came to recognize that were occurring in all of us as we worked through the issues which had captured our attention.

Such definitions of the feminist research agenda as grounded, as interactive, and as emancipatory, fit in well with the goals of the agenda I had begun to envision as vital for teacher–student research. Teacher-research is a political struggle similar in many ways to feminist research: a movement toward teachers controlling the discourse which exists about their own classrooms, discourse which has traditionally belonged to outsiders to those classrooms. In part, because we practice what Clifford and Guthrie call "a feminized occupation" (328), teacher-researchers look to give voice to those who traditionally have been rendered voiceless, calling for teachers and students to tell the stories of their own lived worlds and to reject the ready categorizations created by those who don't occupy these worlds. At the same time, drawing connections between the two research projects raises questions. Many of the notions inherent in the feminist research paradigm assume a unique role for the woman as researcher and woman as researched: The assumption present in such a paradigm is that women are uniquely able to explore the experiences of other women because of the marginality they share, an assumption whose implications leave me uncomfortable for a number of reasons. Do I, as a woman researcher, necessarily have an immediate connection to and understanding of the experiences of my female students—simply because we share gender? Should I then look solely at the experiences of my female students and disregard the experiences of the male students in my class? Must my male colleagues well-versed theoretically and practically, intellectually and emotionally, in the feminist agenda be shut out from practicing research with female students? Do the notions inherent in a feminist paradigm only work if the issue under investigation involves what is generally recognized as a woman's issue (i.e., abortion; rape; women's voting trends; in my case, women's writing)?

Such notions are fraught with problems. They rely on a view of representation discouraged by Tyler and others, a view which posits that shared social conditions and experiences are sufficient to warrant the assumption of shared understandings. While Tyler grounds his critique of this assumption in a rejection of the notion of representation, some feminist scholars such as Adrienne Rich reject it in terms of its naive understanding of the pronoun *we*. In her essay "Notes toward a Politics of Location," Rich rethinks her position on the subject of representation, questioning her own ability, of which she was at one time convinced, to adequately speak for the feminist movement. She begins her essay in this way:

> A few years ago I would have spoken of the common oppression of women, the gathering movement of women around the globe. . . . I would have spoken these words as a feminist who "happened" to be a white United States citizen, conscious of my government's proven capacity for violence and arrogance of power, but as self-separated from that government, quoting without second thoughts Virginia Woolf's statement in *Three Guineas* that "As a woman I have no country. As a woman I want no country. As a woman my country is the whole world." (7)

She sets her task in this essay and beyond as a "need to understand how a place on the map is also a place in history, within which as a woman, a Jew, a lesbian, a feminist, I am created and trying to create" (8), a questioning of the tendency by scholarly feminist women, like herself, who have had easy access to means of publication, to lay claim to the representation of others: "The problem was that we did not know who we meant when we said 'we.' " (11). Throughout her essay she plays with this notion in interesting ways; while she feels a responsibility to limit her presumption of understanding of the lives of others (she particularly speaks of the difference of experience of black women) and thus to think in terms of "we" less often in her writing, she recognizes the paradox of this stance since "there is no liberation that only knows how to say 'I.' There is no collective movement that speaks for each of us all the way through. And so even ordinary pronouns become a political problem" (16).

Rich cautions me, as does Tyler, to be wary of my attempts at representation of others, despite obvious connections I might have with those I'm researching: other women, other teachers, other writers. But what she also tells me is that the connections I necessarily make with those I research in this collaborative way are very real in some sense, and that without such connections, the truly emancipatory nature of the research would be lost. Her caution leads me to think in this way. No one can ever truly represent the experience of another person completely; neither can anyone speak for another in any real ways. Women who research women, students who research each other, teachers who research students in their classrooms, all fall prey to the same problems even as their particular situations allow them to open up new spaces and new connections for all involved. As a woman when I research with another woman, or as a writer when I research with other writers, I begin with some added connectedness by the very nature of our positions, connections which make understanding easier in some ways but more difficult in others. I cannot rely on the commonalities as some kind of panacea, because by doing so I will miss the differences that necessarily exist between any two people, and I cannot presume that the commonalities allow me to speak for anyone else. Too much assumption of sameness because of some connection results in the dilemmas in which Rich—and a host of other white feminists—have found themselves.[3] And so, while a certain amount of connection among researchers and the re-

---

[3]See, for example, Audre Lorde's critique of Mary Daly in "An Open Letter to Mary Daly." In that essay Lorde condemns Daly, and by implication a host of other white feminists, for assuming that their experience can speak for black women.

searched may make possible collective action, we must constantly work to find a balance between the interactive nature of this research and its emancipatory possibilities.

Cautions aside, a focus on feminist research adds to the notions of ethnographic and phenomenological research in some important ways. In keeping with the most important elements of all three paradigms, I see the possibility of a paradigm for teacher-research—a grounded research which finds its basis in the personal, in the local, in the anecdotal; an interactive research which looks *with* rather than looks *at,* actively seeking connections between researcher and researched even as it refuses to see those connections as permission to speak for another; an emancipatory research which recognizes critical reflection as its primary purpose and which celebrates active changes in the status quo as its desired outcome.

As Susan, John, and I began our research, we set ourselves the task of looking at Susan's and John's writing: both the actual compositions they had produced for the Argumentative Writing class and the act of composition itself, from their own writing background and influences to their visions of themselves as writers. In so doing, we quite consciously positioned ourselves as a particular kind of researchers. We chose to focus on the personal, on our individual experiences as writers; we worked to blur the lines between the researcher and the researched, committing ourselves to analyzing and writing up our findings together; we tried to realize, in fact, celebrate, that our work might result both in changes in how they saw themselves as writers and in how they went about their writing after our research had run its course as well as in changes in how I saw myself as a teacher and how I would now go about my work with student-writers. Beginning with the personal, we tried through a variety of means to get at their individual experiences as writers: All three of us composed our own writing histories, complete with anecdotes and analyses of the various influences on us as writers; we all wrote about what we look like when we write, trying to get at the processes we follow as writers; we all made lists of the characteristics we value in good writings. All this was preliminary in some ways to the major part of our work, our reading and analyzing together the essays Susan and John had written in response to my first two assignments of the previous term, fairly general assignments that asked them to analyze the techniques of various authors we had read who were writing on the subject of language and racism.[4] We took turns reading these essays aloud and talking about our reactions to the essays at a number of levels: the content, the form, and the style, thematizing as we went and coming to some agreement as to the similarities and differences Susan and John showed as both writers and readers. Because we had in our research group two writers who, in their approaches to composing, illustrated many of the themes about male and female differences raised by Annas, Gilligan, and others, it seemed easy to move from the individual to the more global, to consider those differences primarily in terms of gender. John, we soon agreed, tended to value what he called earlier straightforward logic, clear-cut proof and a rational approach in the professional essays he had read as a basis for his writing in the course, generally appreciating a factually supported stance and voice from a particular author even when he disagreed with him or her. These values translated into his own writing as well: In his writing, he seemed to strive for logical connections, piled high with examples and proofs from numerous sources, com-

---

[4]The specific language of the assignments was as follows:

Assignment 2

At this point you have read a number of pieces which, while they are on the same general subject (language and racism), differ in some important ways: their stances toward their subject, their forms, their intended audiences, their tones, their general purposes, etc. Your task in this assignment is to pick any two pieces which we have read so far and which you see as having some similarities as well as differences and to compare the two. You can either focus on one area of difference or try to deal with several areas; just make sure that you don't try to deal with so much that you spend all your space on surface level comparisons. I want you to dig beyond what we were able to cover in class discussions.

As in the last paper, you should feel free to do some experimentation if you want to; at the very least try to make the papers as interesting to this reader as they are informative!

Assignment 3

Now that we've spent some time talking about specific argumentative techniques and styles, you will have a chance to evaluate the sorts of arguments we've read and discussed. In this paper, I'd like you to talk about the kind(s) of arguments that worked well for you as well as those that did not work so well, and to try to explain why. . . . Try to move beyond saying simply that article 1 worked because of x, y, and z to a statement that arguments of a certain sort work best in general because of certain characteristics; in other words, I want you to try to understand the specific argumentative techniques and styles of each article and to then expand from there into some kinds of generalizations about argumentative writing as a whole.

posed in a voice that worked to convince its reader through its strength and factual tone. [See Appendix F for the essays written by John and Susan that we considered in our study. See also the next section of this chapter written by John which lays out the specific differences we gleaned from our readings of both of their essays.]

Susan's relationship to her reading and writing at first struck all of us as more problematic. While she valued personal experience, emotion, and a personal style in her reading of professional essays, we could at first only identify glimmers of these qualities in her own work. What we saw immediately was that she was prone to write in somewhat standard, some would call logical, patterns of organization and style; hers was neither a narrative approach nor what Cixous and other French feminists would call "writing the body." But as we talked through the differences between her approach and John's, we began to see a number of variations. While John wrote with a kind of linear logic, an "A leads to B leads to C" rendition, Susan wrote in a more immediately connected way, an "A, B, and C all relate to D" rendition. Susan seemed to strive as well for a balanced approach in her writing, giving credit even to those authors with whom she found fault and focusing heavily on what she called the "sound" and the "flow" of the finished product.

The kinds of writing we saw valued and practiced by John and Susan readily seem to support those easy explanations of men's and women's writing posited by such researchers as Farrell and Hiatt and those played out in more complicated fashion by Annas and Gilligan. Gilligan, for example, in her work with Kohlberg on his six stages of moral development, came to recognize that two different voices emerged from her extensive interviews with boys and girls, men and women. Starting with the responses of two eight-year-olds, she explains that "While Jeffrey sets up a hierarchical ordering to resolve a conflict, . . . , Karen describes a network of relationships"(33). Describing two eleven-year-olds' responses, she finds that while Jake "sets himself apart from that world," Amy "locates herself in relation to that world" (35). Again and again, Gilligan saw these kinds of responses from men and women of varying ages, leading her to conclude that women cast relationships into "a nonhierarchical vision of human connection. Since relationships when cast in the image of hierarchy appear inherently

unstable and morally problematic, their transposition into the image of web changes an order of inequality into a structure of inter-
connection" (62). The notions Gilligan recognizes in women's
thinking have been echoed by teacher-researchers like Annas who
have studied women's writing. Annas sees a woman's method of
writing as "inclusive; it connects rather than separates, assumes
complexity, is circular rather than linear." Using Virginia Woolf's
writing as a starting point, she looks at how Woolf "mixes genres,
using narrative, characterization, and image to construct an argument." Other characteristics of women's writing she notes include
the grounding of an argument in personal experience, the elevation
of the process of reasoning, the placing of responsibility on the
audience, rather than the author, for reaching conclusions (365).

As I have read and thought about the themes we uncovered in
John's and Susan's writing—themes reflected in some of our readings of others' understandings of these issues—I am struck by the
relation of these notions of gender difference in writing to the
issues of literacy of which I have written elsewhere. My own developing understanding of literacy and its connection to issues of
form lead me to read these themes in somewhat different terms,
terms which again draw upon the teachings of Bakhtin. If men and
women do indeed write differently, perhaps we can find reasons in
a kind of gendered relationship to the conforming and in-forming
literacies I am convinced surround the emerging literacies of all
people. While, as John told us in a meeting one day, "I had to
conform also when I came here [to the University of Michi-
gan] . . . It's not women only who have to conform," I've come to
believe that men and women have to conform differently. I look
back once more to Bakhtin's words and I see in them a way to
think about the unique kind of conforming women have to do to
meet the demands of a school discourse which is structured around
what he calls "the authoritative word."

> The authoritative word demands that we acknowledge it, that we
> make it our own; it binds us, quite independent of any power it
> might have to persuade us internally; we encounter it with its
> authority already fused to it. The authoritative word is located in
> a distanced zone, organically connected with a past that is felt to
> be hierarchically higher. It is, so to speak, the word of the fathers.
> Its authority was already *acknowledged* in the past. It is a *prior*
> discourse. It is therefore not a question of choosing it from

among other possible discourses that are its equal. It is given (it sounds) in lofty spheres, not those of familiar contact. Its language is a special . . . language. It can be profaned. It is akin to taboo, i.e., a name that must not be taken in vain. (342)

The conforming literacy I have spoken of elsewhere, a literacy which is situated in the forms of school discourse, is in many ways the same authoritative discourse of which Bakhtin speaks here.[5] It stands separate from, "higher" than, he says, other discourses—in particular, what he sees as "internally persuasive discourses," what I have referred to as in-forming literacies. If we look from this perspective at the forms and genres accepted and taught in the schools, we can see their grounding in certain structures which Gilligan, Annas, and our own research group have identified as more common in the writing of men. As teachers we teach from textbooks that stress logical thinking and form, logic defined in linear terms: topic sentences at the beginning of each paragraph, followed by proof (the more the better) gleaned from outside sources, ending with a conclusory statement which forms some kind of transition into the next logically derived point. We tell our students that to be overtly emotional in their writing is bad, and that while personal anecdotes are fine for "personal essays" and narratives (generally taught at the beginning of the term as the "easier" genres for students to master—and I use that word intentionally), by the time they move on to argument, the mainstay of our writing programs, they must think in terms of Aristotelian or Rogerian arguments and keep first person camouflaged. I exaggerate only a bit, I think, to make the point: What most teachers stress to their students is a way of writing that is firmly situated in the authoritarian discourse Bakhtin speaks of, a discourse which has little room for other approaches, particularly those which are of the in-forming variety. While the conforming literacies leave out the individually derived literacies of all students, the problem such omission creates for female students is unique: As "the word of the fathers," authoritative discourse systematically denies women's ways of thinking and writing from any participation. The development of an individual ideology which Bakhtin sees as a struggle

---

[5]For a fuller explanation of my understandings of informing, conforming and reforming literacies, see my essay in Robinson's *Conversations on the Written Word.*"

between authoritative discourse and internally persuasive discourses becomes an unfairly weighted battle as far as most women students are concerned: Their own in-forming literacies, for the most part, are given little or no space to coexist in most writing classrooms. Bakhtin further tells us that this struggle which he believes will always liberate the voice of the individual is of utmost importance: "An independent, responsible and active discourse is *the* fundamental indication of an ethical, legal and political human being" (*Dialogic Imagination* 349–50). What are the results if the struggle is weighted so unfairly? Where does this leave our women students? Yes, all students are subject to the conforming literacies of the schools, literacies that, of course, shift in terms of their demands from high school to college; but women students are hit with a kind of double whammy, resulting in a struggle that may not lead to the liberation Bakhtin suggests—unless they encounter a classroom situation which specifically sets its sights on creating a space for female students to work through the struggle.

In this research we did together, Susan, John, and I attempted to create such a space. By opening up our conversation to include those issues of a conforming and in-forming literacy and by looking hard at Susan's and John's writing, we made an opportunity for both discussion of writing difference and changes in writing, if that seemed appropriate. The space which we occupied for a term has not been without its problems, but, as I think you will see, it helped us all move toward re-forming our ideas of what literacy can and should be—for both men and women.

*John's Turn*

*How Susan and I Read and Write: A Study of Our Papers and Discussions*
Throughout the course of our study on emancipatory research and the alleged differences in male and female writing, I have played the role of devil's advocate. I was uncomfortable with the feminist research method to the extent that it relied so much on Susan and myself as "evidence." I am accustomed to doing research in the library, not in my mind. Midway through the term it occurred to me that perhaps what we were doing was all contrived, that we were looking too hard for something that wasn't there or something that we couldn't find. I noted that:

> We're setting out to prove that there's differences between male
> and female writing, right, and so this could lead to us trying to
> find things that aren't there. And so when Susan writes in a
> masculine way, we can attribute that to socialization, you know,
> but then again, this is where our study's screwed up because we
> can never determine the extent of socialization, the effect. And
> another thing that's gonna screw it up is the nature of the assign-
> ment. . . . I think Susan's required to rag, cause you've got to go
> to extreme opposites to like, this is good and this is bad. So
> there's so many different factors we're dealing with, like there's
> socialization, the nature of the assignment, that kind of stuff so
> our study's going to be pretty screwed.

Cathy then rebutted with this to say:

> I don't think that that means that it screws up what we're trying
> to do at all—in a lot of ways, but . . . one way is that in spite of
> the assignment I see real differences here between this one [Su-
> san's paper] and yours [John's paper]. So I think that's part of it.
> Yea, we can never tell what's socialization and what isn't, we can
> never tell that. We could always be looking for something that
> makes it feminine as opposed to masculine . . . These could just
> be differences between you two as writers that might not have
> anything to do with whether you're male or female. Just could be
> the way Susan writes and the way John writes. So everything we
> say has to be couched in a lot of these terms, but I do
> think . . . we see support for some of these things from some of
> the stuff we're reading about male and female writing. So you
> can never really conclude that Susan is definitely a feminine writ-
> er because she does this and John is definitely a masculine writer
> because he does this, but what we can say is John seems to be
> doing these certain kind of things very differently from what
> Susan seems to be doing, and this stuff seems to be supported by
> stuff we're reading in the literature about what other people have
> said are differences in male and female writing.

Indeed this seems to be the conclusion that we have settled
upon. Now that we have reached the end of our research, I appreciate the way I was able to learn more about myself in a direct
manner through the feminist research method. This is something
that was really important for Cathy. She felt that meaningful research requires that each participant should learn and grow from
the experience. The advantage of emancipatory research is that it
allows one to interact with the evidence, to learn from it directly, as

opposed to traditional methods where one must relate one's experiences to abstract concepts. This kind of feminist research method is more humanistic. It encourages an environment where personal beliefs can be expressed and evaluated. The self-validating effect of emancipatory research is shown through Susan's experience this term. Through the freedom and encouragement that this type of research fosters, Susan was allowed to find her natural writing style. As she explains more fully in the section she wrote for this chapter, the section following this one: "I am sure I am not alone in the problems that I have with expressing myself on paper, but because my experience cannot be the same as anyone else by virtue of human individuality, I hereby exercise the license to expound upon my writing as a unique process."

I too have benefited from the research that we have done this past term. I had to examine my writing style and the motivations behind the way I write. I was able to use Susan's writing as a reference point, a thing to compare my writing to. Although I feel much of my writing style has been reinforced, that I did not go through the massive changes that Susan did, I have learned to understand and accept styles of writing different than my own.

We discovered that our ideas about good writing influenced the way we read and the way we write. I like clear purpose and organization in the essays I read. I like to be presented with firm positions from which to decide my own stance. Another aspect of our writing involved strategies towards prospective readers. I don't write for anyone in particular. I don't aspire to actively involve the reader. When I do acknowledge the reader it is to make a statement such as this: "now that we can clearly see the validity of this point, . . . " I use the word *we* as a way to manipulate the reader; I tend to manipulate the reader into granting my points by writing very confidently and making "factual" statements. My style is consistent—support, evidence and examples; it is not written as much for a particular reader. This is reflective of what I believe to be good writing. Susan noted that my style stemmed "from a stereotypically masculine viewpoint which is hungry for hard facts based upon hard research which should lead to hard results." This seems to be the criteria I use to judge other people's writing. We could see this from the ways in which I critiqued professional authors in the essays I wrote for the course. For example, at one point in a piece I wrote about essays by Langston Hughes and

Ossie Davis, I wrote the following: "Despite the fact that Hughes did [provided examples] what Davis failed to, he is unable to justify his thesis due to his lack of real evidence." I don't emphasize the technique of someone's writing as much as the quality of the ideas behind the writing, I don't focus on the "writing" aspect of papers. I expect my ideas to stand on their own merit. I do try to make things clear, I just don't worry about flow and body.

Susan's writing seems different from mine. Susan stated at one of the meetings of our research group that "I really seem to favor a balance . . . I don't really talk about generalizations of what an argument should be, but one of the general things is that somehow it should be balanced in some way." What better way to give the reader a sense of balance than the way she writes: delineating the issues in a quick stream of ideas, making a statement, then qualifying it and then moving on to another point to requalify it. This keeps the reader actively participating to see what's coming next. Susan stated that she keeps the type of audience in mind when writing. She fashions her writing for a particular point, making sure her paper is in tune. She noted "that when I write, I'm really concerned with certain things, I'm really concerned with the way it sounds, and with the way it all flows together. Just like, the whole basic composition of the thing as a shape." She adds that "that's very feminine, whereas what you're talking about with wanting to make this point and that point and being really subject-oriented, that seems kind of male." This doesn't mean that the quality of thought that goes into a paper isn't important for Susan, it just means that in addition to the potatoes, there had better be a smooth gravy.

What we have found in our research is that the way we as individuals read influences how we write, and the way we write influences how we read. If we find a style of writing effective and we use it ourselves, then we favor that style in our assessment of other people's writing as well, both professional and student writers. We saw this in three sources: the essays we composed for the Argumentative Writing class; the transcripts of the recordings of our talk about that writing; our writing about our reading and writing, done for this project.

<u>Susan's preferences</u>: Susan likes several things in the writings of others that she reads: emotion, an attempt by the writer to involve the reader, a push for social change, and balanced arguments. She

told us, "To me an argument works best when it bridges the gap between author and reader." We saw this in paper 2 when she wrote, "Because Angelou has the element of emotion deeply embedded in her argument and challenges the audience to analyze racist aspects of education in this country, it has more of an impact by conveying a message directly to the reader."

What we saw in the group:

CATHY: One of the things I really saw . . . it's almost as if in the piece that she's reading she's defining good writing as active and not passive and so that the reader has to enter into it and be an active participant in it. Which seems very different from how John you seem to be defining it which was they needed to give you all the facts that you needed to have in order to reach a conclusion.

Susan's dislikes: Susan dislikes arguments that are factual to the point of being dry and writing that uses too much elevated language. When she reads, she says, "I like to feel as though I am on equal terms with the author, and pretentious language can only serve to alienate the audience." We saw these dislikes in her writing about others' arguments:

In addition to overuse of emotion in writing arguments, the choice of language and expression of voice are also key elements which act to either draw the audience in, or shut the members out. Usually, unless a piece is written solely for academic purposes, a more conversational, relaxed style often works best because it puts the reader at ease. No one wants to waste time looking up unknown words the author has chosen most likely to impress the audience. Elevated language, especially when more commonly used words could express the presented concepts better, can be indicative of an argument which is inherently weak. The essay "Language and Experiences" by James Britton is a fine example of an overly academic style which is often condescending or pretentious. This essay also tends to be very repetitive whose length could be greatly reduced as a result. Repetition in an argument may further insult and bore the audience, whereas an essay that is lucid and to the point draws a more positive reaction.

(from paper #2)

Susan's own writing: One characteristic is that she uses visual imagery:

What exactly does Susan French look like when she finally sits down to write a paper after worrying profusely about it for at least three days? She sits staring at a blank screen with her elbows firmly planted on the table and her face laying heavily upon her palms. Some cells will probably get chewed off at this point inside her mouth, and provided that her nails were not terminated at an earlier hour, they will soon end up detached from her body.

(from her section of this chapter)

Susan also uses emotion in her writing. She's more willing to give credit to views that she disagrees with, and she writes in a circular manner—both issues that I will talk about later.

<u>John's preferences</u>: I like clarity, good use of evidence, examples, unique ideas. I appreciate emotional appeals as long as there is also some sort of evidence or reasoning to support the claims.

<u>What we saw in the group</u>:

CATHY: Then you come back to "This wouldn't be so bad if he had any decent arguments or proof to support this assertion." So it seems to me that you always come back to that same thing. Even though you're talking about emotionalism or talking about this, it's always emotionalism as supported by arguments or proof. Or manipulation as supported by arguments or proof. So the bottom line and this makes it similar to the other paper, the bottom line always is emotionalism works, manipulation works if you've got arguments or proof to support those assertions.

<u>Johns' dislikes</u>: I do not like radicalism. I do not like it where an author will make all sorts of claims and then leave it unsupported.

[Davis] asserts that "[those] who [use] the English Language as a medium of communication [are] forced, willy-nilly, to teach the Negro child 60 ways to despise himself, and the white child 60 ways to aid and abet him in the crime." The evidence for his assertion is weak enough already, especially if one were to use common sense and realize that all of the connotations he listed are applicable to the real world, but he also fails to support his thesis that these 'negative' connotations actually have any adverse effects on the black race. He seems to imply it, but he leaves too much to the reader. His lack of examples of real world usage of these "negative" connotations renders his essay worthless.

(from paper #2)

<u>John's own writing</u>: I use evidence:

It is a fair assumption that all people have preconceived notions on various matters. That is to say, everyone has an opinion or prejudice concerning specific issues. "The evidence from both psychology and history overwhelmingly supports the view that decision makers tend to fit incoming information into their existing theories and images. Indeed, their theories and images play a large part in determining what they notice. In other words, actors tend to perceive what they expect." (Robert Jervis, "Hypotheses on Misperception, " *World Politics* 20, no. 3, April 1968)

(from paper #3)

Whereas I use evidence to support my points, I expect the same from others. If quality evidence is not used, clear and logical reasoning is acceptable.

The major problem is that on examining *Roget's College Thesaurus* (1978) there are discrepancies concerning Davis' listings. These discrepancies could perhaps have been explained if Davis had bothered specifying the year for the *Roget's Thesaurus* he used. He claimed that there were 134 synonyms for white, 44 of which were favorable and then listed words such as immaculateness, cleanness, honorable, trustworthy (for this word he added "a white man's colloquialism"). In the thesaurus that was examined for this paper there were only 32 synonyms under the heading whiteness, of which the four above mentioned were not listed. He also claimed that there were 120 synonyms for black, 60 of which were unfavorable and then listed words such as threatening and sinister. Again, the thesaurus used for this paper did not list these words and only contained 23 synonyms under the heading black. The words included were words such as black, ebony, coal, darkness, midnight, and inky. There were no derogatory connotations.

(from paper #2)

Davis, in other words, failed to impress me due to his faulty evidentiary claims as well as his lack of solid reasoning.

We saw from both our outside reading and from our whole class discussions the stereotypical notion that masculine logic tends to be linear and that feminine logic tends to be circular. Without making any qualitative claims as to masculinity or femininity, I will examine myself and Susan's writing to determine if there are any traces of linear or circular methods of logic.

Through the course of our research, we found that I tend to write in a very "linear" manner. It is clear in my writing that point A leads to point B leads to point C, the point being that I favor that kind of logical progression of ideas. This is clearly seen in paper #3 where the assignment was to discuss methods of writing that we found effective and those which we did not find effective. There I wrote, in part:

> In "Aria" Richard Rodriguez makes effective use of personal experience, emotion, and manipulation to support his belief that bilingual education is wrong. Using personal experience he paints a poignant picture of a family that is deeply affected by their children's learning of English. They lost the closeness they once had, however he portrays it as a great triumph. Indeed before he learned English he never felt as if he had a public identity. He appreciated the shame of not being able to communicate and function well, especially where his parents were concerned. "Hearing them, I'd grow nervous, my clutching trust in their protection and power weakened." Rodriguez draws us to his side through his emotional anecdotes. We feel bad that their family lost so much of their intimacy, however he feels that the advantages he gained from learning English and establishing his public identity were more important. Now that we are on his side, celebrating in his success story, he manipulates us into believing that bilingual education is bad. After all he didn't have one and look how well he turned out. He actually felt that if he weren't forced into learning English exclusively he would have delayed forever. He slowly and skillfully convinces his audience of his point.

Cathy and Susan had this to say about my writing in paper #3:

SUSAN: I'm not sure what exactly linear logic is as opposed to circular, but I think that that kind of moving from the fact into the support and then he kind of generalizes it . . . the last sentence kind of ties the whole paragraph together.

CATHY: Yep. That's good. A leads to B leads to C kind of reasoning . . . what I looked at, in every single paragraph of proof then, what you do is you have a first paragraph, you have a topic sentence that lays out what you're going to do in each paragraph. "In 'Aria' Richard Rodriguez makes effective use of personal experience, emotion, and manipulation." So that's how your paragraph runs, first you talk about experience, then you talk about emotion, then you talk about manipulation. And then you end that paragraph with sort of a concluding statement. "His approach is subtle . . ." Next paragraph—same organization format. "In 'What's Wrong with Black English', Rachel Jones effectively uses personal experience, emotion and examples . . ." and then you do those three things and

then you end that paragraph with a summary statement—"Her subtle approach allows the reader . . ."
S: It's a super organized paragraph.
C: Yea, it's super organized. And after you read the first two you pretty much expect that the third one is going to be in that very same format and then it is. "Ossie Davis utilizes an extreme point of view, manipulation and emotionalism." And then you go through and you talk about those three things. So, in terms of the organizational format of this, I think what you said that linear reasoning really shines through here. I mean, I didn't put that term on it yet, but that's exactly right. That's what it is. Here are the three things I'm going to say, and here they are. Very linear. When you get to the concluding statement in each one, yes of course you conclude that statement because you've shown me those three things.

Interestingly enough we noted that Susan tended to write in a more "circular" fashion, weaving in ideas at various points, moving from being specific to general and then back to specific, inserting support and example from different topics. For the same assignment, here is part of what she wrote:

> Because an author usually chooses topics s/he already has strong opinions on, the emotion expressed in the paper may often work to the author's advantage, but on the other hand, extreme opinions may repel some of the intended audience at an early point in the essay. Take for instance the piece by Ossie Davis whose tone is condemning and bitter. He approaches the topic of racism very pessimistically and uses the synonyms for blackness and whiteness from Roget's Thesaurus as the only support for his argument, which is narrow in its scope to begin with. Sometimes brevity can be a source of strength for an argument as proven through a personal statement by Langston Hughes focusing on the alienation felt by existing in an all white world as a black student. Davis however, attempts to shove his argument down the throat of the reader through a rapid-fire style of listing, which only succeeds in giving the reader a sense of guilt and helplessness. The conclusion is void of any feelings of hope or suggestions for improvement which sharply contrast the endings of both the Angelou and Miller/Swift essays. In short, an essay should not solely convey an author's anger and frustration regarding an issue through verbal temper tantrums or condemnations, techniques which in effect make the audience respond negatively.

We concluded the following about Susan's paper #3:

> JOHN: . . . [Susan's] more careful to point out that this is a bad way but that there's several other good ways of doing it. So she's more careful, she stretches that more. She's more giving that way.
>
> CATHY: And that might go back to what Susan was saying earlier as a linear versus circular kind of argument style. I'm not sure if that's true, but I'm wondering in this paragraph since we're on this paragraph if that's partly what's going on. John starts off with Ossie Davis does this, or whatever and goes on about that. You start out with the topic and go on to Ossie Davis but then also Langston Hughes does it this way and then Angelou and Swift do it this way, so it's like going all around "the thing" instead of just going from point A to point B to point C.
>
> SUSAN: Yea, cause John said Davis is this, this and this and then I kind of talk about what authors generally do and how it's gonna work in each way, like for each audience and for each author . . .
>
> C: I'm not sure circular reasoning is the right term for it, anymore than I'm sure linear reasoning is the right term for the other thing, but there sure seems a difference in the structure of the paragraphs.
>
> S: Yea, circular reasoning for me has some negative connotations, because it's circular, it seems like it wouldn't be as effective because you're going from this thing and you're kind of taking a long time and going this roundabout way to get to your point. Um. but I don't know, can you redefine circular reasoning in a way that—
>
> C: We can redefine it any way we want to. Connected reasoning as opposed to—
>
> S: More complex reasoning? (laughing)
>
> C: No, I don't think it's more complex. I don't want to put value judgments on that, maybe. But, more connected and more single-minded? I don't know that we should try to think of terms to talk about it, but I see a big difference between you two.

One can start to see the differences between our two styles of writing. I tend to write very compact and specific paragraphs, where one point leads to another (linear). Susan on the other hand writes paragraphs that contain a bundle of ideas that link to prove her point (circular).

Another interesting occurrence we found was that in papers where the assignment called for comparing and contrasting or making qualitative judgments Susan tended to be much more open and willing to give some sort of credit to both sides, as opposed to what I would do, supporting one side fully and taking an absolute stand, giving no quarter to the opposing view. For example, here is what she wrote in part for paper #2:

> The Schulz piece is the exact opposite of a personal account in that her tone is condescendingly informative. This essay conversely does not attempt to bridge the gap between audience and author. The reader instead comes away from the writing feeling like a computer that has just endured a session of routine data entry. She is extremely clear in getting her point across, but she inevitably sacrifices originality and creativity for this clarity. Her paragraphs tend to be rather short, with one basic idea presented in each followed by a listing of supporting evidence in the form of related terms and phrases. Whereas Angelou leaves much of her argument for the reader to interpret, Schulz employs a straightforward, academic style which makes it easy to get a general feel for the argument as well as the supporting points.

It is clearly seen where Susan favors a balance. She indicates that she has a personal preference for one style over another, but she is willing to note the good qualities of the other style as well. This contrasts with my own writing strategy, shown in this excerpt from my paper #3:

> Preconceived notions are very important in the way people deal with new information. If the input is compatible with existing beliefs it will be readily accepted. However if the input disagrees with existing beliefs the person will tend to want to ignore the new input. He/she will be very skeptical in considering the information. Rodriguez and Jones were successful in their use of argumentative techniques because of the tactful way they presented their arguments. They were subtle and clever enough to get the reader's support. Davis and Raspberry were not successful because they violated people's beliefs in such an overt way and belligerent way as to turn them off from taking seriously their works.

If one were to examine the paper I wrote, it would be clear that I gave no credit to either Davis or Raspberry, while fully supporting Rodriguez and Jones.

The effect of our ideas about good writing on our reading is as follows. It was interesting to note on the matter of emotion, that Susan and I emphasized opposite requirements. For Susan emotion, originality, social significance and the like were paramount. In support of these qualities, elevated language and the standard dry approach of using massive evidence were justified. Whereas for me, that academic approach was key, and in support of good evidence, personal experience and creativity could be employed. We found this when Susan criticized Britton heavily for his academic approach, while allowing this in Smitherman: "Although her [Smitherman's] essay might be criticized for its academic approach, I feel that the originality of the topic justifies her own scientific analysis of the issue and that this is necessary to convince the audience of her argument." Although that defamed academic approach, in my opinion, is a necessary foundation for good writing, I did appreciate emotion and originality as was the case in "Aria" by Rodriguez because of the good mixture of academics and emotion.

*Susan's Turn*

*How John and I Differ As Writers: Our Influences and Backgrounds*

A large portion of our group research involved discussion of the various influences on our writing, which were undoubtedly manifested in the papers we analyzed. Cathy, John, and I independently compiled materials talking about our writing histories from early elementary school to present, noting the changes in form and levels of comfort throughout the years in our writing of different genres. We then looked closely at our own personal ideas of the elements that constitute quality writing, and studied the effects of these biases toward our judgments as readers. Using techniques outlined by a feminist research model we were able to move toward an understanding of ourselves as writers within the basic framework of our respective gender and life influences.

Although John and I compiled information stemming from identical topics in order to have a common basis for comparison, we emerged from our research with very different feelings and ways of knowing about our writing. We found that many of our personality characteristics influence the way we write, which are in turn reflected in our biases for and against the writings of others. Cathy played an integral role in this process, serving as a mediator directing the goals of the group to broaden the overall shape of her dissertation in a general sense, as well as validating our findings and self-discoveries on a more local level. John and I both came away with knowledge and changed perceptions as a direct result of our research, but in very different ways. Over the course of the entire project which began in September, I rose to a level where I could fully celebrate many of the differences between men and women, especially as they carry over into writing, the existence of which I had vehemently denied up to that point. I became a strong proponent of "the feminine style" of writing which had profound effects both on myself as a woman writer and the ways I interpreted writings of others. John, perhaps due to the feminist approach to our research, emerged holding strong to many of his preconceived notions of writing. If anything, our research in a sense reinforced his biases toward his definition of quality writing, which will favor him in his field of interest—Political Science. However, his perceptions of writing in general have been broadened to include many different cross-sections of analysis, through which he was able to develop these preconceived notions. John concludes his paper [first draft of paper written out of our research] with a paragraph reflective of these ideas:

> I have been required to dig into my psyche; to understand the motivations behind my own writing style. I have become exposed to the problems of women in a male-dominated world. I have learned to appreciate the more subtle, giving, and patient approaches of some women's writing. I hope to be able to perhaps find my own unique style of writing. This attempt will certainly be difficult because I usually write only for classes, and as I stated above when it counts, I tend to have an extreme case of masculinitis. I find that when I write in journals or letters that my writing style is much more relaxed and that words and ideas just flow from my mind. This does not lead to a smooth and flowing letter however. When I write, I tend to put more emphasis on the ideas and not the way they are conveyed. This is something I would like to improve in my writing. I would like for my writing to flow through the use of smoother transitions and a better connectivity of ideas. I would like to shift my focus a bit. This is not a desire to move from the male-side of the continuum to the female-side, as I am comfortable with the attitudinal aspect of my writing, but rather an aspiration to improve my writing independent of any gender issues.

A valuable medium of recording and analyzing our research was through written transcripts of our meetings. Although the tone often could not be expressed, the content of our verbal interactions served as a valuable source for analysis. In a discussion between myself and John about our first drafts referred to earlier, as taken from transcripts, we learned about the different effects our research had upon us as individuals.

> J: Well that's the thing, I don't know what to write it for. All I wrote down was ok, I analyzed my writing—there it is. That's it. I don't know if this is what you're looking for.
> S: Did it help you, though? Did you learn about your strengths and weaknesses at all?
> J: Well, I learned something about my writing.
> S: Well, so it helped you. Or not? Or do you think that you just kind of did it and you feel really detached from it?
> J: From what I wrote. What I wrote is me. It explains me a lot. But I know from having done this research that all I've really done is sort of reinforce the way I write already. But I've learned a lot about the way I write, so definitely I'm getting something out of this group. So I'll read mine now if you guys really want to see what little I've gotten out of this now.
> C: Wait, wait, it isn't how little you've gotten out of it.
> S: You're being a negaholic.
> J: I am, cause I don't know where to go . . . I just need some direction though.

This excerpt is exemplary of a couple elements of John's personality which consistently affected his approach to writing. Task oriented in most situations, John expresses his frustration at having to develop a paper without a defined goal in mind at the start. Because our research was largely theoretical, and rejecting of a male-oriented notion of empirical research, John often felt displaced in discussions and in completing assignments that were not goal-oriented. Similarly, when John writes, points are stressed above all else. He believes that his ideas are strong enough to stand on their own, and is willing to accept the consequences of sacrificing flow and transition between thoughts in order to maintain his notions of the elements that comprise quality writing. With regard to this point he says,

I don't flow, I don't know why. Cause I remember one of the things you [Cathy] listed [taken from an earlier meeting in a discussion of what constitutes good writing], was that the paper had to sound good, you know as far as the flow and each sentence was like a note maybe or something like that, and I don't worry about that. I mean I put it in really awkward sentences and it doesn't bother me. I mean I know it sounds funny, but. Ok this is the thing that got the ball rolling. When she [Susan] was talking about the way to write. Sometimes I have a dull feeling in my head that this sounds pretty awkward. But that's it, that's the extent, it's not developed, that's it. I mean I, it's not like musical stuff—I play the piano and all that stuff. It's just something in my head that isn't really developed, that I don't really care about that, that the writing sounds good. I don't know, it's funny. I don't know why I can't flow.

In contrast to John's self-understanding, at an earlier point in the transcript I say,

Yea, that's an idea that I tried to convey in this. That when I write, I'm really concerned with certain things, I'm really concerned with the way it sounds, and with the way it all flows together. Just like, the whole basic composition of the thing is a shape. And I think that that's very feminine, whereas what you're talking about with wanting to make this point and that point and being really subject-oriented, that seems kind of male.

From these chosen spoken excerpts we see that John and I approach writing quite differently. Cathy and I often had the same goals in mind when we wrote in contrast to John, and as a result John sometimes interpreted his writing differences as weaknesses, especially when discussing flow. For John, flow is something he tells us he cannot do, or is not interested in, but that his ideas can stand well on their own. Looking back upon our meetings, I noticed that we came to critique our own writing ability with a strong bias in favor of feminine writing characteristics. We progressed from looking at masculine and feminine characteristics in a neutral fashion to viewing feminine characteristics in a more favorable light. I never interpreted my secondary commitment to ideas as a weakness, whereas John saw his secondary commitment to flow as such. Somehow, certain writing characteristics became more worthy than others in the group, and because Cathy and myself were strong proponents of the feminine style, John was forced to interpret his writing against a new standard which did not celebrate his writing style.

John comes to grips with his own issues with regard to writing forms, paying specific attention to how his psyche and experiences have helped shape his writing style, which often sharply contrasts my rendition of self-influences. He begins his paper with a general statement:

> It is fair to state that a person's writing is, to some extent, reflective of his/her personality. Discounting perhaps an advanced writer's use of unique methods to achieve a specific reaction, even putting conditioning aside, I think that a person's personal writing style will emerge. How else can we explain the numerous styles of writing we see, even if they are all somewhere along the feminine-masculine continuum. Supposedly all people are conditioned to write in a masculine style. The degree to which they were successfully conditioned is one factor in the different styles observed. Even after considering this, it seems logical that there is another explanation for the variety of styles outside that which is explainable by simple masculine vs. feminine writing. I believe this to be personality.
>
> The psychology behind my writing style: I tend to write not only in an opinionated, confident, arrogant, absolute way, but I also try to write academically, using elevated language. This it occurs to me is manipulative because in doing so I hope to convince the reader of my point by impressing him/her with my style. Perhaps I intend for the reader to simply accept my points without reflecting on them. This doesn't grant that my argument is weak, but rather I wish to assure the reader of my confidence. When I write "we" or "the reader" it will tend to be to try and draw the reader in with me, not really trying to involve the reader as much as to convince him/her of my point (manipulation). Susan pointed out that I try to legitimize my points by making strong statements (make my opinion seem as it were fact). Another reason I use elevated language to an extent is to demonstrate my literacy in English. I am Korean and have been in the United States since I was one but I still carry a bit of a chip on my shoulder- I fight the stereotype of the immigrant who struggles with English.
>
> Although I am very opinionated and authoritative, I can be open-minded if in the right situation—when no stakes are involved such as pride, grades or status. I am able to participate in discussions if in the right situations and moods, but normally

inclined to pursue an adversarial role. I have been conditioned by interactions with my father and my sister to participate in one-way communication-interactions.

The following is the pattern I follow when I write. I read the relevant material. I consider the possible questions. I then consciously choose the question which seems most arguable in an absolute way. I skim over the readings again, noting important passages relevant to the paper topic. I make an outline and figure out where evidence from the readings will fit into the outline. I then proceed to write the paper, revising as I go along. Rarely do I ever rewrite a paper.

Influences on my writing. I remember in sixth grade we had a creative writing elective. I am extremely uncreative in a lot of ways. I preferred not to do the homework and to get in trouble, having to write sentences over and over as punishment. I didn't learn how to really write an essay until tenth grade. It was the standard three part paper containing five paragraphs. In eleventh grade my A.P. History teacher reinforced this standard form through the essays we had to write for his class. Same stuff in twelfth grade. English 125 taught me to focus and be clear in my writing. English 225 has encouraged me to work on smooth transitions as well as making my papers more reader-friendly. The biggest influence on my writing however goes back to first term freshman year. I had Political Science 101. My T.A. and I worked out the following pointers to improve my writing because I was having problems writing for the class: propose solutions, discuss/explain evidence, state personal opinions, make sure things in paper/paragraphs advance or support the point of the paper, turn implicit points into clear points, overlook assumptions and prove premises, avoid summarizing too much, restate instructions for paper briefly spending more time developing arguments. The point to all of this was to deal more with advancing arguments than trying to prove this or that was said. To write at a higher level. Debate and Political Science (my major) base everything on proof and logical links. Both are inherent to the way I write and what I look for from others. It only seems natural to justify opinions with examples, evidence, and analogies.

My writing is never very unique or creative. I'm not a creative person, I've always known that. My writing is pretty standard and I don't feel free to be creative. The way I dictate when I write certainly seems to be modeled after our "banking" system of education. I/teachers deposit knowledge without regard for a true discussion or exchange of ideas.

John elaborated on Paulo Freire's banking concept of education again during one of our meetings, making a link between this idea and how it might relate to issues of form. That section of the transcript reads:

> And also just going back to something else that I've been hitting recently, just about our style of education. I kept hitting this in my Project Community. They have these articles about this banking system of education, the way the teachers just feed the stuff into the students and students don't think and that kind of stuff. Well, maybe we're just conditioned to do the same kind of thing when we write, not to be interactive or anything like that. If we give credit to the banking concept, that's just one possible thing I was thinking about.

From John's brief rendition of the "Banking Concept," the question of exactly how our style of education relates to our learned style of writing is raised. After a careful study of the findings of Pamela Annas, Carol Gilligan, Mary Hiatt, and others, as a group we were able to posit our own conclusions with regard to form, often by just talking through ideas waiting for results to arise from those discussions. We chose this style as opposed to formulating theories and hunting down subjects in order to prove them, which is indicative of the traditional male-dominated positivist research. Knowing that students are taught at a young age to think and behave in certain ways, we shared our experiences with the ways in which we were trained to write especially during high school. John and I had common experiences; the five paragraph essay was beaten into our heads, and we became aware that a student's success at writing was primarily based upon how well she/he wrote in the standard form. In a male-dominated world from which this standard arose, we wondered whether women were naturally at a disadvantage when forced to fit between such narrow parameters, the definition of acceptable form. Assuming that Freire's banking concept of learning held true for writing, we came to the conclusion that such rigidity of expectations discriminated against everyone who could not write in the standard way, the added element of gender differences placing women at an even wider disadvantage.

Most interesting in the development of my understanding of gender differences in writing was the existence of a transitional period I found myself struggling through. We live in a society which systematically discriminates against women in many professions, resulting in part from standards which have been set and maintained by men throughout history. Because of this fact, it would seem logical that if in fact women's cognition and/or writing style was naturally different from that of men, these differences would be interpreted in a negative manner. For this reason, at the commencement of our research I was defensive about the mere existence of differences, holding that the perceived differences were based solely on stereotypical male versus female behavior. After reading "A Woman's Place in Man's Life Cycle" from *In a Different Voice* by Carol Gilligan, I began to see the idea of gender differences in a new light. Gilligan celebrates many typically feminine characteristics—a perspective that I found empowering as a writer as well as a feminist. Once I got over this hurdle of denial, I was able to redefine my personal expression of feminism, and am now a strong proponent of "the feminine style."

I am sure I am not alone in the problems that I have with expressing myself on paper, but because my experience cannot be the same as anyone else's by virtue of human individuality, I hereby exercise the license to expound upon my writing as a unique process. What exactly does Susan French look like when she finally sits down to write a paper after worrying profusely about it for at least three days? In choosing to write in the third person for this section: she sits staring at a blank screen with her elbows firmly planted on the table and her face lying heavily upon her palms. Some cells will probably get chewed off at this point inside her mouth, and provided that her nails were not terminated at an earlier hour, they will soon end up detached from her body. Writer's block now manifests itself partially due to a fear of failure. Susan has always been a good writer, but she cannot help but think that this time, she will not have anything intelligent to say. Compounding this fear is another inhibition which tells her that if what she is about to write is not top-notch, then why bother?

Faced with a self-defeating mindset she begins to peck at the keys after a considerable time of inactivity. The hardest part is always the first paragraph—since high school she has been taught that a paper might as well be graded solely on the strength of the thesis statement. To fail here will surely spell demise. Everything Susan has been taught about "proper" form as dictated by a society created and run by white males paralyzes creative thought process and alternative forms of expression to a large extent. Any deviation from the norm is taking a great risk; will the professor buy it? Better be safe and stick to my usual is what she generally ends up saying. After all, she has been known to get A's in the past, so why mess with what is already working? Slowly the first paragraph unravels itself from what she is sure is just a garbled collection of thoughts. She then rereads the beginning several times, and finds herself recharging with every read because it sounds pretty good! Void of any real notes aside from a scribble here and there, never having used an outline, she keeps struggling until at last she hits a point where thoughts begin to flow with ease and her speed typing is put to good use. The flow of a paper is very important to Susan as a writer; certain sentences cannot be left alone until they sound right. She generally has an idea of where a paragraph is heading, and a good sense of when that paragraph should taper to a graceful end. Not a great deal of revision follows the initial writing task, most is done within sentences as they are being typed with a good deal of mental manipulation of wording going on in the interim. Sources are quoted to strengthen argument, and the final product is moderately organized both between paragraphs as well as within them.

John also has some problems when it comes to writing, but he expresses them in ways very different from mine. He tends to procrastinate a great deal, but when he actually sits down to get some work done, the procrastination ends. Even when he is not completely comfortable with his knowledge on the topic he "just writes," and does not worry about how it sounds or if his ideas flow. John generally is confident that his ideas are strong enough to stand on their own, therefore any other aspects of writing are superfluous. Because of his confidence with regard to content, he is generally less inhibited as a writer than me, and generally quite comfortable with his present process and style.

What does all this say about writing process? Pamela Annas spends a portion of "Style as Politics: A Feminist Approach to Writing" talking about the kinds of problems women characteristically experience with respect to writing. She mentions such blocks as "perfectionism, fear of criticism or judgment, depression, numbness or blankness, fear of taking risks, fear of knowing oneself, and discomfort with the mechanics of writing and organizing a paper" (366). I felt that her article was in some bizarre way speaking directly to me, and then I realized that women must have sets of relative experiences which in effect stifle us as a group when it comes to writing. She writes, "As women writers we have walked a fine line between objectivity and subjectivity, between self-censorship and self-indulgence, silence and noise, rigid control and little or no control" (369).

So many times in my writing I have found myself torn between wishing to express my thoughts in one genre but then settling for another because I am afraid of my more creative impulses. The most pervasive criticism of my work has been that it is too dry and does not take risks. I have always had a problem with exposing too much of myself to others, and for this reason have had an aversion to creative writing. Expository writing is the genre that I have always felt most comfortable with possibly because it is the most advantageous academic form. Annas writes, "We may value women's creative writing while at the same time feeling that it is very different from expository writing, the actual essay or research paper, which on the other hand we have been trained to think should be based on what the authorities say rather than on personal experience, and on 'hard' data rather than 'soft' " (360). Perhaps I have acclimated myself to a grade-oriented version of success which did not reward the feminine style enough, or my failure to validate my own personal experience has had a self-defeating effect on my creative impulses. John is similar to me in that he can appreciate different genres, and can agree with an argument presented in a style which presents the personal as opposed to the factual as proof, but both of us tend to shy away from this form in our actual writing, John more so than me. We concluded that this is probably the result of conforming to a masculine standard of writing taught in early high school which effects both men and women.

This process that I have grown accustomed to is one that was shaped throughout my years as a writer, progressing from the compositions I completed as a first grader, to meeting the demands of higher-level writing at present. My early writing experiences were mostly characterized by an encouragement to merely complete the assignment, and be creative as possible. I never felt anything but proud of the stories I wove which usually ended up on the good work board, along with many other papers. Looking back, positive reinforcement in student confidence was the goal of these exercises, and at this age, everyone seemed to feel good about their writing accomplishments.

As my schooling progressed to the high school level, expectations became much more rigid upon the introduction of the five paragraph essay. Teachers at this point were interested in the student's ability to clearly organize main ideas and pieces of supporting evidence into an introductory paragraph, conclusion, and a body consisting of the remaining three paragraphs. Inadvertently, this push toward organization had detrimental effects upon my previously developing creative skills, but because I desperately wanted to achieve academic success, I humbly agreed to write in whatever way was demanded of me at the time.

John reports similar indoctrination—the ugly five paragraph essay also presented as the model in his high school. This form places the skill of backing up thoughts with factual support and organization above all else, a form that our research group has described as "masculine," which would seem to favor John's natural writing tendencies at this time. However, the line between the natural and the conditioned is often blurred; therefore, we may never know what style of writing is more natural for John and me. High school is certainly a critical period for the development of writing in some capacity, and our group was concerned that if women were forced to write in a style that by virtue of innate gender differences was foreign to them, then would women have an even harder time making the transition between genres than men?

Making the transition between high school and college level writing was a big step for me, as I am sure it is for many students. The dryly organized, undercreative style that we mastered in high school was now worth about a C on a University staff assigned paper. I remember completing my first assignment which was a Music History paper the first semester of my freshperson year. Using the techniques of compiling and processing research that served me well up to that point, i.e. rehashing the material in a way that I now consider plagiarism, I completed my paper on Mahler Symphony #1 and received the shocking grade of C+. After being convinced that I would never survive in such courses, a closer examination of the present expectations of student writing I began to see that I had to acclimate to this new form. My English 125 course helped me a great deal to realize that within a structurally sound paper, my voice and creativity also had to shine. Basically, I found myself combining writing styles of elementary school and high school, taught separately with respect to age, as a groping technique to meeting these new demands which were frightening and strange to me at the time. Perhaps this difficult transition could have been lessened if these two forms had been equally incorporated in my writing training throughout early education.

In a group discussion of the various transitions we are forced to make as writers, I share my self-perceptions, lifted directly from the transcripts:

> For so long, I've been writing in a very specific way. With very formulated paragraphs. In every essay I've written probably since English 125, the first paragraph has been very compact—you know how I write. And it's all there and it reads pretty well, but it's just, it's dry . . . I'm trying to get up to that next rung in the ladder, I guess. And also, imagery. I don't know, something, I'm just really doing a lot of experimentation with that. And sometimes an image will just come to me.

After having achieved success in writing freshman compositions, I was met by a whole new set of challenges upon my enrollment in the course from which this research project was born, two semesters later. This course placed the skill of expository writing on yet another level. I now had to have an audience in mind and design a form accordingly. I learned to present my ideas in this chosen form as argument, after having expanded the definition of the term to include everything from fictive experiences to the most academic, boorish style. Through our workshops and work in peer groups I was encouraged to take risks, and to experiment with different types of argument that I had previously avoided. Coming up with original perspectives on racism and sexism was challenging on top of shaping argument by our newly created definition. At this point I was still a bit inhibited as a writer, and even when making an effort to break out of this shell, I held fast to my concrete, conservative forms with which I was most comfortable. John holds fast to concrete forms that he is most comfortable with as well, and in contrast to me, is often adamant about changing aspects of his writing even in response to a teacher's request. In more advanced writing courses, more flow and transition were common suggestions for improvement, but John's notion of argument as factual and idea-centered made him opposed to incorporate these additional points. In courses where students are encouraged to write in other forms, especially English and writing courses, perhaps John is at a disadvantage because of his learned style, in the same sense that women are inhibited by the five paragraph essay in high school.

At the present time, I have not yet let go of all of my writing inhibitions, but still have made substantial progress even in comparison to last semester. I think the strongest catalyst for opening creative channels has been our group research discussions centering around feminist methodology and writing forms. Actually seeing successful examples of women's writing which adheres to this foundation has empowered me to use such techniques without as much fear in my own writing. I now attempt to replace passive voice with active voice as much as possible, which personalizes my writing, making it more meaningful to the reader. A conflict of voices is still evident in much of my writing, but I feel that I have triumphed in being able to recognize the point I am at, and realize my potential for growth. Often, I begin papers in a very distant, non-conversational style subconsciously, which may or may not be replaced with a more personalized style later in the paper. For example, in my composition of this paper I did much revision especially at the beginning, attempting to establish conversational form at the onset to match this tone evident later in the paper. I foresee having to press onward, mastering more writing forms and developing my voice to its full value probably for the rest of my life. Although these are challenges which will be difficult to meet, I look forward to the point in my life where I will be able to use every ounce of knowledge I have acquired to nail down a writing style which is distinctly mine. Perhaps this level is unattainable though, whereby the more a person studies her self applications, the more complicated the general picture becomes. I have a feeling that only through years of additional experience will I be able to come to grips with this question.

I have noticed profound differences in my most recent writing, which I largely attribute to my emancipatory writing effectively as a feminist, ideas stemming from our group research. Dialogue between John, Cathy and me reflects this growth:

> S: You're weaving in strands. [talking about women's writing in general]
> C: You're making the strands blend. But you know what else I think. I don't think Susan could have written this paper [an earlier draft of this section] 6 months ago.

S: Probably not. Definitely not. Maybe not even a couple of months ago.
C: Yep. I would say that you would not have handed a paper like this in to me.
S: I'd be too scared. I'd be way too scared to start typing stuff like that and going to third person and talking about some stupid gold block, but now you know, it's just so weird, because when I did write that page and a half of Sue's paper, [a paper I will explain shortly], I just sat down at the computer and you know, I don't know what happened, but because it wasn't mine, because it didn't matter what I wrote, it was creative and it was good. And the same with this paper. I didn't sit down at the computer with the intent of getting an A, with impressing my paper, doing this, that and the other thing to get an A. I could be free. I was unleashed!
C: What about the other papers you're writing this term?
S: I don't think I've written one yet. I really haven't. I have a psych paper due soon.
C: What do you think you're going to do?
S: It's going to be different, it's going to be different. I'm going to be more bold and more, I'm going to at least think about taking risks more. I'm not going to say that I'm going to do crazy stuff in every paper. And that was even pretty conservative. I mean who are we kidding here. But um, it was a leap for me.

One of the ways in which I have changed as a writer as a result of our group research has been in taking an active role in finding a voice within myself which is completely unique to me. Students everywhere begin their studies as perfect blocks of gold unadulterated with inhibitions and filled with an incredible natural potential to write in ways natural and comfortable for each individual. As each student progresses, the once perfect, yet malleable block of gold is pounded and gouged taking on a convoluted, impure state. Often, what is meant to be a nurturing process by educators instead becomes a wrecking ball which serves to inhibit the natural, and constrict what should be a wide range. In her work with adolescent girls at a Boston boarding school, Carol Gilligan has attempted to answer the question of why young women are confident at eleven yet confused at sixteen. What are the inner-workings of developing girls which foster such a decline in self-efficacy? In a lecture on behalf of the Tanner Series [University of Michigan, March 1990], she shed some light on the subject by sharing with her audience an observed teacher-student interaction in response to an assignment completed by this student. The young woman had compiled an analysis of a poem in a way that was brilliantly fresh with creativity and voice which was undoubtedly genuine. Upon reviewing the piece the teacher dismissed the young woman's interpretation as wrong because she did not incorporate the theme of "carpe diem" into the assignment. A harsh conflict instantly emerged due to a disparity between the teacher's rigid guidelines with respect to form and a young student in the midst of the exciting process of self-discovery. The teacher's insensitivity toward development was evident to those introspective of the situation, yet the implications of this filtration process are widespread and detrimental especially to women.

In my writing experience over the past few years, I know that I have grown a great deal as a writer; a process which will continue throughout my adult life. At this point I have a fairly good idea of my strengths and weaknesses in writing and possess the motivation to reshape my style in a way which allows me to develop my "different voice." A child who loved to write stories and share them with others, I believe that somewhere along the way my creative talents were sequestered. When I look at my recent work, the times that have encouraged me to tap into this creative reservoir, I see a pattern which almost speaks for itself. Over Spring Break I was with a friend in Florida who was procrastinating over a ten page paper on the Criminal Justice System. She was having a terrible time starting the paper, and since I did not have anything to do I felt compelled to help her out in any way I could. With only a basic knowledge of the subject I sat down at the computer promising to write the first paragraph. I asked my friend a few questions about her actual experiences in the courtroom, and came up with the most creative, original beginning I have ever concocted. I developed my idea for a page and a half incorporating some vivid imagery and even tossed in a little humor. My point here is that because it was not my paper and I was free of all responsibility for that paper, my creative juices finally began to flow after countless dryly written opening paragraphs. This was indeed a personal triumph for me because I proved to myself that I was not restricted to one style of writing from a lack of talent for other form. My friend eventually did finish the paper and it was returned a week later with a rash of positive comments about my portion; reinforcement from an authority figure which further bolstered my self-confidence for writing creatively.

Another way I find myself able to write creatively is when I can somehow distance myself from the active subject. When I can achieve this comfort zone I can work to meet the reader half way. I do not always have the reader in mind in the same sense that Cathy makes a conscious effort to flow and "make it easy for the reader to understand what she has to say," but I am concerned with the way my paper reads and sounds to others. I see myself as being midway on the reader-friendly continuum, where John and Cathy are on the extreme ends. John says that he never writes for anyone in particular, and is never concerned with inviting the reader to play an active role in what he has to say. Earlier in this paper, I spoke in detailed imagery of my actual writing process, but wrote in the third person in order to feel comfortable with this form. Even as I write this paper I am discovering a great deal about myself. Another confession I have at this point is that because this paper will not be scrutinized with a fine-toothed comb and stamped with a letter, I feel much more comfortable experimenting with different forms, and therefore can learn much more about myself as a writer. I have come to the conclusion that years of evaluation and wanting desperately to succeed has blocked some of my potential, which can only be regained by such analytical self-examination in conjunction with a challenge of former writing training. Also, by having students keep a journal of free-response writing and complete assignments which attempt to regain a lost sense of freedom by allowing them to determine appropriate forms is an affirmative step in the right direction. All of these alternative approaches to encourage natural writing places a great demand on teachers, who could perhaps benefit the most from these findings.

Because my writing is changing rapidly, in addition to the way I view the writings of others as a direct result of this project, I sense that the next logical step is selling this heightened awareness to others. Unfortunately, many persons of power and esteemed members of the University community have a very narrow definition of appropriate writing forms. Our research group last semester branched off into the various colleges within the University and attempted to get a feel for the academic expectations with respect to form characteristic to each field of study. The general consensus was that the more male-dominated fields were less open-minded to alternate forms, i.e. "the feminine style," thus perpetuating a silent type of discrimination against women. I do not wish to sound accusatory, because most of this discrimination is unintentional, but the fact still remains that experts in the field of form posit that the feminine style is alive and well. Whether the University will continue to maintain patriarchal standards of writing which foster the exclusion of women in these fields, or whether newly found research will some day become common knowledge thereby equalizing validity of styles, will hopefully become an issue of deserved importance in the future.

## Cathy's Turn

### Notes Toward a New Kind of Research Program

I am left with the not-so-easy task of making sense of this exhausting yet enlightening eight-month project which has left each of us at various times frustrated, exposed, rejuvenated, and excited. We've seen in Susan's section some indication of the variation in response between herself and John as to what they gained from their participation in the project. For Susan, the work was a safe-house of sorts, a place to feel free to think, reconsider, and experiment, resulting in a renaming of herself as a woman writer. For John, the work reinforced some of his beliefs about writing, even as it opened his mind to the possibility of difference between the writing of men and women—and a rethinking about what that might mean for his female peers. What I want to write about at this point has to do with what I, too, have learned from this experience, something to do with the new possibilities I am envisioning for teacher-research.

As I look back over the very different responses of Susan and John to our work and look as well at the transcripts of our meetings, I am reminded of some of the problematic questions posed by the two of them at different points in our research, questions both of them raised again in their composition of the two previous sections of this chapter: John wonders about the validity of this kind of research approach; Susan worries that how we describe what we find might factor into a continuation of the old stereotypes about women. These questions are, for both of them and for those of us interested in research, very real questions, questions which seemed to have been answered at least on the surface either by me directly or by all of us more indirectly as the project progressed. Reconsidering their questions at this point, however, allows me a way into thinking more generally about some of the issues of research which have haunted me from the very start of my forays into teacher-research. What their questions raise for me has something to do with the interrelation between the three elements I have come to identify as keys to the research paradigm I am advocating for teacher-research: research as grounded in experiential knowledge, research as collaborative in both conception and practice, research as emancipatory action. Let me begin by posing their two questions once more and showing the connections I see between them.

As we saw, Susan's recognition of the differences between her writing and John's at first caused her some discomfort, particularly because of the terms we used to describe such writing and the connotations she associates with such terms. "Circular reasoning for me has some negative connotations," she told us one day as we were discussing the differences. She explained why: "Because it's circular, it seems like it wouldn't be as effective because you're going from this thing and you're kind of taking a long time and going this roundabout way to get to your point." This discomfort echoed her initial fears about the possible misunderstandings which might result from speaking in generalities about women's ways of writing as being somehow different from men's. She, you may recall, at first actively resisted any kind of research study which would separate writing in these ways, fearing that such a study might find "that females do write more passively than men and don't drive their point home enough or whatever," reflecting the fear that many others have seen in the kinds of studies which reduce a gendered look at writing to essentialist ideas about men and women, and which thus end up settling for answers in less complicated fashion than they may actually occur. In an almost opposite stance, John at first expressed an equal amount of discomfort in terms of the local nature of our studying, worrying that our focus on gendered issues in writing at an individual level could do little to prove notions of difference at a more global level. As John recalls in his section:

> JOHN: We're setting out to prove that there's differences between male and female writing, right, and so this could lead to us trying to find things that aren't there. And so when Susan writes in a

masculine way, we can attribute that to socialization, you know. But then again, this is where our study's screwed up because we can never determine the extent of socialization, the effect. And another thing that's going to screw it up is the nature of the assignment. . . . I think Susan's required to rag because you've got to go to extreme opposites to like, this is good and this is bad. There's so many different factors we're dealing with, there's socialization, the nature of the assignment, that kind of stuff. So our study's going to be pretty screwed up.

Susan discovered answers to her own questions later in the term in our group meetings, answers which speak indirectly to John's concerns as well. Susan began to see many of the characteristics of female writing as we and others had named them in a new light, at one point renaming the actual terms in more positive ways. She resaw "circular writing," a term with negative connotations for her, as writing which "weav[es] in strands," a positive—some would even say feminine—image of her writing.[6] This renaming of terms led her toward an acceptance and a celebration of the possibility of a woman's way of writing—an idea which begins to seem a freeing one for her. Susan had admitted at various points in our work that she had been criticized in the past for being a dry writer. In her newfound excitement about women's ways of writing, she began to see that characteristic as a somewhat inevitable end to the structured way of approaching writing she had formerly considered "correct" and now considered "male" in nature. Rejecting that male construct as the only possibility became a freeing notion, one that gave her a kind of permission to approach her own writing in a different way. The results were wonderful to see:

> March 20
> SUSAN: Basically when I write now, I'm completely aware of everything we're talking about in this feminine versus masculine style. . . . I'm almost pro-feminization of writing now, and so I tend to be now writing more in that style—and knowing and trying to write in that style.
>
> March 30
> SUSAN: I'm so excited! Writing this paper [a paper which summarized what had happened to her thinking about writing and

---

[6]Mary Daly in fact uses that image throughout her feminist tract *Gyn/Ecology.* She speaks of feminists as "Spinsters," saying, "We can weave and unweave, knot and unknot, only because we hear, what we hear, and as well as we hear. Spinning is celebration/cerebration. Spinsters Spin all ways, always" (424)

writing itself over the course of our research] was probably the easiest time I ever had in writing a paper. Discoveries in writing; I really discovered a lot while I wrote this paper . . .

JOHN: So many things are striking me. First of all, Susan and I both talked about how the lack of pressure makes her free to be creative, makes me free to be more open, but Susan has such good self-awareness. She comes out with such vivid understanding of why she writes this way or that way, being able to describe herself. I understand the psychology behind my own writing, but it seems that over this past year she's gone through this process of finding herself.

CATHY: What about other papers you're writing this term? . . .

S: It's going to be different. I'm going to be more bold; I'm going to at least think about taking risks more. I'm not going to say that I'm going to do crazy stuff in every paper. And that was even pretty conservative. I mean, who are we kidding here? But it was a leap for me . . . a big leap.

J: Why is it that you keep referring to it in a negative? Crazy stuff and this and that? Why don't you say you want to be more creative?

S: Because for so long, I've been writing in a very specific way. With very formulated paragraphs. In every essay I've written probably since English 125, the first paragraph has been very compact—you know how I write. And it's all there and it reads pretty well, but it's just—it's dry. I'm trying to get up that next rung in the ladder, I guess. And also imagery, I'm just really doing a lot of experimentation with that. Sometimes an image will just come to me. . . . I never really did that before.

C: No, I never saw that in your papers before.

S: And. . . the whole issue of trying to reclaim this style which is probably natural to me . . . a style that I'd like to have and like to be able to use successfully.

Susan's ability to reclaim a style, as she calls it, seemed to arise from her studying her writing and John's at a local level; then moving from that understanding to a more global understanding, one that situated her experience within the experience of others she'd read about, in order to return once more to the local level, manifested in terms of her own self-conscious attempt to change both her approach to her writing and the actual product she composed. This identification of the problem in terms of the personal allowed her to recognize and accept it more clearly in the experience of others and gave her a kind of green light to transfer that knowledge back once again to her own experience.

John's objection seems to speak in some ways to a similar issue of concern—that of "what counts" as evidence. For Susan, someone who had expressed suspicions about the more global kind of research based in empirical "proof" about which she'd been reading, basing a study in her own experience as a writer allowed her both a way into understanding the general concerns raised by others as well as a kind of freedom to act. For John, on the other hand, this basing of a study in individual experience seemed insufficient to be considered a "real study." What we consistently had seen him count as evidence in his own reading and writing was empirical, factual evidence. It came as no surprise, then, when he felt uncomfortable with a view of research which went against his view of what counted as proof. For John, individually derived, local knowledge simply was not enough; he wanted us to produce a research study which could find a way to isolate a single factor about gender difference in writing, a factor which could then be proved by massive, in-depth research: talking to professors and looking at numerous papers from other male and female writers, for example. Valuing personal, local knowledge—one's own experience—as "real" evidence proved to be more difficult for him.

At the time of his question, I posed an answer for him, an answer based in my own belief in particular research techniques, an answer he quotes in full in his section of this chapter, and which he admitted satisfied at least his immediate needs. But as I think more about his question and about Susan's, as I think more about the role of local knowledge in research and its relationship to more global understandings, I want to repose my answer in a more complete way, an answer that will speak to the ties I am seeing among local knowledge, collaboration, and emancipatory strategies. In short, I want to look at John's and Susan's questions as a way of raising some of the important connections that must take place in order for this kind of research to be successful.

John's raising of the issue of what should count as research relates, I think, to his disappointment expressed in our last sessions that, while Susan seemed to have gained something by this study, John's understanding of his own writing really hadn't changed all that much; in terms of the emancipatory nature of our work, Susan was somehow "getting more out of it." He said at one point, "I was getting jealous about the way she could write so vividly about her own writing. That was really good. While she was reading I was really starting to get down on myself; [saying] I can't do that." And earlier that same day: "Because before last term she was totally against any differences, now she's totally celebrating it and I'm the same person." John recognized that this focus on the personal was a freeing one for Susan, and was disappointed that the focus on the individual didn't turn out for him in quite the same way. For Susan, the project had become a personal triumph, a forum for her to think with other interested people about issues already important to her and a place to try out her developing attitudes about issues of writing: both in talk and in writing. As a woman and as a feminist, Susan's stake was very personal; it didn't take much for her own grounded experience to let her feel ownership in the project. John's history in the project is quite different. John involved himself in the project originally, he told me, because it seemed like fun and because he liked to talk about issues. And as long as our work together stayed mostly at the level of talk, John's stake in the research slowly grew. He saw his role in many ways as the "devil's advocate," he says, keeping us honest about attributing too much to gender difference, using his own writing as the basis for his objections. But as we began the hard process of putting together our work in a collaboratively derived form, John's commitment seemed to wane, reflected in both his increased silences at our last few meetings and his constant disclaimers that his written contributions were not as thoughtful as Susan's.

Why is it that John at the project's close feels less ownership over our work than either Susan or I? What is it that makes this kind of collaboration in some ways unequal? What are the implications of unequal participation in an approach to research that stresses the importance of collaboration, that pushes for a change in the status quo?

Clearly, there seems to be a connection among the focus on local knowledge to which we subscribed, our individual contributions to the collaborations, and the emancipatory possibilities we uncovered as a result of our participation in the research group: Susan, who found a focus for her work in her own experience and who found that experience valued in the group, admittedly did change radically in her thinking about her writing and significantly in her own writing style. For her, an emphasis on the local gave her a strong voice in the collaboration. For John, the changes were much more subtle. Despite his disappointment at the end in both himself and in the group's work that he was not contributing as much as Susan and I were, John himself admitted to some changes in a paper he wrote in part summarizing his reactions to our work together. He explained that he has begun to rethink his own approach to writing (although that hasn't led to many actual changes in the writing itself) and has learned more about writing in general and women's writing in particular:

> I have been required to dig into my psyche; to understand the motivations behind my own writing style. I have become exposed to the problems of women in a male-dominated world. I have learned to appreciate the more subtle, giving and patient approaches of some women's writing. I hope to be able to perhaps find my own unique style of writing.

Perhaps in comparison to Susan, these seem like small changes to John. From my perspective, they show a large change in the status quo: John is thinking differently about writing and will most likely be a different kind of reader and participant in discussions as a result of this work. And I see other changes as well, for both John and Susan, changes which occurred, I think, because of the grounded approach to research we espoused. When I look through the pages of transcriptions, I see a pattern. I see early meetings in which I talked a lot, setting up the terms for analysis and leading the way to our identification of themes. In the later transcripts, this pattern changes appreciably. Discussions seemed to have no single leader and the back-and-forth questioning that occurred especially between John and Susan about their writing occupies most of the pages of the transcript. Without conducting substantial discourse analysis into the kinds of turns and responses each of us took, I can attribute the change in this way. When the project began, the research belonged to me—despite my attempts to involve everyone in its design and in how it would be carried out. Because the project's major write-up would be in the form of a chapter in a book I was writing and because at least a portion of the chapter's emphasis would be on issues I had spent the last four years exploring, the project remained mine. As both John and Susan learned more about their own writing and took ownership of the knowledge they were gaining, their relationship to our work and the nature of the collaboration itself began to shift. In important ways, the work began to belong to all of us, albeit to different extents at different points. Susan, by the close of the project, confident of her own understanding of our work, took on an almost teacherly role, questioning John about his own writing and his reactions to hers ("Why is it great? . . . Why do you do it that way?"). John took his own work on with a new seriousness, showing a self-awareness as he questioned his own approaches and examined why he writes as he does ("I just slapped the stuff down like a grocery list and I figured when I saw that that I'm a pretty lazy writer. . . . I really expect my ideas to shine through regardless of how horrible my writing is.").

The responses of Susan and John to this work lead me to believe that focusing research at the local level creates a form of knowledge for those who participate in the research that is different from the knowledge gathered when one studies ideas more in the Big R research style. The knowledge Susan and John gained, a kind of personal knowledge, lets them respond to outside readings and ideas in a heteroglossic fashion, reflective of Bakhtin's requirements of an individually developing ideology. Because students come to an understanding of an issue primarily from their own experience, they take ownership over that issue: They come to look at what they read in terms they establish from their own experience. As students become authorities on the subject under consideration, they become authors in their own right about issues that rightly belong to them. And as authors of the work, as subjects of the research, they enter into collaboration at an active level. The work no longer can belong to one researcher, and no one researcher can represent their experience. Seeing themselves as subjects capable of creating new grounded knowledge allows them to shape the project collaboratively. This new ownership further gives its members the freedom to accept or reject what other so-called authorities tell them—a necessary rethinking of the status quo.

But what of the notion of unequal collaboration? Does unequal participation mean that this kind of research does not work? Because Susan and John clearly put in and got out different amounts from our work, was this a success for Susan and a failure for John? Is Susan's obvious ownership and equally obvious change a more important result than John's subtle shifts? I don't think so, and I think therein lies the heart of this approach to research. Paulo Freire, in talking about the teacher-student relationship, tells us participation can never be, should never be seen as equal. "The dialogic relationship does not have the power to create such an impossible equality," he explains (Shor and Freire 92). We can expand that understanding to the dialogic relationship among students participating in this kind of collaborative student–teacher-research. If we believe that such research begins with individual experience, we already are situating ourselves in a celebration of individual difference, and thus must realize that each participant will bring a different kind of knowledge base into a project. A celebration of difference tells us as well that some of the experience they bring will fit into a particular part of a project more readily than other experience, but that it is the knowledge of the participants—at whatever level—that is the basis of our work. Despite John's discouragement about his contribution, for example, our project could not have progressed as it did without his important participation based in his own experience as a writer. Just as his shifts in understanding are in part a result of Susan's participation, her changes are in part a result of his contributions. Part of the job of the teacher-researcher, then, must be to draw out the varying experiences and to help students see how their own knowledge fits with the knowledge of the group, how each student has a contribution to make to the research project. Beyond that, every project will result in unequal excitement, unequal gain, if by "gain" we mean obvious shifts in understanding. Emancipation and empowerment are not items to be measured in quantitative terms, and clearly will not look the same on the surface to be of value to individual students. Collaborative student–teacher-research, in other words, is not a race in which the student wins who runs the farthest distance; student–teacher-research should be a way of life in the classroom in which critical reflection and action are an exciting result of an ongoing look into what makes a particular classroom work as it does.

John and Susan approached this project with different needs, put in different amounts of time and energy, and will walk away from the experience with different perspectives. Both were clearly collaborators, though, who came to work from their own grounded knowledge base and helped to create a new understanding of the issues at stake for themselves, for me, and for those who will read our work.

CHAPTER 6

# *A Postscript to* Composing Teacher-Research: *A Work in Progress*

My work with students and teachers over the past decade and my reading into a number of disciplines have helped to inform my understandings of the possibilities for teacher-research, and have helped me re-form the perspectives and even the methodologies which drive my practice. Each time I've reconsidered the work in which I've been involved, asking myself hard questions about the particularities of the research and the pedagogy which surrounds it, assessing what was successful and what wasn't, I've been able to push myself toward a better understanding of what teacher-research might be—in its most imaginative and empowering sense.

As I read and reread the four case studies which make up the body of this book, I see differences in my attempts to do teacher-research. As I think about the teacher-research I will do in the future, I already anticipate shifts in my methodology as I continue to rethink how to do research in a way that will help me learn with my students in order to effect change in our classrooms. I know now, though, that what will remain constant in my attempts at teacher-research is my sense of it as exploration. I know I will continue to question what I've done and use that questioning as a way of refining what I might do next. I also expect that when I write up the research I conduct—either alone or with others like John and Susan—the literature I compose about it is more likely to be exploratory than summative. My writing will continue to take shape in essays like these—that is, in attempts—and it is likely to reveal my uncertainties as well as those of my students.

I know also, though, that my attempts at research will be driven by the three questions which I have come to see as central ones to my continuing growth as a classroom teacher, questions raised at first for me in the work of Clifford Geertz. As he asks: Is this kind of research even possible? If so, is it ethical? And to these I add a question of my own—one pertinent, I think, for me as a teacher who sees myself also as a researcher: If we can do such research, and do it in an ethical manner, does it help create better pedagogy for our students and ourselves?

Research which is *possible*. Research which is *ethical*. Research which *centers on pedagogy*. As goals to strive toward, these are fairly lofty ones, I know. My work with John and Susan and my reading of Tyler helped me realize that in order to at least move closer to these goals, I had to first move away from the ideal of representational research which had been so much a part of my understanding of what research is. Any of my research projects whose major purpose was to represent others, I learned, failed to be truly ethical and didn't make sufficient strides toward improving pedagogy.

The further question for me, then, has become how I can "do research" that is not representational. And, as I mention in the last chapter, as John, Susan and I came to talk about our own research, we arrived at three characteristics which seemed to be informing ones about what research might be like in a move to be evocative rather than representational, to be *possible, ethical,* and *centered on pedagogy*.

*First, evocative research emerges from local experiences.* Locally derived research relies on the experiences of its participants as its informing center. Additional voices, which enter because of the reading one or more of the participants brings to a discussion, are, of course, important but only in how those voices help the participants understand their own experiences more fully. When we've started with the words and experiences of the participants in the research, our voices are not muffled by the strong and convincing voices of the experts we read. Our voices serve as the center, our experiences as the issues for the research. By listening to these voices and experiences and trying to make sense of them as experiences (and not as explications of someone else's theories), we have learned to see what was in front of us all along—and to be theory makers ourselves.

*Second, evocative research explores the nature of its collaboration.* Research, of course, is necessarily collaborative—even traditional research involves at least two people, the researcher subject and the researched object. I think teacher-research takes on another ethical level, though, when those who are participating explore what it means to collaborate with another person in order to make sense of the lives of those involved. Such collaboration becomes reciprocal as all participants talk and learn from each other, and the roles of researcher and researched become almost interchangeable; such collaboration becomes a part of both the research process and the product, so that participants are involved with the research from conceptualizing the question to writing up their understandings of the experience, making the research something that is informing for them. Exploring the nature of collaboration leads the questioning teacher-researcher and student-researchers to think about the role of audience in that collaboration as well, anticipating who the audience for the work might be and how they might write up their experiences in ways that will speak to the multiple audiences of selves and others.

*Third, evocative research orients itself toward praxis.* When all those who participate in the research reflect critically on the experience, they logically make changes (in their writing, in their curriculum, in their understandings) accordingly. As I learned with Susan and John, though, such change is not a race in which the person who learns the most wins. Rather, praxis-oriented research encourages people to change in their own ways, according to their own needs and their own abilities/desires to make sense of the research that was collaboratively practiced. Again, questioning student- and teacher-researchers will probably wonder how such praxis impacts on the audience beyond the primary participants. A truly praxis-oriented research project will see a collaborating audience inserting its experience into the equation and making adaptations as well.

This sense of how research can be collaborative and praxis-oriented primarily for the participants in the actual research but secondarily for another set of participants—the outside readers/responders to the research—is one of the issues that fascinates me about the possibilities for classroom research. Such considerations lead me toward a rethinking of genre and a pondering of what genres might be the most expansive and ultimately satisfying ones for those of us who practice classroom research. My interpretation of Tyler's musing on the postmodern ethnography resulted in one satisfying kind of genre, I think: a piece in which all participants were able to speak in alternating, lengthy sections in which conflicts, contradictions, and agreements all emerge. Such an approach, I believe, reflects quite accurately the process that evolved in our research. Each of us got to reflect and speak about our experience, and each of us relied on the experiences of the others in order to compose our sections, showing our reliance on local experiences and a collaborative process and ultimately expressing the changes each of us felt within ourselves as a result of the project.

But do I think this specific way of researching and writing up our research is the only way? Definitely not. In this particular scenario, I worked with students who chose to participate because they were fascinated by the topic that had evolved. These students worked diligently to be able to articulate their understandings and were able to write lengthy pieces reflecting that diligence. We worked many hours over the course of two semesters to be able to refine our understandings to the point that we felt we could write about them, and the final piece reflects, I believe, the luxury afforded us by that time and reflection.

Given a different set of circumstances, a different teacher, and different students, I think the genre would evolve quite differently. As Tyler says in the piece that so informed my thinking, "The point is that questions of form are not prior, the form itself should emerge out of the joint work of the ethnographer and his native partners [sic]" (127). As I consider the possibilities for various genres for teacher-research, I believe that a number of ways of researching and writing up that research are possible—provided such research sees itself as local, as collaborative, and as praxis-oriented.

Patti Lather, in her book *Getting Smart: Feminist Research and Pedagogy With/in the Postmodern*, speaks of "the textual staging of knowledge." From her perspective, the best way to present research is to tell some kind of story, in order to "vivify interpretation as opposed to 'support' or 'prove.'" She continues:

> Turning the text into a display and interaction among perspectives and presenting material rich enough to bear re-analysis in different ways brings the reader into the analysis via a dispersive impulse which fragments univocal authority. Such writing works against the tendency to become the locus of authority; it is writ-

ing that probes the blind spots of the interpretaters' own concep-
tualizations and attends to its own constitutive elements. (91)

This quote, I think, captures the challenge for teacher-researchers:
to find a means to present to others the *context-full* texture of the
classroom and to do so in a way that allows others—both those
others who participate in the creation of the text by their presence
in the classroom and those others who participate in the creation
of text by their reading of it—to see the material differently. By
pushing for this kind of interpretation and reinterpretation and
reinterpretation by any number of others, a very full and rich
picture of a classroom can occur. To go back to the words Ann
Berthoff used to describe teacher-research over a decade ago, "RE-
search, like REcognition, is a REflexive act. It means looking—
and looking again. This new kind of REsearch would not mean
going out after new 'data' but rather REconsidering what is at
hand" (Goswami and Stillman 30).

My purpose in this chapter, then, is to describe some of the
ways in which teachers might explore and even invent some new
genres that will go far toward answering this challenge. My recent
reading into the research of others has led me to think hard about
the ways in which some others have been "pushing the envelope"
of research genres. In this chapter, I first will talk about three
approaches I have encountered in my reading since the time I
completed my work with John and Susan, approaches which are
helping me rethink my own work. In the last part of the chapter, I
will talk about a true work-in-progress, a classroom research project in which I am currently involved, in which those of us participating are self-consciously trying to put Lather's display metaphor
into use.

## STOCK: "THE FUNCTION OF THE ANECDOTE IN TEACHER RESEARCH"

Patricia Lambert Stock begins her essay "The Function of the Anecdote in Teacher Research" by telling the story of a conversation
she had with coteacher Jane Denton about an incident which had
just happened in their fifth-hour class. Stock and Denton discuss in
amazement Gilbert's participation in class that day. Gilbert, a stu-

dent who never did homework, had actually responded to a teacher assignment in which students were asked to write out a family story. Gilbert "sort of" did the assignment; he brought in a tape he had recorded of his mother's rendition of their family history, and volunteered to be the first in class to share. "We, as a family, the Sanchez," began his mother on the tape, and the class listened in rapt attention at the tale Gilbert's mother had spun. The questions students subsequently raised led to an unexpected and exciting teaching and learning moment for both teachers and students.

Stock, in narrative fashion, captures the two teachers reimagining the classroom moment; she sets the scene of the now studentless classroom and recreates the dialogue of the two teachers recounting their memories of what had just occurred. As she does so, she invites the reader, too, to imagine the classroom, the teachers sitting in it, and the conversation that ensues. She then recaptures another version of the anecdote as it evolves with another audience: two more teachers who come from down the hall to share the planning period and indulge in some teacher talk, who join in the discussion and respond to the telling of the anecdote by adding their knowledge of some of the students involved, asking questions for clarification, and suggesting possible interpretations. As they talk, these teachers imagine how Gilbert's tape and the students' discussion of the tape might be used to develop some lessons about narrative structure. As the classroom anecdote is subsequently told and retold to two other groups of teachers (and as Stock retells those retellings in her essay), it is reshaped. In the retellings, "we preserved and deleted details we had collected in our first shaping of the anecdote and added new ones" ("Anecdote in Teacher Research" 180). The anecdote grows and changes as the teachers who particpate in a discussion of it ask questions, tell related stories of their own about other teaching-learning moments, and imagine its significance as a way of rethinking curriculum. Out of this anecdote, then, comes more than good teacher discussion. Participating in the anecdote helps teachers reimagine their own classrooms and curricula.

Stock sees a definite purpose of teacher anecdotes like this:

> That teachers tell anecdotes when we discuss our teaching is common knowledge. What is not generally recognized are the functions that the shaping, reshaping and rehearsing of anecdotes play in the research we informally—and I would claim—

systematically conduct into our practice. For example, when Jane and I began to shape the anecdote . . . we gathered pertinent information about a teaching-learning interaction. We collected data, if you will. When we reshaped the anecdote for colleagues, first in one setting, then in another, we selected, deleted, organized and analyzed the information we had gathered—for a particular purpose: to effect better teaching and learning. . . .

In our professional talk, we teachers allude to the library of anecdotes we share. . . . Sometimes we begin by testing the dimensions of an anecdote one of us has told the others: Telling and retelling it, we place and replace it in contexts that enrich its meaning. As we add and subtract details, we teachers translate the anecdote into an event, a significant occurrence within one of the larger narratives that define our teaching practice. . . .

All the while, of course, we interpret and reinterpret them in the light of the larger narratives that shape our professional practice. Situating specific teaching-learning moments in the material circumstances in which they occur and reflecting on them in their own terms rather than in another, specialized discourse, we replay them, inviting colleagues who have not experienced those moments with us to examine them with us as we re-search them.
("Anecdote in Teacher Research" 184–5)

As Stock describes the life of this particular anecdote and explains the function of anecdotes in general for teaching and learning and their place in teacher-research, she explores a new genre for the profession. Too often, teacher talk has been critiqued as idle chatter at best, as destructive to students at worst. The implication has been that when teachers tell tales about students, they are merely venting, blowing off steam. As Stock chronicles the importance of this particular anecdote, she elevates teacher talk to the level of research; teacher talk—at least this teacher talk—became not only a systematic way of learning more about a particular student but also a systematic means of analyzing a classroom moment as a way of reshaping the teaching and learning that goes on in a classroom.

Stock's retelling here seems to me to fulfill the challenge of Lather's display metaphor, even as it serves as an example of an evocative means of doing research. She begins with local circumstance, telling a story about a particularity of the classroom; she expands the traditional notion of collaboration by involving not only the two coteachers of the classroom, but also several groups of teachers whose interpretations and reinterpretations of the incident helped reshape the actuality of the anecdote. And she recognizes the implications of this anecdote for praxis: The retelling and the reshaping of the anecdote led to curricular discussions, as the teaching-learning moment of the anecdote became a focal point in revising the classroom curriculum specifically in two classrooms, and more generally in the revised thinking of the many teachers who participated in the many discussions about the anecdote's implications.

The anecdote goes beyond that, though. In Stock's retelling of the retellings in the essay, her narrative rendition of what happened at each step allows me as reader to join in the conversation. As I read, I felt part of the expanding life of the anecdote: I, too, raised questions and suggested possible interpretations in my marginal scribblings. Because the story of the anecdote is told in an open way—without recommendations as to what I am supposed to think—and because the material is presented in its contextual fullness—so that I can imagine the participating characters and hear the conversations in my mind—I feel like a participant in the teacher talk which comprises the text. Just as the teachers involved most directly in the making of the text revised their curricula in response to their participation in the anecdote, I, too, as reader now anticipate changes in my own teaching.

Stock's piece is a short essay and one that focuses on a single moment in a single classroom. The power in it, for me, lies in her ability to recapture the anecdote as it grew and changed, to recreate for readers the responses and reactions to that moment, and to enable readers to imagine along with the actual participants in the text.

## SCHAAFSMA: *EATING ON THE STREET*

David Schaafsma's book *Eating on the Street: Teaching Literacy in a Multicultural Society* is a story of what he calls "collaborative myth making" (196). At the center of the book is an event involving the seven teachers and some of the thirty students who were part of the Dewey Center Community Writing Project, a summer writing program for middle school, mostly African-American, students in Detroit. The event: As the teachers and students walked through the streets of downtown Detroit on a field trip one day, several of the students pulled out snacks and proceeded to eat as they strolled along. For some of the teachers this incident had no particular significance; for others it seemed a sign of disrespect and general bad manners. As one teacher in particular later raised the issue at a teacher meeting, suggesting that something should have been done about the students' eating on the street, the discussion became heated, serving as an emblem, it seemed, for the different pedagogical stances and misunderstandings that existed between and among the teachers in this project: those who were Caucasian and those who were African-American; those who were experienced teachers and those who were fairly new to the profession; those who were from Detroit and those who were not; those who saw themselves as whole language teachers and those who did not.

In the text, Schaafsma uses the event as a way of getting at some of the differences in perspectives among these teachers. In lengthy transcripts taken from interviews with the teachers after the summer project, he asks the teachers to tell their versions of what happened that day, as well as to describe some of their own history as teachers and their beliefs about the place of Black English dialect in the classroom. For Jeanetta and others, letting children eat on the street signified liberal do-gooding at its worst: if African-American children eat on the street, it looks bad to others, they believe, allowing others to make generalizations and judgments about the "sloppy behaviors" of African-American children and thus contributing to racial stereotypes—ultimately stigmatizing these students. Teachers who allow such behavior are helping to further these stereotypes. In related fashion for some of these teachers, allowing Black Dialect to be used in the classroom signifies the same kind of disrespect; when students aren't expected to use standard English, believe these teachers, others can make the same generalizations about the sloppy and uneducated language of these children, again resulting in stereotypes and ultimately in a denial of opportunity for them.

Juxtaposing the teachers' stories two at a time, all of which are infinitely more complicated than I have summarized here, Schaafsma establishes a case for looking at multiple perspectives as a way of coming to any real understanding, recognizing his own position as the ultimate storyteller in this book. He explains:

> To hear Jeanetta's story, her history, is to begin to understand what a constructivist perspective on the social nature of self and Other might mean. Jeanetta Cotman's story, and every other teacher's story I tell in this . . . is one voice in a story—my

story—without an absolute, without an essence or a center, just as her own story contains echoes, voices, from many sites or historical moments in her own history as a teacher. . . .

I needed to look at situations from her perspective in order to understand eating on the street, to construct my own story about how to teach better in multicultural settings. (62–63)

Schaafsma recognizes that by layering story upon story told in some depth by the storyteller-teachers, he—and ultimately we as readers—can move toward a fuller understanding of what it means to teach in a multicultural setting. Each participant provides a slightly different perspective on both eating on the street and on teaching in this particular setting. By celebrating the differences in these stories and in the storytellers themselves, Schaafsma sends a clear message: Solo understanding can only ever be partial. It is only through what Gadamer calls a fusion of horizons that we can begin to come close to a full picture of students, of classrooms, of teaching and learning.

Schaafsma further complicates the picture he paints by embedding the stories of the teachers within the larger story of teaching in Detroit in general and in the Dewey Center, the alternative whole language school which was the site for this summer project, in particular, providing histories of both. As the narrative histories of these teachers and their commitments come through, embedded in the stories of what it means to teach in Detroit and at that school, the picture of what it means to teach literacy in a multicultural site becomes more complicated. Jeanetta's background as a teacher necessarily differs from George's, which differs from Toby's and Dana's. Jeanetta's stance as an African-American woman from the South and a long-time teacher in this particular building, before it became a whole language magnet school, informs her perspective on eating on the street—just as Dana's stance as an African-American and Detroit native, a young woman just graduated from college, who espouses many of the new approaches to teaching and learning she had just been taught, informs hers. Schaafsma emphasizes these complications as a way of making a point about the nature and purpose of collaboration. The deep-rooted responses of some teachers to what may seem to others an insignificant incident become significant. As Schaafsma listens to these teachers and questions along with them why things matter to us in certain ways and why we teach what we teach, it is clear that the very act of placing your own commitments alongside the commitments of others makes for praxis: Critical reflection necessarily occurs; action is inevitable.

What Schaafsma accomplishes in this book is a model for classroom research. Although, like Stock's piece, this book focuses more on teachers than on students, the lessons are applicable. By taking a single incident and letting it serve as the starting point for discussion and by including lengthy chunks of teacher talk, Schaafsma allows for the creation of new knowledge: for himself as researcher, for the teachers as collaborators, and for us as readers. Without instructing us as to what we're supposed to see, he lets the stories speak for themselves, and the richness of the transcripts, along with the richness of the histories he writes of the city and the school, lets the message through: Collaboration is sometimes messy, and multicultural education is much more complicated than some would have us believe, yet the teaching and learning that can occur when teachers speak honestly about their backgrounds and commitments make a case for a dialogue among those whose differences may help inform each other. Schaafsma's research begins with the local, the stories of these teachers; complicates the notion of collaboration; and integrates praxis throughout—all the teachers involved see teaching anew as a result of their work together.

In an evocative manner, he involves the reader in these stories as well. Perhaps because the transcripts are so long and full, I felt myself a part of the conversation, too, ready to add what I think about the issues. And as I read the histories of these teachers, I felt myself stretching my beliefs to try to understand more fully these teachers' commitments as well as the commitments of other teachers that I know, wondering whether if we all took the time to work through the seemingly innocuous incidents that are so much a part of our teaching, we would discover their importance and the implications they hold for our pedagogy.

## LATHER: *GETTING SMART*

Patti Lather's book *Getting Smart: Feminist Research and Pedagogy With/in the Postmodern* ends with an intriguing rendition of a course she taught in Feminist Scholarship. Used as an example of the kind of research about which she theorizes in the rest of the book, the rendition takes shape in what she calls four "tales": a realist tale, a critical tale, a deconstructive tale, and a self-reflexive tale—tales which help her explore "what it means to write science differently" (123). In the final chapter she exposes the reader to her research into this introductory women's study course in which she tried to insert issues of student resistance into a liberatory curriculum. Intrigued by what she calls "the crisis of representation" and "postmodern writing strategies" as well as by "the many different directions I could have gone with [the writing in this chapter], the gulf between the totality of possible statements and the finitude of what is actually spoken," she decided to "craft four narrative vignettes, to tell four different 'stories' about my data" (123–24).

The stories serve as different readings of the material gathered from the class, each reading taking a different kind of critical perspective. In the "realist tale," she tells basic information about the class and the way she and her co-researchers gathered data (through interviews and pre-/post-surveys). In the "critical tale," she takes one student's journal and "reads" it through the critical frames of Marxism and deconstructionism. In the "deconstructive tale," she explores how and what emancipatory pedagogy means in her classroom setting, as she "moves against stories that appear to tell themselves" (129). In the "self-reflexive tale," she composes a "playlet" from the words of the doctoral students who conducted the research with her, words which are occasionally in conflict about the meaning of the research.

Each of the vignettes allows her to reexamine the material she elicited in her research. Unlike traditional research, in which data is pulled together in just one way in order to tell a single version of "what happened," Lather's writing works to decenter the notion of a single truth or reality. Like the pieces by Schaafsma and Stock, Lather celebrates the multiple means of interpreting what is in front of her, relying on the differing approaches to reading her research as a way of reducing the authority of a single text or author.

Such writing is necessarily evocative rather than representational. She begins with the local—the information she gathered through surveys, inverviews, and journals—in order to craft tales about her students and classes. Complicating the notion of collaboration, she in fact collaborates not only with her undergraduate students and graduate teaching assistants (and co-researchers) but also with herself as she inserts her own multiple readings of her students' responses. And basing her study upon emancipatory practices in her classroom, she recognizes this work as praxis-oriented.

What is significant for me in her approach to this research is her focus on how the research might be told differently from these four different perspectives. Like Lather, I am often overwhelmed by the number of directions in which I could go with the material I gather in my classrooms; the possibilities seem endless. Her various readings of the same class are intriguing then: By offering the reader different versions of the same material, her stance as all-knowing researcher is diminished, inviting us as readers to insert our own experiences into the equation and to come up with other readings based in our own backgrounds. In this way, we can see research as possibility, as an invitation to open up to the multiple means of seeing into a classroom, with the implication that there may, indeed, be unlimited ways to "read" our classroom research.

## COMMON THREADS

As I read these three pieces, I reveled in them for what they taught me about doing research in new ways. Each uses a different genre for the presentation of its research and each relies on a different process for conducting the research. Stock writes a fairly straight-forward essay with a beginning, middle, and end, an essay filled with narrative moments alternating with more traditionally analytic ones; her research process is based on the telling and retelling of an anecdote. In so doing, she recognizes the power of the many teacher voices who heard the anecdote to help shape and reform its meaning. Schaafsma's book combines a number of genres: transcripts, narratives, analyses, and histories, among others. His many methods of research are reflected in his alternating sections of prose: transcripts juxtaposed with histories; analyses juxtaposed with narratives; teacher voices juxtaposed with student texts. By alternating these methods and modes, he elevates the impact of all of them as important pieces necessary to complete the puzzle. Lather, in her final chapter, self-consciously reads the research she gathered in different ways, creating a piece in which her alternative stances toward the material recreates the classroom and the students in it each time. The four treatments she employs allow her to create different voices and different stances toward the class and the research, exposing readers to the multiplicity of means of reading any kind of research.

Despite the differences in mode and method, these three pieces are woven together by some common threads, threads which can help teacher-researchers like me imagine changes in how they, too, can do research. First, in each of the pieces, the researcher is unmasked. In each case, the researcher/author is introduced as an "I" and is a self-conscious participant in the making of the text, the teller of the tale which makes up the piece of work. Second, in each case, the research is integrally connected to pedagogy, an emancipatory or critical pedagogy in which praxis becomes the goal: using the student's anecdote to reenvision the curriculum, using the teachers' conflict about Black dialect to rethink how to help students with their writing, using rereadings as a way to rethink feminist scholarship. Third, while each piece is composed by a single author, each relies heavily on co-researchers. Stock's writing depends on the co-researching teachers; Schaafsma centers on the seven teachers with whom he taught; Lather integrates the work of her undergraduate students and her graduate assistants in her writing. Finally, each piece looks to involve the reader as another kind of co-researcher. Because the author is unmasked and not seen as sole authority, and because each is written in a genre that moves away from the traditional hypothesis/proof mode, readers are invited to place their own experiences alongside the experiences discussed in the texts: Stock's growing anecdote begs for us to add our questions to help it grow even more; Schaafsma's teacher dialogue asks our stance on the issues under discussion; Lather's readings encourage us to add more interpretations.

The vision of these pieces has added to the reconfiguring I've been able to do about my own work as a result of stepping back and looking critically at the research in which I have been involved. As I continue to move toward a more evocative stance in the research I undertake, I have tried to incorporate some of the common threads my reading of these authors has suggested. In the work I am involved in at present—a true work in progress—I have attempted once more to put some of these ideas into practice. This current research project has taken many stages and is, as I write this, reaching one of its most important steps. I don't know yet exactly where it will end up, what genre it will take as it gets more complete, what understandings it will help yield for those of us involved. But I offer it here as yet another way to see what research can be when it is conceived of in the ways I have tried to do in the pages of this book.


## THE EMERGENT CASE STUDY: A WORK IN PROGRESS

In the winter of 1993, as a professor at Eastern Michigan University, I joined with my colleague Russ Larson and former student Ahren Lenhert to try to develop a case study of a composition classroom to be used to help preservice teachers understand some of the complexities that exist in a classroom. The three of us certainly came from different perspectives, and we decided that by joining together to develop this case, we could use those varying perspectives as a way to expose new teachers to the complexity and context of a classroom. In Russ's section of a conference paper we presented in the early stages of our research, he explained his reasons for pursuing this kind of multivoiced approach to case study:

> How do I help my students understand what's involved in teaching before they are actually in the classroom? I've been reflecting on this issue for over twenty years, and I'm still wondering. How can a student understand classroom dynamics from the perspective of a teacher before the student actually switches roles and becomes the teacher?
>
> One strategy that seems to be getting more attention right now is the teaching case. Cases aren't new; I've used them successfully in technical writing and business communication courses. In these courses the cases present actual workplace situations and require students to respond appropriately. For example, students are given the details surrounding breakdowns in service at a major hotel and write a proposal for restructuring the service. Or students are given the facts about substance abuse treatment in a specific locale and then write a report examining the feasibility of a hospital opening a substance abuse program. A response typically involves researching the problem, developing a strategy for solving the problem, and writing a report. Although these cases are somewhat open-ended, the student responses can be evaluated according to the facts given in the case, the principles taught in the course, and the practices appropriate in a specific community. These cases require students to respond

as practitioners and thus to apply the principles and practices their teachers have taught them.

Such cases would seem to offer the same possibilities for preparing teachers, but the few I have tried over the years elicited poor responses from my students. The cases seemed contrived. Instead of being a dramatization of a specific teaching situation, instead of providing a springboard that would lead students to reflect on teaching principles and practices, they seemed designed to lead to a specific solution or to illustrate a specific practice. They, in other words, seemed to ignore the richness and complexity inherent in actual teaching situations.

Should I have been surprised that cases worked better for preparing students in technical writing and business communication than for preparing teachers? Not really. Practitioners in business communication and technical writing operate within clearer limits. They tend to produce documents, not teach students.

And then I experienced some cases that worked for teachers.

During July 1992 I attended the Penn State Conference on Rhetoric and Composition. At that conference I participated in two sessions presenting teaching cases, and I was impressed. These cases stimulated significant discussion of teaching issues; they seemed to be based in actual classroom situations, and they helped people understand principles and practices. I can still recall the discussion of a case involving two teachers who used peer groups in dramatically different ways, one as a method of empowerment and the other as a strategy for getting students to make specific revisions. And every time I respond to writing from students whose primary language is not English, I remember a case based on a paper written by a refugee from Ethiopia.

In September when I returned to teaching at Eastern Michigan University, I had the opportunity to become involved in a case writing project set up by the American Association for Higher Education. Pat Hutchings, the person in charge of this initiative, set up a two-day retreat to which I and other participants brought drafts that we thought might evolve into useful teaching cases. . . . When I attended the retreat . . . I brought drafts for three cases, and one of them did take final shape that weekend. The theme that I chose, the breakdown of a class because of a racial conflict, seemed a natural one. I had never had a class break down this way, but racism and anger can bubble beneath the placid surface of any class. To write my case, I pulled together specific students from several different classes—a young outspoken black woman; a white male jock who liked to play devil's advocate; an intense white male who felt that his family had suffered from reverse discrimination; a fortyish black policewoman who was married to a white policeman—and then I put them together in the same hypothetical classroom and let their emotions surface. The well-intentioned white male instructor made some tactical errors, and by the end of the narrative, the accusations of racism were out in the open, and a very angry black woman had slammed the classroom door, shattering the placid surface and challenging the instructor's practices and his philosophy of teaching.

Was the case a success? It was published through a case studies project at Pace University, and I still like the way it reads (Larson 1994). The narrative flows smoothly, the tension builds toward the explosion, the conflicts and characters seem genuine, and at the conclusion the issues are left hanging there like handmade ornaments on a Christmas tree just waiting to be talked about.

But I'm still not satisfied; I'm troubled by my original question of authenticity. The case seems credible enough to everyone else who reads it, but for me, it is a short story. It is a carefully formed version of something that could happen but never did. Does my case bring forth solid teaching issues, or does it exploit fears that students and teachers have regarding explosive issues and classroom conflicts? (Fleischer, Larson, and Lehnert 1–4)

Russ's dissatisfaction with case studies as he knew them led him to want to try something new. As he talked to me about the dilemmas he had found in writing case studies, he convinced me to join with him to pursue a different approach, one that would retain the positive features case studies offer as a pedagogical strategy for beginning practitioners but one that would be more authentic: that is, a case study that would reflect the actualities of a real teacher in a specific classroom rather than the imaginings of a composite teacher in a created classroom. I then introduced to the discussion my interest in evocative research and multiple perspectives. The issues I have raised throughout this book were the issues I raised with Russ, and together we tried to find ways we could move away from the representational nature of much case study research, to find ways instead to evoke meaning through multiple voices. We then were able to have Ahren join our discussions, through his response to an Undergraduate Assistantship Program at our university which matches students with professors to pursue joint research projects. Ahren, an English major and prospective teacher, had taken his Introductory Writing class with me the previous year and was interested in learning more about teaching techniques, especially in composition classrooms.

Together we designed our project to be something that each of us could learn from and each of us could respond to differently. What we decided was this: Over the course of an entire semester, Russ and Ahren became participant-observers in my English 121 (Introductory Composition) class. Each of us took running notes and kept a journal about what we saw happening in the class; we audiotaped all the classes and videotaped a few of them. Through the transcripts and our reflections, we hoped to be able to compose a case study that would recreate a fairly ordinary class, but one that would raise some of the pedagogical concerns that were real for us as teachers in the classroom and that we suspected would raise pedagogical concerns for other prospective teachers.

The case study that we are still composing relies on our concern for multiple perspectives, both the perspectives of those of us who participated directly in the class and those who might read and respond to our writings. We see it not as a narrative rendition of the class but rather as a layering of understandings, what we have termed an "emergent case study." At the first layer we have the transcript of one class session, a session in which students were conducting a whole class workshop in response to one of their peer's papers (see figure 1). At a second layer we have what we call Multiple Perspectives from the Inside: First are background statements from Ahren, Russ, and me about our participation in the project, our reasons for participating and our hesitations or concerns; second are our critical readings of the transcript, readings in which we each try to identify what we thought occurred in the classroom that day. To those readings we added a response from the student whose paper was the focus of the class that day. The

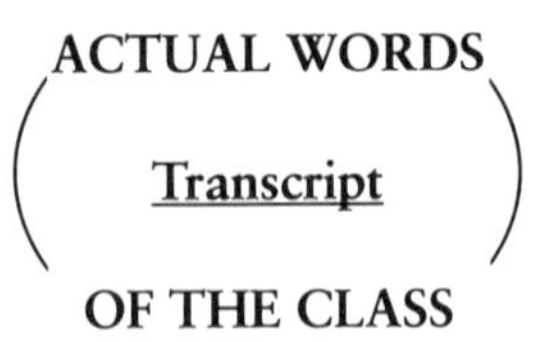


Figure 1

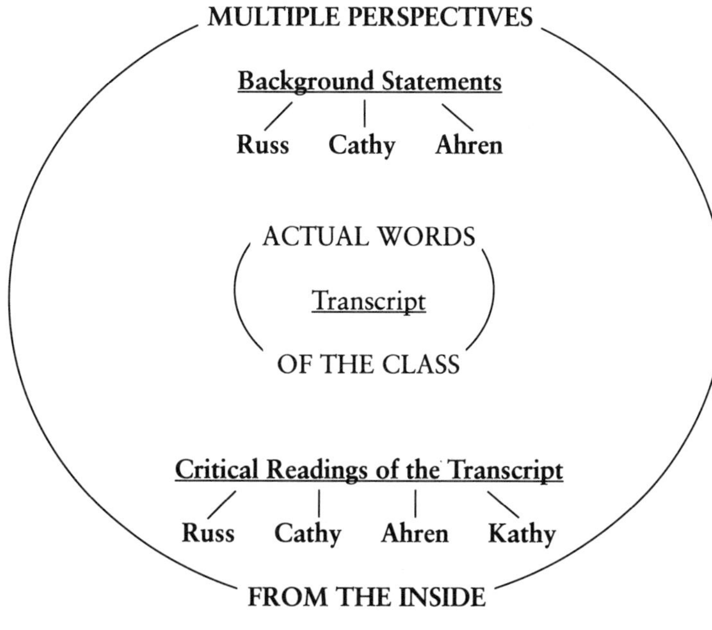


Figure 2

issues the readings raise range from concern about who controls the classroom discourse to what strategies for revision are included and omitted (see figure 2). At a third level we have what we call Multiple Perspectives from the Outside, critical responses to the transcripts from two sources: a group of teachers who responded to our work at the NCTE conference and a group of prospective teachers who were students in Russ's Teaching College Composition class in the Winter of 1994. New issues of concern were raised by these responses, adding another level of understanding to our emergent case, concerns about teacher and student roles and about silence in the classroom (see figure 3).

Seeing this case study as emergent, seeing our research as the confluence of multiple perspectives, seeing our work as evocative, has helped us create a teacher-research project which is possible, which is ethical, and which is tied to pedagogy. We relied on local circumstances, allowing the issues to emerge from the context of the classroom rather than determining the issues beforehand or letting our reading of others' works set our question. We see our work as appropriately complex in its collaborative nature, work which relies on a number of voices in its making—voices which

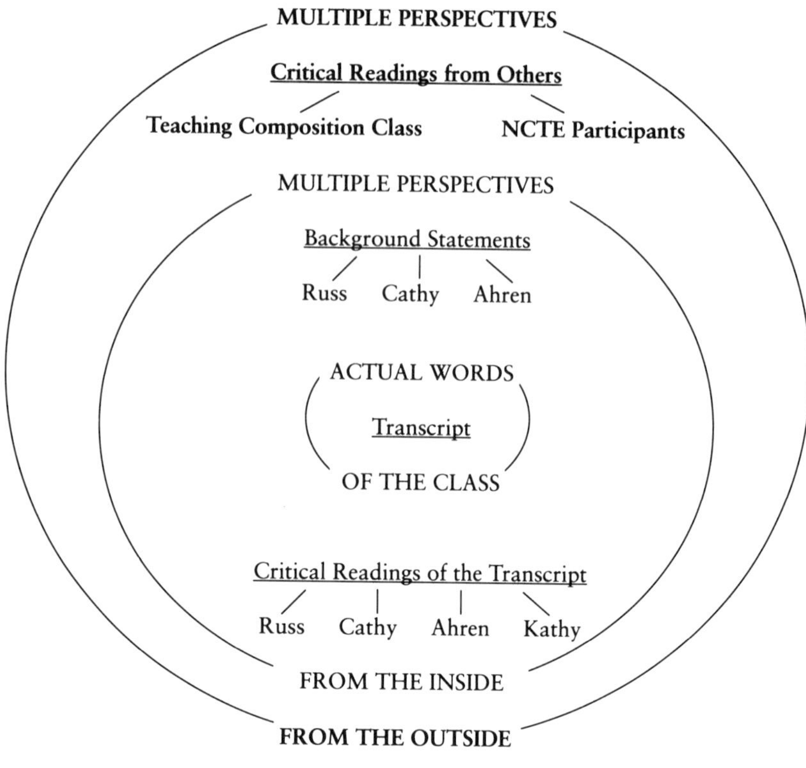


Figure 3

expose differences in perspective—and which does not seek consensus as its necessary end. The collaborative process we highlight in the work relies on voices from the inside and the outside as a way to expand all of our understandings. We also see our work as praxis-oriented, both for those of us who were members of the classroom and for those who participate by reading and writing responses to the case: Ahren as prospective teacher, Russ and I as experienced teachers, the experienced teachers at NCTE, the prospective teachers in Russ's class.

And as is appropriate for teacher-research, the form of this case study emerges from the participants and the nature of the research itself. And the genre continues to emerge. At the two conferences at which we have presented pieces of the case, our form has included written and spoken material: the transcript, summaries of our introductions and critical readings, writing by the audience. For its inclusion in Russ's class, the form looked a little different:

Students there read the transcript, wrote their own responses, read in full our background statements and responses, and then talked and wrote other versions of their responses.

The layers of this case continue to grow; the genre of presentation that will emerge for subsequent renditions of our work will most likely change again. The freedom we felt to experiment with genre for this project was integral to the project's success, I believe. Once we moved away from doing case studies as usual, we were able to expand our notions of what case studies could be.

## "THE END OF THESE NOTES . . . "

My journey thus far as a teacher-reseacher has led me down a number of paths, all of which have in some way helped me toward the place I now find myself occupying. I recognize, though, that this place is only a temporary stopping point. As my conceptions about the possibilities for ethical and pedagogically sound research continue to evolve, so, too, will my practices develop and change. While I don't know where these new understandings will lead me, I do know certain things. I know I will continue to conduct research with students, to share research with students and colleagues, and to read into bodies of literature to inform my work. And I know that such work probably will not be any neater or any more linear than the work I have conducted so far. I have learned that teacher-research is necessarily messy and sometimes confusing, and I am certain that much of my writing about it will continue to be as exploratory and sometimes contradictory as my writing thus far has been. But I do know I will continue to look critically at my work in order to further my growth as a teacher-researcher and as a way to help the prospective teachers with whom I work to see teacher-research as a way of life in the classroom.

What I also know is this: I will continue to be a teacher-researcher, to conduct research from my perspective as a classroom teacher, because I am committed both to improving my teaching practice and to benefiting my students' learning—and because teacher-research is the most powerful means I know of enabling those commitments.

And so, to return to the line from Adrienne Rich which closes chapter 1 and which allows me once more to pause in the story of my research, "This is the end of these notes but it is not an ending" (21).

# APPENDIX A

# AKEMI'S WRITING SAMPLE

*First Free Write*

It appears to me that stress is rather good for a person. However unreasonable amounts of stress can cause some mental anguish. I write this because at this moment I cannot think of nothing stressful that has happened to me. I am only fifteen (15) years old and I have not yet experienced stress in its full force.

As I think about all the problems that children my age are facing, such as: rape, divorce, child abuse, unwed mothers or fathers, poor, welfare, I see how much I am blessed by not having this stress upon me.

But I do recall one stressful time in my life. I was in the fifth grade. It was winter and my cat came home sick. He (his name was Cinderella) had a small bruise on the top of his head. i didn't think much of it at the time and I went ahead and fixed his mild for him to eat. Cinderella stayed to the house that night and died right out on our back porch. When I cam downstairs the next morning my cat was just as hard as a brick and cold as ice. It took almost a week for mom to get me another cat. Not exactly stressful but it is a situation.

*Second Free Write*

I remember having alot of stress on me last week. My U.S.H. Teacher have given out a class project about two weeks before. But me and my partner had not quite finished ours yet.

I had already finished the written report, a graph and two political cartoons. Catrina, (my partner) had done the maps. But we forgot all about 2 more political cartoon, and the slogan which was to be done on a big sheet of cardboard. So the day the project was due we went to the library at lunch time where half of our class was, doing their projects. Valerie gave us an extra sheet of cardboard. While I did the slogan Catrina did another map.

When we made it to class, I finished coloring in the slogan while Catrina started on a political cartoon. Afterwards I did the other political cartoon while Catrina organized our work. By the end of the hour, we had finished our project and turned it in.

*First Try . . . Prompt*

It appears to me that stress is just another form of fear. Almost everyone has one fear or another. These fears put pressure on you which causes anxiety and stress. But stress isn't always harmful to a person. Stress can make a person's life more accurate. However many don't believe me.

The adults I know seem to think that a teenager's life is free of pressures. I used to believe that statement. But now as I am looking back over my life it is really not stressful compared to the stress I will feel later on in my life. Talking on the phone, getting new clothes, or traveling really doesn't mean nothing to me. I feel is I better myself, I can deal with all those little minor problems that I will be faced with.

Right now I do have a small fear. This fear is that I am sitting here and writing on stress and I have absolutely nothing to write about. Cathy from U of M is sitting here ready to read what I have wrote and yet I have nothing. I personally believe that I have really never had any large amounts of stress put upon me and this is what causes me to have so many blank pages.

# APPENDIX B

# DIERY: KATY

June 16, 1916
Dear diery

Mama gav you to me to-day for my sixth burthday. Mama said I shuld tell you al of my seekrets. My biggest seekret is about my brother Willium. I was hidding in the bushs in the yard and I saw Willie barry a seekret treshure. He digged a very bit hole and putted in the treshure. They he barryed it with dirt. Willie is ate years old and he calls me a crybaby when I cry. I wonder what the treasure is. Maybe it mite be a wedding ring or a dimon. I wonder if I shuld tell Mama about Willies seekret treshure.

with fond admurashen
Katy
This is how Omi uste to sine her letters. Omi is my Grandmother

July 4, 1916
Deer diery

Mama said to-day is independents day. Mama said that means that many grate men had a grate huge fite to save are rites so we culd hav freedum of speech and make are own laws. I wil make my laws be blew and red. I asked Papa if he was one of thoze men in the fite becauze Papa is a verry grate man. Papa smiled and pikked me up into his arms. He gave me a grate huge hug. papa say Katybug your Papa was not born in time to fite in that war but if he had bin Papa wuld hav bin in the verry front and if his cuntry called on him he wuld go. Willie and Jacob hav a grate huge bocks of fir drakers for to-nite when it is late and the can lite them off and they will asplode. I am verry ecksited for tonight and Mama said we all mite stay awake late to-nite if we finish all of are chors and milk the cows. Jacob is my brother who is nine. To-morrow is his birthday. He is going to be ten years old.

With fond admurashen
Katy


September 30, 1916
Deer Diery

Tomorrow is my first day of skool. I will walk to skool with Willie and Jacob after we milk the cows and do are chors. I am verry ecksited to go to skool and to meet the teecher. mama uste to be a teecher and I can reed and rite letters. Mama teeched me to reed and rite when I was sik of the small poks and had to be in my bed all the times. The dokter told Mama I wuld die but I am not dead. yesterday papa hiched up the teem after we pult up the weeks in the potatos and he tuk Willie and Jacob and me to get new shews at the stor for us to go to skool in. My new shoes are verry nice and have buttons all the way up the side.

With fond admurashen
Katy

P.S. I got a new dres but Gussie my sister who is three dint get a new dres or new shews becauz she isnt going to skool. Gussie wares my old close.


October 19, 1916
Deer diery

I am verry hapy at skool and I luv my teecher verry much. She is verry good and nice and pritty and she wares nice joolery. I am verry good quite when my teecher tells me to study my lessins and when she is teeching my grad I am verry good and I lissen and I don't wiggle in my seet lik sum of the boys. One of the boys is verry bad and he wispers when he shult be quite. he is all ways having to sit in the corner with the DUNCE cap on his hed. His name is Fred Jacobs. My teechers name is Miss Quinn and she all ways smels pritty lik flowers. She has pritty brown hare and she wares pritty close. Yesterday she wared a pritty blew dress that made a swishy noyse when she walked.

With fond admurashen
Katy


November 27 1916
Deer diery

Today is a tarrable day. I am verry heart-broked. It was verry pritty this morning while I was milking the cows and doing my chors but then it got tarrable. My first grad clas was over and we wented to are seets and it was time for the thurd grad class to have there lessins. Willie is in the thurd grad. Then I hurn Miss Quinn say WILLIUM verry loud and she told Willie to put out his hands so she culd hit them with the pointer. But Willie dint want to and he was skared but he putted them out and he was trying not to cry and his hands were shaking. And I culdnt help it and I said no dont do it verry loud and Miss Quinn putted me in the korner with a DUNCE cap on and she hitted Willie with the pointer on his hands verry hard and I was crying. When I wented home at the noon hour to milk the cows, I told Mama about what happint and she said she was sad to hav to such nawty childrin. I felt verry bad. Why did Mamn say I am nawty. I wonder. How come Miss Quinn hurted Willie and made him cry and made me cry. Is it bad to take care of your brother. I don't lik waring the DUNCE cap on my hed.

With fond admurashen
Katy


January 4, 1917
Deer diery

To-day I wented to the frozen pond with Lydia and Lena. Lena is six and Lydia is all most seven. They are my bested frends. To-day we wented to the pond to wach the boys play shinty. They putted a tin can down on the ice and were hitting it with long bended stiks for a game. It was a lots of fun to wach until sumone got hurted. It was Fred Jacobs. The boys were hitting stiks to gether then hitting the can and Fred got hitted in the hed by a stik. He felled down and dint get up so we all runned out there. He got took to the dokter and he had a kinkushen on his hed. Fred had to go home and he culdnt come to skool to-morrow or the next day.

With fond admurashen
Katy

January 18, 1917
Deer diery

To-day Fred Jacobs did a tarrable thing. he washt my fact out with snow. It was the noon hour and Willie and me and Jacob had just gotted back from home to milk the cows and Fred said to me Katy I got a suprize for you and I said what is it Fred Jacobs and he washt my fact with snow. I was mad. I was so mad I cryed. When I wented home after skool I told Mama what Fred did and Mama said I shuld stay away from thoze nasty boys who do that to little girls. I gess that I hav to stay away from all the boys in my grad then becauze they all lik to wash girls faces with snow.

With fond admirashen
Katy

February 6, 1917
Deer diery

I have been verry sick. I feel hot and I hurt all over. Mama said it mite be namonia or it mite be a floo. Mama keeps putting a cloth with hot oats inside of it around my nek. This makes me feel better iksept I don't like it becauze it is hot and ichy.

With fond admurashen
Katy

April 25, 1917
Deer diery

It is springtime and Miss Quinn is helping are skool to pur-form a play. I am the part of the good farry who saves the little girl who is losted in the forrist and has a magic wand. Mama made a costum for me and it is verry pritty lik a farry waves. Fred Jacobs is the part of the woodsmen who chops the magic tree. Jacob and Willie cant be in the play becauz they hav to stay on the farm and help Papa when he is thrashing the wheet. jacob and Willie hav to run in front of the thrasher and take out the stones from its way. I am not old enuf to do that but I will be when I am ate years old.

With fond admurashen
Katy


May 11, 1917
Deer diery

Today is Saturday, so I'm helping Mama wash are weekday close. To-morrow is Sunday but we cant wash close then becauz Mama said Sunday is the Lords day and we hav to rest. On Sunday we go to church. Our paster is Paster Schmit he is tall and nice and he has spektakles and he rides a mule to church. Paster Schmit talks in German all thru church and we sing German to. Even when I sneeze my frend Lydia said Gazoontite to me. At home Lydia has to all the times talk German to her family so she nos a lots more German than me. She started lurning English wen she came to school.

With fond admurashen
Katy


June 16, 1917
Deer Diery

Mama gav me a new diery to-day for my seventh burthday. To-day we made ice cream and it was verry good. Gussie and I were the ones who got to stir it and turn the handel. We ate watermellin to. Good-by diery.

With fond admurashen
Katy

# APPENDIX C

# MOTIVATIONAL FORCES

In the world of Thucydides' *The Peloponnesian War*, the Ancient
Greek world in which Athens and Sparta were the battling super-
powers, there arose in smaller countries the need to form alliances.
Some countries managed to stand alone for some time, yet eventually even they had cause to ally themselves. In this tumultuous time
of wars, debates, conventions, and treaties, alliances were frequently being made and dissolved, Why did these countries join
together, what made them remain obedient to central authorities,
and what made them break thes alliances and treaties?

Many decisions of this sort were based upon considerations of
utility. Especially just before the onset of a war, countries become
aware of their weaknesses and vulnerabilities. They feel the need to
strengthen their position in preparation for the war, and the most
efficient way to do this is to secure allies. Not long before the
beginning of the Peloponnesian War, "The Athenians tightened
their hold on their existing allies and sent embassies to places in the
neighborhood of the Peloponnese, realizing that they could carry
on the war all round the Peloponnese of they could establish firm
and friendly relations with these places."(II,7 p.128)

After listing the member countries of both the Spartan and the
Athenian alliance, Thucydides says, "These were the allies on each
side and these their resources for the war." (II,9 p.129)

Without these other countries as their allies, the strength of the
Spartans and the Athenians would be greatly lessened.

Another of the primary motivating forces behind all political
and diplomatic decisions is goodwill. When Corcyra wishes to
leave alliance with Corinth and place itself under Athens, one of
the arguments it uses to sway Athens is that "if you (Athens)

welcome our alliance at this time, you will win our undying gratitude." (I,33 p.55)

They argue that "an act of kindness done at the right moment has a power to dispel old grievances quite out of proportion to the act itself" (I,42 p.61) and try to convince Athens that "to have us coming over voluntarily into your camp, giving ourselves up to you without involving you in any dangers or any expense,"(I,33 p.55) will promote among the allies of Athens a feeling of goodwill and will make them more willing to remain subjugated to central authority.

When the Mytilenians entered an alliance with Athens following the Persian War, it was with the understanding that "the object of the alliance was the liberation of the Hellenes from Persia, not the subjugation of the Hellenes to Athens." (III,10 p.198)

A feeling of goodwill between the Mytilenians and Athens caued them to remain content within their alliance. "So long as the Athenians in their leadership respected our independence, we followed them with enthusiasm." (III,10 p.198)

Not until Athens began their attempt to take them over did the goodwill dissipate. Then, the Mytilenians turned to the Spartans in hopes that they would act in goodwill. "You should take us into your alliance and send us help quickly, thus revealing yourselves as people capable of helping those that should be helped and at the same time hurting your enemies." (III,13 p.200)

Yet, goodwill is not the largest cause involved in treaty and alliance making. As the Mytilenians said, "In most cases goodwill is the basis of loyalty, but in our case fear was the bond, and it was more through terror than through friendship that we were held togther in alliance." (III,12 p.199)

Perhaps this fear, this terror was the greatest of all factors in international and political relations. Wars are usually begun as the result of some fear or another. "Fear played a greater part than loyalty in the raising of an expedition against Troy." (I,9 p.40)

In the Spartan-Athenian clash, "what made the war inevitable was the growth of Athenian power and the fear which this caused in Sparta." (I,23 p.49) Fear in this case causes war, not an alliance.

When faced with the necessity of revolt, Corcyra looks upon its previous policy of no alliances "as a lack of foresight and as a source of weakness." (I,32 p.54)

"They (Corcyraeans) urged Corinth not to start a war, saying that, if she did, they themselves, through no fault of their own, would be forced in sheer self-defense to make friends elsewhere and in quarters where they had no wish to make friends." (I,28 p.52)

In the face of a possible war, Corcyra decides to ally with Athens. Thus, fear not only causes war, but the fear of war can lead to alliances. "In Corcyra, the news of the preparations provoked alarm. They had no allies in Hellas . . . they decided therefore to join the Athenian alliance . . . to see whether they could get any support from that quarter." (I,31 p.54)

Fear, akin to awe and respect, not only plays a large role in causing wars, but also in the prevention of war and revolt.

> "This fact will make your enemies
> think twice before attacking you; whereas
> if you reject us, however confident
> you may feel, you will in fact be the weaker
> for it, and consequently less likely to be treated
> with respect by a strong enemy."
>
> (I,36 p.57)

Fear, the fear of punishment or retribution, can be used by central authorities to subdue their allies. "Make an example of them to your other allies, plainly showing that revolt will be punished by death. Once they realize this, you will not have so often have to neglect the war with your enemies because you are fighting with your own allies." (III,40 p.217)

The consequences that occur should the power holding authority lose its ability to incur fear would be a possible revolt of its allies and a weakening of its forces.

When Melos approaches Athens and asks to be considered as an ally and an equal, Athens replies, "If we were on friendly terms with you, our subjects would regard that as a sign of weakness in us, whereas your hatred is evidence of our power." (III,95–97 pp.402–3)

Fear, fear of domination, can also cause a revolt among allies. "When we (Mytilene) saw that they (Athens) were becoming less and less antagonistic to Persia and more and more interested in enslaving their own allies, then we became frightened." (III,10 p.198)

In a world so dependent upon alliances, treaties, and revolts for their protection or freedom, it is essential to recognize and utilize these forces. It is important for the central authorities as well as their allies to see utility, goodwill, and fear for what they are and to employ them in all political, marital and diplomatic actions.

# WHAT FOURTH-HOUR
# STUDENTS WRITE

Subject matter—

Sentence structure (phrases/sentences?)—

Overall structure (paragraphs/lists/etc.)—

Point of view (personal/distanced/etc.)—

How connections are made?—

Purpose of piece?—

Genre (story/report/etc.)—

In or out of school? For what subject?—

Anything else you notice?—

# A P P E N D I X  E

# C H A R A C T E R I S T I C S  O F

# W R I T I N G

| Form | Characteristics |
|---|---|
| 1. Notes | incomplete sentences<br>sloppy<br>organized for self<br>usually 3rd person<br>sometimes assignments (and then they're different) |
| 2. Definitions | list form<br>neater<br>assignment<br>word for word from somebody else |
| 3. Story | usually complete sentences, paragraphs<br>1st or 3rd person<br>tells event<br>fiction or nonfiction<br>title<br>can have moral |
| 4. Summary | paragraphs<br>own words, but not opinion<br>assignment<br>sentences<br>3rd person (but sometimes 1st, depending on teacher) |

5. Journal        do it daily
                  sentences or 1 word, paragraphs, phrases, run-ons
                  letter to self
                  you come up with subject matter
                  1st person
                  in or out of school

6. Reports        long
                  complete sentences
                  detail
                  1 subject (most important part)
                  both your own and others' words
                  research
                  3rd person
                  often whole class does same subject

7. Poems          sometimes rhyme
                  a lot of thought
                  feelings
                  like a song
                  phrases
                  capital letters
                  often short
                  stanzas
                  titles
                  in and out of school

# APPENDIX F

# SUSAN'S WRITING

*Assignment #2*

While the Schulz and Angelou pieces are both very strong examples of argument, the tone, style and purpose of each work is quite different respectively. Angelou entices the reader's emotional being with an honest personal account of the events surrounding her high school graduation, a technique which sharply contrasts the more dry, academic approach Schulz employs. Beyond the more surface differences of brevity as opposed to length, and clarity of the message being conveyed, these two essays are distinctly different in other aspects which I will cover in the remainder of this paper.

For the most part, Angelou is not openly hostile or accusatory in her piece, unlike Schulz whose style is much more attacking. By sharing a personal experience with the reader, Angelou succeeds in closing the gap between herself and the audience. It does not take long for the reader to feel compelled by her honesty, and welcomed into sharing a single facet of her life from her perspective. Because of this warmth the reader feels immediately, Angelou's argument is already less risky in that she isn't threatened by offending her audience. Because the reader isn't placed on the defensive, she is far more likely to react to the argument for what it says to the reader, rather than condemn it immediately for the way in which an idea is conveyed. This type of argument also increases the chances of the reader's ability to relate to what is being presented because it may trigger a similar situation in his past or present. This technique allows him to feel empathy towards the author's personal account which in turn increases the attractiveness of the argument.

The Schulz piece is the exact opposite of a personal account in that her tone is condescendingly informative. This essay conversely does not attempt to bridge the gap between audience and author. The reader instead comes away from the writing feeling like a computer that has just endured a session of routine data entry. She is extremely clear in getting her point across, but she inevitably sacrifices originality and creativity for this clarity. Her paragraphs tend to be rather short, with one basic idea presented in each followed by a listing of supporting evidence in the form of related terms and phrases. Whereas Angelou leaves much of her argument for the reader to interpret, Schulz employs a straightforward academic style which makes it easy to get a general feel for the argument as well as the supporting points.

A good argument needs to hold the reader's interest from beginning to end, otherwise key points presented in a particular argument may be dismissed as trivial, unrelated bits of information. Even though the Schulz essay is far shorter than the Angelou, because Schulz tends to be boorish with a repetitive, listing of information approach, she loses her ability to captivate and maintain an audience from beginning to end. Angelou employs a literary style full of detail and imagery, which stimulates the formation of animated visual pictures. This type of writing is far more enjoyable for most people to read, and therefore creates the impetus for the reader to continue. Schulz in my opinion has her style working against her because its repetitive nature bores the reader, making reading the entire piece somewhat of a chore.

There is also a marked difference between the two pieces in the way they conclude. Angelou's tone is rather optimistic and inspirational at the end, and despite a solid argument for her ideas, Schulz seems rather accepting of language injustices instead of trying to convince others to evaluate their own sexist/racist use of language which surprised me at the end. The reader gets the feeling with the Schulz essay that she is not really taking a position on the issue; but merely relaying her observations of the way people use language to express themselves, justifying these ways in her conclusion. The essay never challenges its readers because Schulz is not promoting social change in any way, shape or form. This lack of conviction in the way the argument is presented detracts from its impact a great deal. Because Angelou has the element of emotion deeply imbedded in her argument and challenges the audience to analyze racist aspects of education in this country, it has more of an impact by conveying a message directly to the reader.

*Assignment #3*

Presenting a sound, lucid argument can be a difficult goal to achieve in itself, but in order to make a truly eye-opening statement the author must take this goal one step further. Thousands of clear arguments have been written on a wide array of subjects, but only a small portion of these attempts are truly effective. It is often helpful to first consider some factors which expressed intentionally or not, detract from the strength of an author's argument. In turn, the general characteristics of an essay in the areas of tone, language, clarity and the manner in which supporting evidence is presented are all interacting factors which determine the overall effectiveness of a piece.

Because an author usually chooses topics s/he already has strong opinions on, the emotion expressed in the paper may often work to the author's advantage, but on the other hand, extreme opinions may repel some of the intended audience at an early point in the essay. Take for instance the piece by Ossie Davis whose tone is condemning and bitter. He approaches the topic of racism very pessimistically and uses the synonyms for blackness and whiteness from Roget's Thesaurus as the only support for his argument, which is narrow in its scope to begin with. Sometimes brevity can be a source of strength for an argument as proven through a personal statement by Langston Hughes focusing on the alienation felt by existing in an all white world as a black student. Davis, however, attempts to shove his argument down the throat of the reader through a rapid-fire style of listing, which only succeeds in giving that reader a sense of guilt and helplessness. The conclusion is void of any feelings of hope or suggestions for improvement which sharply contrasts the endings of both the Angelou and Miller/Swift essays. In short, an essay should not solely convey an author's anger and frustration regarding an issue through verbal temper tantrums or condemnations, techniques which in effect make the audience respond negatively.

In addition to overuse of emotion in writing arguments, the choice of language and expression of voice are also key elements which act to either draw the audience in, or shut members out. Usually, unless a piece is written solely for academic purposes, a more conversational, relaxed style often works best because it puts the reader at ease. no one wants to waste time looking up unknown words the author has chosen most likely to impress the audience with an extensive vocabulary. The argument itself should be strong enough to stand on its own to draw support from the audience. Elevated language, especially when more commonly used words could express the presented concepts better, can be indicative of an argument which is inherently weak. The essay "Language and Experience" by James Britton is a fine example of an overly academic style which is often immediately rejected by readers who see the piece as condescending or pretentious. This essay also tends to be very repetitive whose length could be greatly reduced as a result. Repetition in an argument may further insult and bore the audience, whereas an essay that is lucid and to the point draws a more positive reaction.

Unfortunately, an author may successfully avoid all of the aforementioned techniques which decrease the effectiveness of argument, but still have a product that does not say very much to the audience. In order to have a great impact on an audience, the ideas presented in an essay must be original. Although good arguments have been constructed which merely compile the observations and work of others, they still lack that "eye-opening" quality which makes certain pieces unique. The Smitherman piece which analyzes Black English exemplifies a high level of uniqueness. The author tackles the complex issue of racism from the perspective that Black English should not be considered a manner of speaking which is deviant from standard white English, unique in that she adequately supports a belief not commonly held or even explored by most educated people. Although her essay might be criticized for its academic approach, I feel that the originality of the topic justifies her almost scientific analysis of the issue, and that this is necessary to convince the audience of her argument.

Also necessary to convey a sense of credibility to an audience, the author must somehow show that s/he is knowledgeable enough about the subject to be presenting an opinion in the first place. A good way to convey this sense is to incorporate personal experience into an argument. Both Richard Rodriguez and Maya Angelou successfully employ this technique which in turn draws an audience because it is a highly personalized style of writing. In general, statements about racism and sexism are more credible when they are made by people who have experienced this type of oppression first hand. The perspective of both of these authors is valid mainly because they are directly affected by racism, proven by their personal experiences. Because people do not have universal experiences, writing about things which are merely observed is possible, but in these cases the author must work hard to prove that her/his observations are valid.

Going beyond the mere necessity for rich supporting evidence in writing effective argument, the logic of each successive statement and paragraph as well as the overall shape of the argument need to be considered. "Language and Reality: Who Made the World?" by Dale Spender is a fine example of how a well-constructed argument can be even more effective if its supporting elements flow logically throughout the essay. Each concept presented led into the next and no single piece of information seemed awkward. "One Small Step for Genkind" by Miller and Swift in turn draws strength from its copious examples and logical succession, but falters slightly at the end when a specific suggestion for improvement seems to spring up from nowhere.

Although there is no cookbook recipe which enables an author to write effective argument, basic guidelines still exist of points to avoid as well as techniques to strengthen argument. Basically, the author must first decide what s/he is to accomplish with the piece, and identify characteristics of the intended audience which directly affect the language, tone and style to be chosen. What is considered effective technique for one audience on a particular subject may be quite devastating for another audience. For example, writing in a purely conversational style may not carry enough weight for an audience consisting of professors, and conversely, high school seniors will most likely reject an overly academic approach to argument even if it is a subject of interest. Fine argument must be as convincing as possible, and to achieve this the author must prove her/himself an "author(ity)" on the chosen subject once the basic premise and techniques have been established.

*Assignment #2*

Langston Hughes' "That Word Black" and "The English Language Is My Enemy!" by Ossie Davis express the same message, that the word black carries many negative connotations which adversely affect the black race. The essays contain similarities and differences. Hughes' article is more valid than Davis', however neither is able to justify their theses.

Quickly, what the articles share are audience (everyone), general purpose (make others aware), and thesis (noted above). The importance of these commonalities is that a common ground is provided from which one can compare the successes of the articles in the pursuit of their purposes, relative to each other. With the acceptance of this assumption, one is free to examine the differences in the articles which were responsible for one being better than the other in the pursuit of their common goals.

Davis' essay was very straightforward. The tone was narrow and antagonistic. The language was harsh. The authority which was cited was a thesaurus. The argumentative technique was the shortness of the article, which left the reader to ponder on his/her own, and the way he listed the connotations.

Hughes' essay was in the form of a dialogue. The tone was that of a challenging nature. The language was colloquial. The authority/evidence was common language. The argumentative technique involved use of examples and the dialogue.

Davis listed massive numbers of connotations for whiteness and blackness in order to get the reader caught up in the flow and thus convince the reader that the connotations did indeed reflect racism on the part of the English language, hoping that the reader would accept his value judgments at face value. Several problems arise from Davis' technique. The listing of connotations is consistent with his belligerent and caustic style which can readily turn the reader off. This will tend to render the reader less open and receptive to the piece. The major problem is that on examining Roget's College Thesaurus (1978) there arise discrepancies concerning Davis' listings. These discrepancies could perhaps have been explained if Davis had bothered specifying the year for the Roget's Thesaurus he used. He claimed that there were 134 synonyms for white, 44 of which were favorable and then listed words such as immaculateness, cleanness, honorable, trustworthy (for this word he added "a white man's colloquialism"). In the thesaurus that was examined for this paper there were only 32 synonyms under the heading whiteness, of which the four above mentioned were not listed. He also claimed that there were 120 synonyms for black, 60 of which were unfavorable and then listed words such as threatening and sinister. Again, the thesaurus used for this paper did not list these words and only contained 23 synonyms under the heading black. The words included were words such as black, ebony, coal, darkness, midnight, and inky. There were no derogatory connotations.

He asserts that " . . . [those] who [use] the English Language as a medium of communication [are] forced, willy-nilly, to teach the Negro child 60 ways to despise himself, and the white child 60 ways to aid and abet him in the crime." The evidence for his assertion is weak enough already, especially if one were to use common sense and realize that all of the connotations he listed are applicable to the real world, but he also fails to support his thesis that these "negative" connotations actually have any adverse effects on the black race. He seems to imply that but he leaves too much to the reader. His lack of examples of real world usage of these "negative" connotations renders his essay worthless.

Hughes presents a dialogue from which his character makes the half-way fair statement that " . . . white folks have done used that word [black] to mean something bad so often until now when the N.A.A.C.P. asks for civil rights for the black man, they think they must be bad." Hughes then goes on to list many, common expressions using the word black in a negative way. At first glance this seems very convincing and effective. He provides examples and seems to support the thesis that the negative connotations do in fact hurt the black race. The problem is that the only link between the negative use of the word black to unfair treatment of blacks is the assertion by Hughes' character. Hughes does not provide any concrete evidence that there is in fact a link. Despite the fact that Hughes did (provided examples) what Davis failed to, he is unable to justify his thesis due to his lack of real evidence.

In having read and examined both articles, neither author was able to convince this writer that "negative" uses of the word black detrimentally affects black people. Even considering the common examples given by Hughes, he failed to evoke an image of a black person being remotely involved with the connotations and phrases containing the word black. There are good connotations of the word black out there in the real world, just as there are negative connotations of white. However, it is difficult to prove any association of linguistics to racism. Language doesn't cause racism, but rather racism makes language. This is supported by Muriel Schulz when she says "Language is nobody's enemy. It is simply used to express the hostility and fear we feel toward others. Whether the difference is one of race, or sex, or religion, or behavior does not matter. The human responds to differences with suspicion and distrust, and those responses are going to be expressed in language."

## Assignment #3

It is a fair assumption that all people have preconceived notions on various matters. That is to say, everyone has an opinion or prejudice concerning specific issues. "The evidence from both psychology and history overwhelmingly supports the view that decision makers tend to fit incoming information into their existing theories and images. Indeed, their theories and images play a large part in determining what they notice. In other words, actors tend to perceive what they expect." (Robert Jervis, "Hypotheses on Misperception," World Politics 20, no. 3, April 1968) To this extent it is fair to conclude that when one is confronted with a concept that strongly goes against a personal belief, the method by which the message is conveyed is critical. Argumentative techniques that work in a subtle manner, that tend to make the reader sympathetic are more effective than those that are flagrant and belligerent.

In "Aria" Richard Rodriguez makes effective use of personal experience, emotion, and manipulation to support his belief that bilingual education is wrong. Using his personal experience he paints a poignant picture of a family that is deeply effected by their children's learning of English. They lost the closeness they once had, however he portrays it as a great triumph. Indeed before he learned English he never felt as if he had a public identity. He appreciated the shame of not being able to communicate and function well, especially where his parents were concerned. "Hearing them, I'd grow nervous, my clutching trust in their protection and power weakened." Rodriguez draws us to his side through his emotional anecdotes. We feel bad that their family lost so much of their intimacy, however he feels that the advantages he gained from learning English and establishing his public identity were more important. Now that we are on his side, celebrating in his success story, he manipulates us into believing that bilingual education is bad. Afterall he didn't have one and look how well he turned out. He actually felt that if he weren't forced into learning English exclusively he would have delayed forever. His approach is subtle, his arguments are hidden among his stories. He slowly and skillfully convinces his audience of his point.

In "What's Wrong with Black English," Rachel Jones effectively uses personal experience, emotion, and examples to demonstrate the plight of blacks in American society. Jones was told throughout her life that she "talked white." She realized the implication, "It means that I'm articulate and well-versed." She was made to feel out of place in interacting with both whites and blacks. She realized the situation that since standard English is based on the way whites talk, that Black English is a disadvantage to those that speak it. ". . . It hurts me to hear black children use black English, knowing that they will be at yet another disadvantage . . ." "It hurts me to sit in lecture halls and hear fellow black students complain that the professor 'be tripping dem out using big words dey can't understand.' " She ties us to her argument by getting our sympathy through emotional appeals. Jones also points out that many famous black leaders spoke standard English and that those that had an ethnic dialect would have less power in the marketplace. Despite the shortness of her article, her use of personal experience, emotion, and examples throughout the piece prove her point that being black is difficult due to language. Her subtle approach allows the reader an opportunity to understand without being turned off by a more radical approach.

Ossie Davis, in "The English Language Is My Enemy!", utilizes an extreme point of view, manipulation, and emotionalism in an attempt to convince the reader of his views. He claims that all teachers " . . . teach the Negro child 60 ways to despise himself, and the white child 60 ways to aid and abet him in the crime." It is safe to assume that most of the audience this work is intended for don't hold similar views. Such wild assertions automatically tend to turn the reader off. His radical views overload the readers preconceived notions on the matter and the reader is no longer fully interested in Davis' point. He also tries to manipulate the reader through his reference to a thesaurus. The reader is supposed to be impressed by his citation and the large list of words that show how the whites are favored over the blacks in language. He tries to get the reader to overlook the fact that he can't establish a link between the negative use of the word black and any unfair treatment of blacks due to this usage. Davis does employ emotion in his article, however the emotion he utilizes is one of hatred. He does not look for sympathy, he is out to pick a fight. This wouldn't be so bad if he had any decent arguments or proof to support his assertions. His angry statements are empty. His article is short and very much lacking sound reasoning and proof of any sort. He makes many claims, but fails to get any sympathy due to his caustic style.

William Raspberry, in "Defining in Black and White," uses an aggressive style and manipulation to justify his view that the definition of black people is much too narrow. His bellicose style, as with the Davis article, turns the reader off. He is very arrogant and cynical. "Tell a white broadcaster he talks 'black' and he'll sign up for diction lessons. Tell a white reporter he writes 'black' and he'll take a writing course. Tell a white lawyer he reasons 'black' and he might sue you for slander." These assertions assume a lot and also reflect his use of manipulation. He wants his audience to take these statements at face value and say "Oh my God, he's right." The reader is supposed to be caught up in his reasoning and is to believe everything else he says. He tries to claim sympathy for his cause but fails due to his lack of proof or examples. His antagonistic style turns one away from the content of the article.

Preconceived notions are very important in the way people deal with new information. If the input is compatible with existing beliefs it will be readily accepted. However if the input disagrees with existing beliefs the person will tend to want to ignore the new input. He/she will be very skeptical in considering the information. Rodriguez and Jones were successful in their use of these argumentative techniques because of the tactful way they presented their arguments. They were subtle and clever enough to get the reader's support. Davis and Raspberry were not successful because they violated people's beliefs in such an overt way and belligerent way as to turn them off from taking seriously their works.

# SELECTED BIBLIOGRAPHY


Agar, Michael. *The Professional Stranger: An Informal Introduction to Ethnography.* New York: Academic Press, 1980.

Annas, Pamela. "Style as Politics: A Feminist Approach to the Teaching of Writing." *College English* 14 (1984): 360–71.

Apple, Michael. *Education and Power.* Boston: Routledge and Kegan Paul, 1982.

Applebee, Arthur. "Musings." *Research in the Teaching of English* 21 (1987): 5–7.

Aronowitz, Stanley, and Henry Giroux. *Education under Siege: The Conservative, Liberal, and Radical Debate over Schooling.* South Hadley, MA: Bergin & Garvey, 1985.

Atwell, Nancie. *In the Middle: Writing, Reading, and Learning with Adolescents.* Portsmouth, NH: Heinemann, 1987.

––––––. "Everyone Sits at a Big Desk: Discovering Topics for Writing." *Reclaiming the Classroom: Teacher Research as an Agency for Change.* Ed. Dixie Goswami and Peter R. Stillman. Upper Montclair, NJ: Boynton/Cook, 1987. 178–87.

Bakhtin, Mikhail. *The Dialogic Imagination.* Trans. Caryl Emerson and Michael Holquist. Austin: U of Texas P, 1981.

––––––. *Speech Genres and Other Late Essays.* Ed. Caryl Emerson and Michael Holquist. Trans. Vern W. McGee. Austin: U of Texas P, 1986.

Barritt, Loren. "Reflections on a Change of Mind." *Outlook* Spring (1983): 23–36.

Barritt, Loren, Hans Bleeker, Ton Beekman, and Karel Mulderij. *Researching Educational Practice.* University of North Dakota, North Dakota Study Group on Evaluation, 1985.

Beekman, Ton. "Human Science as a Dialogue with Children." *Phenomenology and Pedagogy* 1 (1983): 36–44.

Berthoff, Ann E. *The Making of Meaning.* Upper Montclair, NJ: Boynton/Cook, 1981.

––––––. "The Teacher as Researcher." *Reclaiming in the Classroom: Teacher Research as an Agency for Change.* Ed. Dixie Goswami and Peter R. Stillman. Upper Montclair, NJ: Boynton/Cook, 1987. 28–39.

Bezucha, Robert J. "Feminist Pedagogy as a Subversive Activity." *Gendered Subjects: The Dynamics of Feminist Teaching.* Ed. Margo Culley and Catherine Pertuses. Boston: Routledge & Kegan Paul, 1985. 81–95.

Bissex, Glenda L. *Gnys at Wrk*. Cambridge, MA: Harvard UP, 1980.

Bissex, Glenda L., and Richard Bullock, eds. *Seeing for Ourselves: Case Study Research by Teachers of Writing*. Portsmouth, NH: Heinemann, 1987.

Boomer, Garth. "Addressing the Problem of Elsewhereness: A Case for Action Research in Schools." *Reclaiming the Classroom*. Ed. Dixie Goswami and Peter R. Stillman. Upper Montclair, NJ: Boynton/Cook, 1987. 4–13.

Branscombe, N. Amanda, Dixie Goswami, and Jeffrey Schwartz, eds. *Students Teaching, Teachers Learning*. Portsmouth, NH: Heinemann, 1992.

*Breakwall*. Student publication from the Huron Shores Summer Writing Institute, 1986.

*The Bridge. Linking Minds: Growing up in Saginaw*. Ann Arbor, MI: Center for Educational Improvement through Collaboration, 1988.

Britton, James. *Language and Learning*. Harmondsworth, England: Penguin, 1970.

Calkins, Lucy. *Lessons from a Child: On the Teaching and Learning of Writing*. Portsmouth, NH: Heinemann, 1983.

Cixous, Helene. "The Laugh of the Medusa." Trans. Keith Cohn and Paula Cohen. *New French Feminisms: An Anthology*. Ed. Elaine Marks and Isabelle de Courtivron. Amherst: U of Massachusetts P, 1980.

Clark, Katerina, and Michael Holquist. *Mikhail Bakhtin*. Cambridge, MA: Harvard UP, 1984.

Clifford, Geraldine Joncich. "Buch und Lesen: Historical Perspectives on Literacy and Schooling." *Review of Educational Research* 54 (1984): 472–500.

Clifford, Geraldine Joncich, and James W. Guthrie. *Ed School*. Chicago: U of Chicago P, 1988.

Clifford, James, and George E. Marcus. *Writing Culture: The Poetics and Politics of Ethnography*. Berkeley: U of California P, 1986.

Cochran-Smith, Marilyn, and Susan L. Lytle. *Inside Outside: Teacher Research and Knowledge*. New York: Teachers College Press, 1993.

______. "Research on Teaching and Teacher Research: The Issues That Divide." *Educational Researcher* 19 (1990): 2–11.

Cook-Gumperz, Jenny, ed. *The Social Construction of Literacy*. Cambridge, MA: Cambridge UP, 1986.

Crowley, Sharon. "writing and Writing." *Reading and Writing Differently*. Ed. C. Douglas Atkins and Michael Johnson. Lawrence: UP of Kansas, 1985.

Daly, Mary. *Gyn/Ecology: The Metaethics of Radical Feminism*. Boston: Beacon Press, 1978.

Donovan, Josephine. "Feminist Style Criticisms." *Images of Women in Fiction: Feminist Perspectives*. Ed. Susan Koppelman Cornillon. Bowling Green, OH: Bowling Green U Popular P, 1973. 341–53.

DuBois, Barbara. "Passionate Scholarship: Notes on Values, Knowing, and Method in Feminist Social Science." *Theories of Women's Studies*. Ed. Gloria Bowles and Renate Duelli Klein. London: Routledge and Kegan Paul, 1983.

Edelsky, Carol, and Kelly Draper. "Reading/'Reading,' Writing/'Writing,' Text/'Text.'" Unpublished manuscript.

Elbow, Peter. *Writing without Teachers*. New York: Oxford UP, 1973.

Emig, Janet. *The Composing Processes of Twelfth Graders*. Urbana, IL: NCTE, 1971.

Everhart, Robert. *Reading, Writing, and Resistance*. Boston: Routledge and Kegan Paul, 1983.

Farrell, Thomas J. "The Male and Female Modes of Rhetoric." *College English* 40 (1979): 909–20.

Fine, Michelle. "Passions, Politics, and Power: Feminist Research Possibilities." *Disruptive Voices: The Possibilities of Feminist Research*. Ann Arbor: U of Michigan P, 1992.

Fleischer, Cathy. "Re-forming Literacy: A Collaborative Teacher-Student Research Project." *Conversations on the Written Word*. Ed. Jay L. Robinson. Portsmouth, NH: Heinemann, 1990.

———. "Re-forming Literacy: Informing Teacher-Research." Diss. U of Michigan, 1990.

———. "Re-searching Teacher-Research: A Practitioner's Retrospective." *English Education* 26 (1994).

Fleischer, Cathy, Russell Larson, and Ahren Lehnert. "Writing the Case Study: A Collaborative Teacher-Research Project." NCTE Convention, Pittsburgh, November 1993.

Foucault, Michel. *The Order of Things: An Archaeology of the Human Sciences*. New York: Pantheon, 1970.

Freire, Paulo. *Pedagogy of the Oppressed*. New York: Continuum, 1970.

———. *Education for Critical Consciousness*. New York: Continuum, 1973.

———. *The Politics of Education*. South Hadley, MA: Bergin & Garvey, 1985.

Freire, Paulo, and Donaldo Macedo. *Literacy: Reading the Word and the World*. South Hadley, MA: Bergin & Garvey, 1987.

Gadamer, Hans-Georg. *Philosophical Hermeneutics*. Trans. David E. Linge. Berkeley: U of California P, 1976.

Gee, James Paul. "Orality and Literacy: From *The Savage Mind to Ways with Words*." *Tesol Quarterly* 20 (1986): 719–46.

Geertz, Clifford. *The Interpretation of Cultures.* New York: Basic Books, 1973.

______. *Local Knowledge: Further Essays in Interpretive Anthropology.* New York: Basic Books, 1983.

______. *Works and Lives: The Anthropologist as Author.* Palo Alto, CA: Stanford UP, 1988.

Gilligan, Carol. *In a Different Voice.* Cambridge: Harvard UP, 1982.

Giroux, Henry. *Theory and Resistance in Education: A Pedagogy for the Opposition.* South Hadley, MA: Bergin & Garvey, 1983.

Goodman, Yetta. "Kidwatching: Observing Children in the Classroom." *Observing the Language Learner.* Ed. Angela Jaggar and M. Trika Smith-Burke. Newark, DE: International Reading Assocation, 1985.

Goswami, Dixie. "Teachers as Researchers." *Rhetoric and Composition: A Sourcebook for Teachers and Writers.* Ed. Richard L. Graves. Upper Montclair, NJ: Boynton/Cook, 1984. 347–58.

Goswami, Dixie, and Peter R. Stillman, eds. *Reclaiming the Classroom: Teacher Research as an Agency for Change.* Upper Montclair, NJ: Boynton/Cook, 1987.

Graves, Donald. "A New Look at Research on Writing." *Perspectives on Writing in Grades 1–8.* Ed. Shirley M. Haley-James. Urbana, IL: NCTE, 1981.

Greene, Maxine. *The Dialectic of Freedom.* New York: Teachers College Press, 1988.

______. *Landscapes of Learning.* New York: Teachers College Press, 1978.

Hairston, Maxine. "Winds of Change: Thomas Kuhn and the Revolution in the Teaching of Writing." *College Composition and Communication* 33 (1982): 76–88.

Harris, Joseph. "The Idea of Community in the Study of Writing." *College Composition and Communication* 40 (1989): 11–22.

Heath, Shirley Brice. *Ways with Words.* Cambridge, MA: Cambridge UP, 1983.

Hiatt, Mary. "The Feminine Style: Theory and Fact." *College Composition and Communication* 29 (1978): 222–26.

______. *The Way Women Write.* New York: Teachers College Press, 1977.

Hillocks, George. *Research on Written Composition.* Urbana, IL: NCTE, 1986.

Himley, Margaret. "'Deep Talk' and Descriptive Knowledge." College Conference on Composition and Communication, Seattle, March 1989.

Holmsten, Virginia L., and the Senior Honors English Class. "We Watched Ourselves Write: Report on a Classroom Research Project." *Reclaiming the Classroom: Teacher Research as an Agency for Change.*

Ed. Dixie Goswami and Peter R. Stillman. Upper Montclair, NJ: Boynton/Cook, 1987. 187–206.

Hoskins, Janet Alison. "A Life History from Both Sides: The Changing Poetics of Personal Experience." *Journal of Anthropological Research* 41 (1985): 147–69.

Hubbard, Ruth and Brenda Power. *The Art of Classroom Inquiry.* Portsmouth, NH: Heinemann, 1993.

Hurlbert, C. Mark, and Michael Blitz. *Composition and Resistance.* Portsmouth, NH: Heinemann, 1991.

Kirsch, Irwin S., and Ann Jungeblut. *Literacy: Profiles of America's Young Adults.* Princeton, NJ: NAEP, 1986.

Knoblauch, C. H., and Lil Brannon. "Knowing Our Knowledge: A Phenomenological Basis for Teacher Research." *Audits of Meaning: A Festschrift in Honor of Ann E. Berthoff.* Ed. Louise Z. Smith. Portsmouth, NH: Heinemann, 1988. 17–28.

———. *Rhetorical Traditions and the Teaching of Writing.* Upper Montclair, NJ: Boynton/Cook, 1985.

Kozol, Jonathan. *Illiterate America.* New York: New American Library, 1985.

Larson, Russell. "Brian Davis." *Case Studies for Faculty Development.* Ed. Rita Silverman and William M. Welty. Series of papers distributed and published by Center for Case Studies in Education. White Plains, NY: Pace University, 1993.

Lather, Patti. *Getting Smart: Feminist Research and Pedagogy With/In the Postmodern.* New York: Routledge, 1991.

Lewis, Magda, and Roger I. Simon. "A Discourse Not Intended for Her: Learning and Teaching within Patriarchy." *Harvard Educational Review* 56 (1986): 457–72.

Lorde, Audre. "An Open Letter to Mary Daly." *This Bridge Called My Back: Writing by Radical Women of Color.* Ed. Cherrie Moraga and Gloria Anzaldua. Watertown, MA: Persephone Press, 1981.

McDermott, Ray, and Lois Hood. "Institutionalized Psychology and the Ethnography of Schooling." *Children In and Out of School: Ethnography and Education.* Ed. Perry Gilmore and Allan A. Glatthorn. Washington, DC: Center for Applied Linguistics, 1982. 232–45.

Macrorie, Ken. *Searching Writing.* Rochelle Park, NJ: Hayden, 1980.

Mies, Maria. "Toward a Methodology for Feminist Research." *Theories of Women's Studies.* Ed. Gloria Bowles and Renate Duelli Klein. London: Routledge and Kegan Paul, 1983.

Mohr, Marian M., and Marion S. Maclean. *Working Together: A Guide for Teacher-Researchers.* Urbana, IL: NCTE, 1987.

Myers, Miles. *The Teacher-Researcher: How to Study Writing in the Classroom.* Urbana, IL: NCTE, 1985.

National Commission on Excellence in Education. *A Nation at Risk: The Imperative for Educational Reform*. Washington, DC: U.S. Department of Education, 1983.

Newman, Judith, ed. *Finding Our Way: Teachers Exploring Their Assumptions*. Portsmouth, NH: Heinemann, 1990.

Nixon, Jon. *A Teacher's Guide to Action Research*. London: Grant McIntyre, 1981.

North, Stephen M. *The Making of Knowledge in Composition: Portrait of an Emerging Field*. Upper Montclair, NJ: Boynton/Cook, 1987.

Odell, Lee. "The Classroom Teacher as Researcher." *English Journal* 65 (1976): 106–11.

Ohmann, Richard. *English in America: A Radical View of the Profession*. New York: Oxford UP, 1976.

Paley, Vivian Gussin. *Wally's Stories: Conversation in Kindergarten*. Cambridge: Harvard UP, 1981.

Phelps, Louise Wetherbee. *Composition as a Human Science: Contributions to the Self-Understanding of a Discipline*. New York: Oxford UP, 1988.

Pinnell, Gay Su, and Myna L. Matlin. *Teacher and Research: Language Learning in the Classroom*. Newark, DE: International Reading Association, 1989.

Ray, Ruth. *The Practice of Theory: Teacher Research in Composition*. Urbana, IL: NCTE, 1993.

Resnick, Daniel P., and Lauren B. Resnick. "The Nature of Literacy: An Historical Exploration." *Harvard Educational Review* 47 (1977): 370–85.

Rich, Adrienne. "Notes toward a Politics of Location." *Women, Feminist Identity and Society in the 1980s*. Ed. Myriam Diaz-Diocaretz and Iris Zavala. Philadelphia: John Benjamins, 1985. 7–22.

Robinson, Jay L., ed. *Conversations on the Written Word*. Portsmouth, NH: Heinemann, 1990.

Robinson, Jay L., and Patricia Stock. "The Politics of Literacy." *Conversations on the Written Word*. Ed. Jay. L. Robinson. Portsmouth, NH: Heinemann, 1990. 271–318.

Rudock, Jean, and David Hopkins, eds. *Research as a Basis for Teaching: Readings from the Work of Lawrence Stenhouse*. London: Heinemann, 1985.

Schaafsma, David. *Eating on the Street: Teaching Literacy in a Multicultural Society*. Pittsburgh: U of Pittsburgh P, 1993.

Schon, Donald. *The Reflective Practitioner: How Professionals Think in Action*. New York: Basic Books, 1983.

Shaughnessy, Mina. *Errors and Expectations*. New York: Oxford UP, 1977.

Shor, Ira, ed. *Freire for the Classroom: A Sourcebook for Liberatory Teaching.* Portsmouth, NH: Heinemann, 1987.

Shor, Ira, and Paulo Freire. *A Pedagogy for Liberation.* South Hadley, MA: Bergin & Garvey, 1987.

Slevin, James. "Genre Theory, Academic Discourse, and Writing within Disciplines." *Audits of Meaning: A Festschrift in Honor of Ann E. Berthoff.* Ed. Louise Z. Smith. Portsmouth, NH: Heinemann, 1988. 3–16.

Smith, Jenifer. "Setting the Cat among the Pigeons: A Not So Sentimental Journey to the Heart of Teaching." *English Education* 23 (1991): 68–126.

Smith, Sheila. "Reinventing the Models and Conventions: Reforming Literacy." NCTE Convention, St. Louis, November 1988.

Stock, Patricia. *The Dialogic Curriculum.* Portsmouth, NH: Heinemann, forthcoming.

———. "The Function of the Anecdote in Teacher Research." *English Education* 25 (1993): 173–87.

———. *The Rhetoric and Poetics of Education.* Portsmouth, NH: Heinemann, forthcoming.

Stock, Patricia, and Jay L. Robinson. "Literacy as Conversation: Classroom Talk as Text Building." *Conversations on the Written Word.* Ed. Jay L. Robinson. Portsmouth, NH: Heinemann, 1990. 163–239.

———. "Taking on Testing: Teachers as Tester-Researchers." *English Education* 19 (1987): 93–121.

Suransky, Valerie Polakow. *The Erosion of Childhood.* Chicago: U of Chicago P, 1982.

Taylor, Denny. "Teaching without Testing: Assessing the Complexity of Children's Literacy Learning." *English Education* 21 (1990): 4–74.

Tyler, Stephen. "Post-Modern Ethnography: From Document of the Occult to Occult Document." *Writing Culture: The Poetics and Politics of Ethnography.* Ed. James Clifford and George E. Marcus. Berkeley: U of California P, 1986. 122–40.

van Mannen, Max. "A Phenomenological Experiment in Educational Theory: The Utrecht School." American Educational Research Association Convention, New York, March 1982.

Weiler, Kathleen. *Women Teaching for Change.* South Hadley, MA: Bergin & Garvey, 1988.

Westkott, Marcia. "Feminist Criticism of the Social Sciences." *Harvard Educational Review* 49 (1979): 422–30.

White, James Boyd. *Heracles' Bow: Essays on the Rhetoric and Poetics of the Law.* Madison: U of Wisconsin P, 1985.

———. *When Words Lose Their Meaning.* Chicago: U of Chicago P, 1984.

# INDEX